STOLEN

STOLEN

LINDSEY UNDLIN

To Sawyer,
I hope you enjoy!
1/15/23

IDUN
NASHVILLE, TENNESEE

Copyright ©2022 Lindsey Undlin

All rights reserved. No part of this publication may be reproduced, distributed, or transmitted in any form or by any means, including photocopying, recording, or other electronic or mechanical methods, without prior written permission, except in the case of brief quotations embodied in critical reviews and certain other noncommercial uses permitted by copyright law.

Names and persons in this book are entirely fictional. They bear no resemblance to anyone living or dead.

Idun is an imprint of W. Brand Publishing

j.brand@wbrandpub.com

www.wbrandpub.com

Cover design by designchik.net

Stolen / Lindsey Undlin—first edition

Available in Hardcover, Paperback, Kindle, and eBook formats.
Hardcover ISBN: 978-1-956906-09-7
Paperback ISBN: 978-1-956906-10-3
eBook ISBN: 978-1-956906-11-0

Library of Congress Control Number: 2021952939

CONTENTS

Prologue .... *vii*

Chapter 1 1

Chapter 2 9

Chapter 3 13

Chapter 4 25

Chapter 5 43

Chapter 6 67

Chapter 7 77

Chapter 8 113

Chapter 9 123

Chapter 10 155

Chapter 11 161

Chapter 12 171

Chapter 13 181

Chapter 14 201

Chapter 15 211

Chapter 16 225

Chapter 17 247

Chapter 18 257

Chapter 19 263

Chapter 20 279

Chapter 21 293

Chapter 22 305

Chapter 23 313

Chapter 24 327

Chapter 25 337

Chapter 26..349

Epilogue 359

About the Author 361

PROLOGUE

Rain poured down over Swallowsville, tapping on the windows of the high school. It was summer, the break was about to end, and the teachers were getting ready for another year.

"It's been awful quiet this summer, barely any violence. It seems too quiet." A tall woman, perhaps in her forties, stalked around a meeting table. "It's been a couple of years since we've had any basketball players go off to succeed in college basketball."

"I think it's fine, they're kids." A man in a black suit sat at the very end of the table. His arms were crossed and he stared out the window. "When you usually pick them, they are freshmen. They're young."

"I feel like I've been failing lately." She sat back down at the table. "Usually, it was every two years that one of my varsity went to the WNBA. Now it's been about five years, I believe."

"You're a great coach. The entire Midwest knows of you. Every school would die to have you coach their varsity team."

"They're doing damned fine with their own coaches; look at Blackridge. They've already sent out one this last year. They're starting to become *basketball central*."

"Swallowsville is never going to lose its name; it's already too well-known." The man leaned forward. "We will always be the better school. Besides, we have that girl you're going to go and try to recruit, right?"

"Keagan Perry? Yeah." She looked down at the desk and shuffled some papers around. "She used to go to Blackridge middle and high school before. She was a top player before her parents took her out of school."

"Is she still a top player?"

"She seems to have been out of the loop for a couple of years, but it's worth a shot, right?" She got up again and stared out the window. "But there is a problem. There would be too many players for my liking. We need to get rid of one player."

"But who would you get rid of? They're all great players."

"None of them are great enough, though. They're all said to be the elite of the elite, but they still can't grasp some simple stuff." She shook her head in disgust. "They all have really interesting backstories, but it has come to my attention that Ruby Aurthur has been on a thieving rampage lately."

"So what are you going to do about that?"

"I think I'm going to move her down to the 'C team.' There, with the innocent kids, she'll change her habits. Ruby is also a jealous, vengeful type. If I kick her down, she'll most likely try to get back at Keagan. Remember what she did to Harlow? She was jealous and you know what she did to her."

"So, you want Ruby to get back at Keagan?"

"And if she doesn't, that flame will be ignited another way." The woman chuckled and turned around. "I know I seem evil, but how else will Swallowsville get attention?"

The man blinked in disbelief. "Are you really this crazy, Talivikki?"

"Absolutely."

CHAPTER 1

The thundering noise of basketballs bouncing was drowned out and suddenly stopped by a coach.

"C'mon, guys." The coach pinched that space between her eyes and above her nose. "Our first game is soon; we just can't keep doing absolutely nothing." The coach spun around to face the ten girls.

"Well, we aren't entirely doing nothing," one of the shorter girls said.

"You just tried to get onto the basket," the coach said, sighing.

"What do you expect from us? We're literally on the 'C team'," one girl said.

"I know, but we at least have to do something so that I don't get fired." The coach spun her whistle around.

A girl watched from the gym's entrance. She was noticeably short with brown hair up in two buns that seemed as alert as her. She seemed too shy to ask to join because . . . she couldn't just *join*, right?

Suddenly, an arm wrapped around her. "Are you thinking about joining the t—" The girl punched this person out of pure shock. "OW! Okay, I see."

The other girl held her nose with one hand and a water bottle in the other. "I'm so sorry, you scared me. Are you okay?"

"Yeah, I'm fine. Anyways, like I was saying, are you thinking about joining the 'C team' or something? Goddamn, you can punch!" the punched girl muttered.

"Well, I can't just join. I don't have any papers or whatever you need."

"Oh, sure you can . . . yeah, you're going to need those papers, but . . ." She put her arm around the other girl once more and walked toward the team. "I'm Ray Eaton, by the way. Who are you?" Ray raised her eyebrows. "I've never seen you in town before."

"Uhm, I don't think I should be allowed to practice," the girl said, ignoring Ray's question.

"Answer the question," Ray said.

"Cali Horn." Cali looked away. "I moved here not too long ago."

"Oh, so that explains it." Ray looked over at the team.

The coach just stared at Ray. "How . . . *where* did this kid come from?"

"This is Cali. I found her standing by the door, watching. She wants to join," Ray laughed and shrugged.

The coach blinked. "You're joking, right?"

"What? She can practice once, right?" Ray looked at Cali. "I mean, you can borrow my other shorts. I hope they aren't too big."

The coach stared again. "Ray. Dude. You can't just bring a random girl in."

"What's stopping her from just joining now?" Ray asked.

She had the face of a twenty-two-year-old woman ... she was tired, a college student, and this clearly had not happened before. She had no clue what to do with Cali. *But we could use another team member. A good one, maybe.* "Okay, fine. You can join; just please have the paperwork in soon." The coach blinked and stood up straight. "I have never seen you before. Are you new?"

Cali nodded. She could feel the other girls staring at her.

The coach looked around. "Well, my name is Milan. You can call me coach or Milan. I genuinely do not care what you call me."

A girl with darker skin and very puffy brown hair held up finger guns and slid over. "Soo 'Cola Woman' is still a go?"

"Twenty laps, Eliza."

"TWENTY?"

Coach Milan nodded.

"Aww, man." Eliza threw her hands up, turned around, and ran.

"Well, Cali, you can borrow Ray's shorts. We just started not too long ago, so it's not like we were doing something." Coach Milan looked at Ray. "Yeah, just take her to the locker rooms."

"Alrighty!" So, off the two went.

Cali could feel them all staring at her, which she did *not* like. She sort of shrunk into herself and looked down. They walked into not the greatest looking of locker rooms. The lockers were beaten up and some didn't even have doors. Cali just stared. "Is this really what you guys have to use?"

"Yup," Ray laughed, but looked slightly sad, too. "The varsity has the best locker rooms, of course." Ray looked around. "Uhm, here's my locker." She pointed at a purple, tough-looking locker.

"How old are these lockers?" Cali asked as Ray opened her locker with a creak. Cali squinted.

Ray laughed, "Daisy told me that they're about sixty years old."

Cali didn't know what to be confused about, so she just nodded. *Who was Daisy, and why did they still have lockers from the sixties?*

Ray pulled some blue shorts from her bag. They were a little long, but they'd probably do. Cali noticed that Ray did have some pretty long, boyish clothes. *Maybe they were hand-me-downs?*

"Oh yeah, I'll introduce you to the team, by the way. Just not right now, you need to hurry up." Ray handed the shorts to Cali and left.

Cali put them on and looked at the very cracked mirror above a sink that looked just like the rest of the locker room—old, broken, rustic. She could still see herself. Her dark skin looked smooth and her hair was perfect. Just like always. Cali took off her sweater, put it on the wooden bench, and walked out.

She did want to join, but felt like it just wasn't her place. She didn't want to take the sport away from her brother, Louie. He died in a car accident a few years ago after attending a party, or so Cali was told. Well, Cali didn't believe it was an "accident" but a murder.

A girl's yelling interrupted her thoughts. "OH MY GOD, JUST DO IT RIGHT! It's not that hard, Justice." This girl was pulling her own red, braided pigtails, in frustration and anger. Her pale, freckled face was red.

The other girl raised her eyebrows and got right into the yelling girl's face. "I'm older than you! You should be respecting me but guess what, Piper? I guess you're too stupid to do that!"

"Why would I respect you? You're a horrible person!" Piper kept eye contact with Justice.

They both stood there, tense, like two feral cats, until another girl came up between them and pushed them apart.

"For God's sake you two, knock it off."

Ray went over to Cali. "Justice is the blonde and Piper is the ginger. They always fight; you'll get used to it."

The girl that pushed Piper and Justice apart walked over and looked down at Cali. "I'm Sienna. Welcome to the team, bud."

Cali awkwardly smiled. "Thanks."

"*Mhm.*"

"Okay, guys, can we get to work here?" Coach Milan came back into the gym with a Cola-Red.

"Of course."

They practiced as they normally did. There were still small fights between the team. Cali didn't understand that. *Why couldn't they just get along? Surely the varsity got along well?*

No such thing. Everything just got worse in the locker room.

"Mel. Justice. SHUT UP." Sienna slammed Justice into her locker.

"Justice, can you just be quiet and act like an adult for two seconds? You two are both eighteen, for God's sake."

Cali looked over at Ray nervously. Ray was just as nervous as Cali. Ray leaned over and said, "Last time, it was a blood bath."

"What?"

"Didn't you notice Justice's ear is ripped?" Ray jutted her head over to Justice and Sienna, who were still fighting.

Ray was right. Justice's ear was ripped. It had stitches too. Everything was coming at Cali faster than she expected. She didn't know the team would be like this. *Isn't a team supposed to work together?* At least, that's what she observed when her brother played.

Cali just ignored the yelling, got dressed, and walked out. Ray followed.

"Hey, I know the team looks bad and all but, it's fun, I promise!"

Cali stared at the ground. "Teams are supposed to get along, Ray."

"Well, yes. We do on the court. Also, that's cheesy, Cali."

Cali nodded. *But I'm right,* she thought.
Ray looked down. "Sorry."

CHAPTER 2

Cali walked up to her front door and looked down. The multi-colored mat read, "Oh, not you again." Her mother was a joker. When her mother got the mat, she put it in the cart while laughing like a maniac.

She bent down, moved the mat, got the key, and went inside her house. The house was quiet and felt numb. Her mother was never home, and neither was Cali's father, and this was her father's house. But she was fine with it.

She was never too stressed; that's what she made herself believe. She was also an only child now and the only thing she had was her drawings and her cat. As Cali walked down the long hallway, she felt her cat rub up against her leg. She stopped, looked down, and crouched.

"Hello, Xife."

Xife. Xife was her favorite character from Cali's favorite book series, *Lions Without Pride*. Xife had a long tail, big paws, big ears, and small eyes. Just like her cat.

Xife purred and meowed. His meow was raspy, old. Yeah, Xife was relatively old. Xife had been there since Cali enrolled in kindergarten ten years ago. Xife was about fourteen years old. Cali dreaded the day she would wake up next to a dead cat, but that surely wouldn't be soon, since the vet said that he was entirely healthy.

Cali stood up and continued walking to her room, with Xife behind her. She opened the door. Her room had very blue lighting coming from the LED lights all around. The room had an art aesthetic; there were unfinished and abandoned drawings piling up in the corner by a desk. The desk was white with a black swivel chair and was cluttered with photos, drawings, notes, and random sticky note reminders. The desk drawers contained clay, paper, paintbrushes, paint, beads, string, scissors, and sketchbooks. Cali liked art, and had for as long as she could remember.

Her bed was next to the window; it had very fluffy, blue blankets, with a pillow just as fluffy. Above her bed, there was a slight slant to the ceiling. The "slant" had posters on it, posters of *Lions Without Pride*, and a famous rapper named Red Fish Blue Fish that was her brother's poster, not hers. There were other posters of people and things she didn't like anymore, but she was too lazy to take them down. Nothing that important except for her brother's poster. She also had a fluffy purple rug next to her bed. There were dressers and other bits of furniture, along with the TV on the side of her room. It wasn't the biggest, but it worked.

Cali was tired, but she went to the kitchen. Down the hall, she passed pictures of her family, pets, and friends. The kitchen was pleasing to the eye. The cabinets were made of darker wood with tile under them. The counter was in a semi-circle around the room, and had dark wood like the cabinets and marble on the tops. There was an island in the middle. It was the same as the counter. The kitchen had everything a chef—or a hungry kid—needed.

She made a peanut butter and jelly sandwich and filled Xife's food and water bowls.

Cali went back to her room. As she put her hand on her doorknob, she looked to her left. It was her brother's door. Still there. As if nothing had happened. As if he still played all types of videos games. *Louie Horn* is what it read on the door sign. It had not been touched since 2014. No one ever went in there except for her mom. It was way too painful for Cali. Her brother was the best person in the world. He always took care of her.

Not today.

She opened her door, let Xife run in, and entered.

Cali awoke in a room. Well, not *really* a room. It was like her eyes were a screen; everything was 2D. There was a bright red light, but it wasn't blinding somehow, and the floor was grey. Suddenly, there was a silhouette. The silhouette looked at Cali, stared, and suddenly a gunshot went off. "Black blood" went all over, and the silhouette fell to the ground, bleeding and groaning. The groaning multiplied as more silhouettes appeared on the ground with either vomit or blood pouring out of them. And some silhouettes had nothing. They were all just struggling and crawling with groaning. Then there was yelling. Lots of it, on top, overlapping the groans. There were now groups of silhouettes. Some fought, and all those fights ended violently, either with severe injury or death. Then she was in a stadium, with the same theme as the room, with people chanting, but she couldn't tell exactly what they were chanting; she just knew they were chanting something. She looked around to see nine other girls. *Another team? Her team? Where was she?*

Then it stopped.

Again, she was in the room. There were two silhouettes. One had an exceedingly long ponytail. The other had curly, long hair. They both opened their eyes, which were completely white, and they drilled into Cali.

Then nothing.

Cali woke up, sweating and out of breath. She sat up very quickly and startled poor Xife, who was sleeping more peacefully. "Sorry, Xife."

Cali looked over at her desk, and at all of the notes, photos, and drawings above it. Then she looked at an empty wall. She got up and wrote and drew things from that dream and put them on the wall beside her dresser and a wall corner. She also wrote down the dream in a notebook and dated it, Wednesday, September 3, 2019. Then she labeled the notebook "Dream Journal."

CHAPTER 3

Cali got no sleep at all after that nightmare. None. She had been up since 4:00 a.m. pondering about the possible meaning behind it. Well, there was a stadium, that meant something about joining the basketball team. *Right?* She was absolutely overthinking it, but she couldn't help but think about it. It was so vivid! She was so exhausted. She wanted to curl up into a ball and sleep in the bushes. Cali heard footsteps behind her.

"CALI!"

Cali looked back. It was Ray running toward her, smiling. "I didn't think that we would meet, *hm?*

Cali slightly nodded. She didn't want to seem rude, but couldn't handle Ray's energy at the moment.

Ray looked at Cali. "Tired?"

Cali nodded again.

"Room too warm? Too awake? Uncomfortable? Bad dream? *Eh?*"

Cali looked at Ray. "Bad dream I guess." Then she looked away.

Ray raised her eyebrows. "What was it about?"

Cali shrugged. "Just some strange shadows."

"Any details?" Ray cocked her head. "Like, I don't know I rarely even dream."

"Well, I saw a basketball stadium," Cali mumbled.

"I'm not a . . ." *She made those stupid bunny ears.* "Dream expert, but what if, *what if,* hear me out . . . your dream was about basketball?"

Cali blinked. She fought against accidentally punching Ray now . . . *maybe she would punch her too hard.* "Makes sense."

"Wait, you said a *stadium*? Only the varsity gets to play in the stadium." Ray raised her eyebrows. "How good are you at basketball, Cali?"

Cali blinked. "My dream probably doesn't mean anything, Ray." She looked down at the sidewalk. Maybe it was just about her brother, she had seen the stadium before, when she was younger. She barely remembered it; she didn't want to remember it. Her brother.

Her brother.

She teared up.

Ray glanced at her and did a double take. "Is everything good, man?"

Cali just continued to stare at the ground, caught in her thoughts and stuck there.

Ray put her arm around Cali. "Did I do something? I'm sorry if I did."

Cali shook her head and looked at Ray. "You didn't do anything." She shrugged.

Suddenly, a pickup full of high school boys rode past them. Their truck was embellished with American flags, eagles, and more patriotic stuff. One kid hanging out of the window called out, "HOMOSEXUALS! YOU'LL HEAR ABOUT US TODAY ON THE NEWS

AT SIX!" the boys laughed until the truck could not be seen or heard anymore.

. . . what?

Ray was confused as well and removed her arm from around Cali. "It's probably the football players."

Cali rolled her eyes. "Ah, makes sense."

They both continued to walk to school. Cali was still extremely tired.

Cali looked up at the school; it had a very modern design. It had three stories and tons of windows. On the grass, there was a blue-and-white sign that read:

Swallowsville
Home of the Swallows
Est. 1943

There were students everywhere, Cali couldn't help but feel claustrophobic and crowded. This was her first day of school, and Cali had not yet become accustomed to the school. She previously went to a much smaller one, and this was quite the change.

She also didn't plan to make any friends. *Ray? Nah, they weren't friends.* Ray was just a girl on the basketball team with Cali. But Ray was the person who got Cali on the basketball team anyway.

"What's your schedule look like?" Ray held up her crumpled schedule.

Cali dug in her pocket and pulled out her neatly folded schedule. Ray snatched it from her hands, opened it and compared. She smiled. "We have five classes together," Ray chuckled. "You really picked . . . art? You like art? That's so cool! You'll have to show what you can do." Ray cocked her head.

Cali shrugged. "What did you choose instead of art then?"

"German."

"German?"

Ray nodded eagerly.

"Why German?" Cali cringed, realizing she really shouldn't have asked.

"Oh, because my great grandparents came from Germany to North Dakota and . . ."

Ray went on and on. She just wouldn't shut up. They walked through the big glass doors; Cali still couldn't get over how nice the inside of the school was. It was like a mall! There were escalators, skywalks, everything. She didn't hear Ray talking about her family and Germany; she was too amazed by the school. There were kids everywhere, all different in many ways, unlike her other school. She had never seen this before. Everyone at her old school used to be so much more . . . *bland*. She was usually so sad about how she lost her brother that she didn't pay attention to the beauty of people. Everyone else seemed to have a brother. She didn't; her family was split, unlike the other kids. She was out of the ordinary.

"Was your old school like this?" Ray waved her hand in front of Cali's face. "If you don't mind me asking, of course."

Cali just shrugged. "Small school."

Ray blinked. "So?"

"Don't worry about it," Cali said as she clenched her teeth.

Ray cocked her head. "Oh . . . makes sense. I bet you're glad to have come to this school! I'll do whatever I can to make you feel welcome."

Cali lifted an eyebrow. ". . . But why? You barely know me."

"I can get to know you, right," Ray laughed. If you let me at least."

Cali fought with herself. *Should I trust Ray or not?* Every time Cali trusted someone, they ended up talking behind her back and bullying her. She raised an eyebrow. "*Eh.*"

Ray frowned and looked away. "Dude. I really don't think you could survive here without me. I could leave and let you struggle, but I won't." Ray looked straight into Cali's eyes and smiled warmly.

Cali sighed, wanting to fire back, she opened her mouth, but nothing came out. Ray raised her eyebrows and just smirked. Ray was . . . right. Ray seemed dumb before, *so how was she right?*

Don't judge a book by its cover, Cali. Her mom's voice rang in her mind. *You need to learn to stop being judgy.*

"I—" Cali snorted like a bull and shut her eyes in annoyance. "I can find my way around here." Cali glanced around nervously.

"Alright, have fun!" Ray then disappeared into a channel of kids. The bell rang just as Ray's smug smile disappeared.

Cali's jaw dropped. She was alone in a new, huge school. Cali swore to herself. Some kid shoved her aside, messing up her nicely ironed sweater. "Move," he glared at her as he continued forward.

Cali glared back. She looked at her schedule. *Period one, Mr. Array, Science.* Cali looked around for someone to help her, but all she saw was the blur of rapidly moving kids. She just stared as reality set in. Speckles of anxious thoughts fluttered around in her head, not willing to leave. Cali looked around, sweating slightly, either from body heat from hundreds of kids or out of nervousness. Cali snuck into a channel of kids. She realized how short and small she was compared to everyone else; she couldn't even see.

Great. This just made everything worse. Where did Ray even go? She really should have kept Ray with her. *Whatever, it didn't matter anymore.*

Then Cali saw the bathroom and instantly ran for it. As she walked in and looked at herself, the bell rang. She sighed. It looked like she would just sit there for the day. Her hair was messier than before, her sweater looked wrinkled and out of sorts. It had to be perfect. She needed to look good so she fit in and didn't look out of the ordinary. Cali stared at herself for what seemed like forever, picking out the small details about herself that made her stand out.

My hands? No . . . no one is going to look at my hands and think I have weird, strange hands. Cali chuckled to herself, laughing at her stupidity. But her smile quickly faded as she continued to pick on herself. She was her own bully now after years of torment.

Cali learned to trust only herself and to always be alert. If she didn't keep her guard up, she would be hurt again. If she kept her guard up, she would not . . . but Cali didn't realize that her keeping herself alert hurt *others*. Cali obviously was the type to only think of herself. Why wouldn't she? She was tormented for everything. Her looks, the way she talked, the way she walked, and even the way she held her utensils when she ate. To others, it seemed as if she was arrogant, full of herself, or even mean in general.

The truth was, she feared being hurt again, so she snapped at any sign of being disrespected, even hurling insults at the person who "disrespected" her. Most of the time, it wasn't disrespect at all, but rather minor criticism or just someone saying they didn't like something she did. Cali didn't realize the way she acted at all because she didn't listen to anyone. She allowed anger to stay trapped in her body. She was like a ticking time bomb and couldn't figure out how to defuse it, as if there was a child inside her using her chest like a door, pounding on it, screaming to be free.

Until she broke.

Cali tried to hold her tears in, but the pain in her throat was too much. So, there they were. She stood there, crying with her head down. Her guard was definitely down.

"You good, man?"

Cali froze.

"Uh . . ." The voice was soft. Cali looked at the mirror. There, she saw a tall, blonde girl in a black sweater vest and white T-shirt. She had a nose ring. She looked like one of those popular girls from those movies. The girl's eyes were a nice, warm ocean blue. They were so beautiful and comforting, hypnotic, even.

Cali nodded, looking down again.

"What's your name?" The girl stood right next to Cali and stared straight at her.

Cali hesitated.

The girl raised her perfectly tweezed, perfectly shaped eyebrows. "Sorry, I should probably introduce myself first. I'm Harlow. Harlow Shaw."

Cali nodded, still frozen.

"Well, what happened? You were crying." Harlow chuckled softly.

Cali, again, stayed silent.

Harlow shifted.

"I don't know you, but whatever is wrong, I can probably help. I know the student council president. She can also help."

STOLEN

Harlow's voice was incredibly soft. She stood with her arms slightly out; she wasn't towering over Cali at all. She smiled; it was strangely comforting.

Cali glanced down. "I can't find my class." She glared at herself in the mirror.

"Which class?"

Cali stood up straight and dug in her pocket. "*Er*, Mr. Array's class?"

Harlow smiled. "Oh, you're super close to it, actually!" She laughed.

Cali frowned, embarrassed. "How close?"

"Here, I'll take you." Harlow pointed behind her.

Cali hesitated again. "You can just give me the directions."

Harlow shrugged. "I mean, if you want me to, it'd be easier for you to just come with me."

Cali sighed. "Fine."

"Alright, just follow me."

They both walked out. Cali stopped and looked around at the hallways. There were absolutely no kids left around. The walls were plastered with posters and art projects, unlike Cali's old school.

Harlow nudged her. "Something wrong?"

Cali shook her head.

"Alright!" Harlow said, half singing the word.

They walked across the hall. Cali looked at the small sign that read, *Mr. Array Room 203.*

Harlow opened the door for Cali and pushed her in, placing Cali in front of her like a proud mom with her child.

"Hey, Mr. Array! This is Cali; she's late," Harlow lowered her head and whispered, "You're a freshman, right?"

Cali nodded slowly.

"She's a freshman, and you know it's the first day, so I'd like you to excuse her."

A tall, bald, bearded, albino man looked over at them. He wore black khakis and a blue plaid shirt with a black tie. Cali glanced around the room. The windows had blackout curtains on them, and the room was dimly lit, but you could still easily get around. Mr. Array chuckled and turned his body to face them completely, with his arms out.

"Harlow, you can't really ask for someone to be excused. You aren't on the student council."

Harlow shrugged and smiled. "Can you excuse her, though?"

Mr. Array smiled at Cali. "Well, of course, just be here on time tomorrow. It's your first day." Mr. Array pointed toward his class. "You can sit where you want; I was just explaining some things."

Cali looked at where he pointed, and her eyes focused on one person, Ray. She was smiling like the Cheshire cat. Smug and mischievous. Cali looked around the room for an open spot far away from Ray. But to no avail, the only seat was by Ray. *God, this was so cliché, of course, the only seat was by Ray.* Cali nodded and went to sit by Ray. She didn't make eye contact with Ray, but could feel Ray staring her down. Cali looked over at Ray. Ray was staring at Cali with her head rested on her hands.

"So, you met Harlow, I see."

"Yeah. Why do you care?"

Ray chuckled, shifted her ponytail to the side, and pointed at her back. "See, it says 'Harlowdog.' She has her own brand and is pretty damned wealthy, dude."

Cali raised her eyebrows. "How wealthy, exactly?"

"Well, millions probably," Ray chuckled. "Everyone wears her brand. You should buy from her sometime. I'll take you to one of her stores. After school how 'bout?"

"Millions?" Cali stared in shock.

"Hey, Cali and," Mr. Array hesitated, "sorry, I don't know the other one's name."

"Ray."

"Cali and Ray, I may be super near-sighted, but I have ears like a hawk," Mr. Array chuckled.

"Sorry." Ray nodded at first. "Aight."

Mr. Array went on with his rules, and normal first day of school things, as you could expect, expectations, that stuff.

Not long after the class ended, Cali and Ray walked together. Cali, with her head down, stared with her cold, dead eyes, and Ray with her head up and tilted.

"So, do you think you need me yet or . . . ?"

Cali sighed but said nothing.

Ray laughed. "You know you'll need me; besides Cali," Ray nudged her with her elbow, "you're going to have to get used to me, we're both on the same team now."

Cali shrugged.

Ray frowned. "Really, Cali, I'm just trying to help you."

"*Hm.*"

CHAPTER 4

Cali went through the crowded hallways that were laced with twists and turns. There was a large lunchroom with round, purple tables peppered all over the room. The cafeteria seemed to be the size of a royal ballroom. There were Halloween dance posters plastered all over the walls. Cali was impressed with how smartly they were placed; right where you would look: on the vending machines, the doors, at the cafeteria line, even some tables. The student council was hard at work . . . a month early.

"I'm guessing your old school was not like this," Ray chuckled as she ate her lunch.

Cali shook her head, and shielded her eyes from the strong sunlight coming through the big windows. "Why would you need a lunchroom this big?" Cali asked, sounding disgusted.

"*Uh*, well, there's thousands of students in this school," Ray said, looking around as if to prove her point. "Isn't that just common sense?"

Cali snorted in offense, "I probably have more common sense than you do." Cali brought her lunch sack up a bit and let it drop, trying to show Ray a bit of pettiness.

Ray raised an eyebrow. "Is your food okay?"

Cali slowly but loudly opened the zipper as she glared at Ray, being sure to not break eye contact.

"Wow." Ray sighed in annoyance. "Look, Cali, I'm not going to hang around you unless you're nice to me. If you don't switch your behavior, I will leave you to suffer."

Cali's ears perked up. "What? Okay, okay. I'll try to stop." She grabbed an apple out of her bag and took a bite out of it.

"So, after school, do you want to go to Harlow's shops or no?" Ray asked.

"I don't have any money."

"I can just use my dad's credit card. He won't know; I do it all the time." Ray laughed.

"Isn't that a bit illegal?"

Ray nervously chuckled. "Probably, but it's only illegal if you get caught, right?"

"No, it's illegal either way," Cali said with concern.

"Whatever," Ray laughed. "Anyways, do you always eat fruit?"

Cali shrugged. "I'd rather not talk about it."

"Oh," Ray looked down for a second, "would you want any of my food?"

Cali shook her head.

"*Hm.* Well, okay. Anyways, we'll go to Harlow's store after school. I heard it might rain, by the way."

The rain raced down to the earth like giant rocks, pelting anyone that came across its path. The barbaric, vicious wind didn't help. Cali and Ray ran through downtown Swallowsville as if they were running through minefields, finding any cover they could, like awnings, garbage can lids, doorways . . . anything they could get their hands on.

"SORRY!" Ray tried to steal an umbrella from a mom and her kid, and Cali yelled at her.

They got to Harlow's store, and Ray opened the door and shoved Cali inside. The entry bells chimed delicately over the hellish weather outside. People looked over at the two, concerned and judgy. Their clothes were soaked. Ray waved awkwardly to a stranger in the scarf aisle.

Ray turned to Cali, "So I see you like to wear sweaters."

Ray pushed Cali toward the sweater aisle. There were sweaters everywhere, in many different colors. One specifically caught Cali's eye; it was blue with a collar. There were small stars on all sides of it on the collar, each tipped away from each other. Cali took it off the rack and held it in front of her.

"It would look nice on you, I bet!" Ray held a thumbs up and smiled in support.

Cali slightly smiled and then frowned. "I feel bad having you use your dad's credit card."

"Cali, it's fine, just trust me."

Cali looked down and finally nodded.

"Is that all you want? We could buy some umbrellas too, and hats." Ray looked around.

Cali nodded.

They walked over to the accessories section, and all the colors were sorted but some of the colors hurt her eyes. Some were softer and more eye-appealing than the rest, those caught her eye.

Ray was already picking out a white hat with a riot of blue polka dots. "Hey, look at this hat, do you like it?"

"Of course," Cali chuckled.

The bell rang as someone else walked in, Ray got curious and looked around the aisle.

"Hi Harlow!"

Harlow looked at Ray and smiled, "Hey, Ray how are you doing?" She then noticed Cali, "Oh, Cali, are you doing any better?"

Cali nodded.

"We were just going to buy her a new sweater," Ray said, excitedly,

"She came from a small school, small town, and she didn't know who you were."

Harlow raised an eyebrow. "Where are you from?"

Ray also looked at Cali with curiosity.

"Yarmen."

Harlow shrugged. "Sorry, I've never heard of that town."

"Me neither." Ray looked up at Harlow, then back at Cali. "Where is that located?"

"By Archile. It's close to the Canadian border." Cali glanced away awkwardly.

"Oh, I know Archile, but never heard of Yarmen. Strange." Ray laughed.

Cali frowned a little.

"Anyways, Cali let's go buy our stuff."

Ray pushed Cali toward the cash register.

"What about the umbrellas?" Cali asked.

She hated how Ray randomly pushed her around.

"Nah, we're good," Ray laughed. "Plus, I decided I'd take you to a restaurant down the street."

Harlow followed them and asked Ray, "Are you using your dad's credit card again?"

Ray looked up and whispered back, "Perhaps."

"Ray, I could pay for you. I don't need it. That would be taking away your own money," Harlow said.

"Yeah, of course, you don't. I know that." Ray laughed. "I'll feel bad if you pay."

As they got up to the register, Ray grabbed the clothes from Cali and laid them out. The cashier looked at Harlow, then back at the clothes, before she started scanning the price tags.

"Ray, I'll pay." Harlow held up her credit card.

"Sheesh, you won't let up *anyway*. So go ahead." Ray rolled her eyes jokingly and chuckled.

Harlow laughed and looked at the cashier.

"Thirty-five dollars." Harlow paid and the cashier put Cali's sweater in a bag and handed the bag to Cali.

"Have a nice day."

"You too," Ray and Harlow said in unison. Cali nodded.

They looked outside to see that the rain had let up a bit, but was still raining a decent amount.

"So, we're going to the Fox Den?" Harlow asked as they walked through the rain.

"Yep."

"What's that?" Cali asked as she put on her new hat.

"Oh, it's a restaurant. It's been around since the 1930s. The Boone family owns it. It's interesting that they owned it during that time considering that the Boone family are people of color."

Harlow looked at Cali.

"I think Swallowsville was very small then, until a bunch of Europeans started to come here because of oil."

"Also be careful of the protesters outside." Ray laughed nervously as she gave Harlow an uneasy glance.

"Why are there protesters?" Cali asked.

"Well, it's just the old white people. The Fox Den doesn't allow any political stuff anymore and it's sparked something in them."

Harlow shrugged. "I don't see why they're so worked up about it."

Cali raised her eyebrows. "Why would they be so mad over politics?"

"It sparked a lot of physical fights. It was mostly younger versus older," Ray explained.

"Actually, there they are," Harlow said.

She pointed to a group of people, some young but mostly older, holding flags that displayed terrible sayings and images. They were all congregated under canopies, sheltered from the rain.

Cali then saw the Fox Den. It was a white, circular building with a lot of windows. It seemed to have been revamped in the 1960s, since there was a drive-in space, even if it was sixty years old it looked like it was used often. There was the restaurant's name on top of the building on a black sign with neon lights spelling "Fox Den." The neon orange fox was positioned over the word "Den" like it was sleeping with its paws hanging off the edge.

"Man, they're out here in the rain too? They won't let up," Ray sighed.

"Let's just go in," Harlow laughed and opened the door.

Cali could hear the roar from the crowd. The inside of the Fox Den was very 1960s-themed. The walls and ceiling were robin's egg blue, the floor was black-and-white check, the tablecloths were red-and-white check like you see in old Italian restaurants. There was a bright red circular bar at the back of the building. There was a black board all around the building with signs of all kinds on it. *Whoa, this is nice,* Cali thought. The three sat down at a table. Ray was already messing with her napkin.

"So, Cali," Harlow looked over at her, resting her head in her hand, "you going to stick to basketball?"

Cali remembered seeing Justice and Sienna fight, and how Ray pointed out Justice's ripped ear. She shrugged. "I'll think about it."

"Please stay, dude," Ray sat up straight, "you're so cool!"

"You barely know me," Cali sighed.

"Oh, I know, one thing I really do like about you and think is really cool, though," Ray laughed, "is I love the two buns on your head. They remind me of bear ears, and bears are cool, right?"

Cali blinked.

Ray smiled nervously. "Hey, would you guys like anything to drink?"

A server came up to them. They had short green hair in a small twirl, dark skin, and friendly brown eyes. Their name tag read, "Frankie Boone." Cali cocked her head.

"Hey, Frankie," Harlow nodded in greeting. "Yeah, could I get a Cola-Red?"

"Same," Ray said.

Cali stayed silent.

Harlow looked at Cali, then back at Frankie.

"This is Cali, Frankie, she's new here."

Frankie smiled. "Nice to meet you, Cali."

Cali just nodded.

"She's just . . . shy." Harlow chuckled.

"What's your last name, Cali?"

"Horn."

"Horn." Frankie glanced away. "Haven't heard that last name in a while."

"A while?" Harlow and Ray glanced at Cali as they spoke in unison.

"Don't worry about it, my family has known the Horn family for a bit."

"I've never heard of the Boone family." Cali looked at Frankie nervously.

"Oh, well. That's to be expected."

"What?"

"Uh, don't worry about it. What do you want to drink?"

"I'll just have water."

Frankie wrote it down in their notepad, "I'll be back in a second."

Cali stared at the table questioning her whole reality. *Did she know the Boone family and just forget? No, she never did. Maybe Frankie has the wrong Horn family. Yeah, that must be it.*

Ray and Harlow looked at Cali, curious. "So, Cali, how would you know Frankie?"

Cali shrugged, "I'm guessing they have the wrong Horn family? I don't know, Horn is probably a common last name."

Ray yawned and leaned back in her chair. "Ah, I wouldn't worry 'bout it. Yeah, you're probably right, Cali."

Cali nodded and relaxed a little, knowing she had some type of reassurance. Harlow, though, still had curiosity in her eyes.

"I don't think Horn is a very common name," Harlow spoke in a more monotone voice, "I'd think something like Smith or Johnson would be a quite common name because it is. Never heard of Horn, though."

"Why are you talking so weirdly, stop using such proper English; you're not around some fancy, big named people, Harlow. Also, she probably has relatives, you ding dong," Ray butted in.

Harlow blinked.

Cali looked out a window to see the "protesters" again. Some were . . . closer. *Wait.* "Does that man have a gun?" Cali's heart dropped as she said it aloud.

Harlow and Ray looked over anxiously, and Harlow nodded with apprehension as fear sparkled in her eyes.

"They won't. Why would they?" Harlow laughed nervously.

"Should we warn people? Should we leave?" Ray asked, looking at Cali and Harlow, then back at the guys with the guns.

"They surely *wouldn't*," Harlow chuckled.

Frankie walked over to them and put their drinks on their table. "Cola-Red, and another Cola-Red. And then some water."

Harlow got Frankie down so she could whisper to them. As Harlow pointed out the window, Frankie's eyes narrowed with anger and frustration that was palpable.

Frankie nodded. "They usually always have guns. I know you haven't been here for a bit but, they won't do anything. You can leave if you want, but they won't do anything," Frankie sighed.

Cali had a gut feeling they should leave, but Ray was already getting up with her Cola-Red. Harlow nodded at Frankie in an apologetic way and got up.

"Yes, you can have that for free," Frankie said. "Have a nice day."

"You too." Harlow prodded Cali to get up. "Let's get going."

Cali nodded and sheepishly made her way toward the exit. As they stepped outside, Cali looked at the protesters. The armed ones were talking to each other and pointing at the restaurant, planning who knows what? Cali felt nauseous, but kept her head up and continued walking.

"Scary stuff," Ray said, taking a sip from her Cola-Red. "Like Frankie said, it'll be fine. It seems like Frankie knows what they're talking about."

Cali and Harlow nodded.

"I just really hope they're right." Harlow looked down and shrugged. "I'd feel horrible if those idiots did something and we weren't there to help."

"Okay, Ms. Super Woman," Ray laughed. There was a twinge of nervousness that overtook the sarcasm by just a hair.

Harlow laughed, also with a little nervousness.

Cali stared at the sky, uneasy. She couldn't help but feel super horrible; something would happen before the black engulfed the orange the sky. Before the stars came out, those people would be up there with the stars.

"You want to come to my house?" Ray offered.

Harlow nodded and looked down at Cali. "Would you want to come?"

Cali shrugged. Harlow and Ray were still like complete strangers to her. *Why would she go to Ray's house?*

"Look, Cali," Ray laughed. "I know what you're going to say, 'oh I don't know you guys well enough, and you are complete strangers!'" Ray said in a mocking tone. "We won't be complete strangers if you just let us get to know you."

Harlow nodded in agreement.

Cali sighed in annoyance, hating that Ray was completely right. "Fine."

"Awesome," Ray said, again sipping her Cola-red.

As the three arrived at Ray's house, Cali couldn't help but notice how poor it looked. It wasn't *that* bad, but it wasn't what Cali expected. She thought Ray's house would be nicer. The house was a sickly white with grungy, dirty windows with dead flies on them. The roof was slightly damaged, probably from a storm or something. The paint was chipped and falling off, revealing the wood underneath. The door was white also. It was more damaged than anything, and looked like it had been beaten and burned before.

Cali looked at Harlow, concerned.

Harlow's eyes had one message, *Be nice, Cali.*

Cali looked ahead of her to see Ray proudly holding the door open for them. "I know my house looks bad, but it's not bad on the inside."

Ray was right; the inside was clean. "I do this all myself, so tell me if I missed a spot. No one is ever home, so I don't exactly have to clean for anyone. Oh! But I do clean for my birds!"

The walls were a pale grey. They were also stained, but other than that, they looked like they were precisely cleaned, like the rest of the house, just like Ray said. They seemed to be in the living room by its looks, and the kitchen was in the next room. The living room was small; smaller than Cali's. The couch and recliner were scratched up and torn by who knows what. It sounded like Ray had only birds.

"Do you have any siblings?"

Ray shook her head. "No, I'm an only child."

There was a brick fireplace in front of the couch with a decent size TV above it. Over on the right was an old recliner. The coffee table stranded in the middle of the two things was chipped and looked ancient. There were water marks from leftover bottles spread out all over the table, engraved there forever. The carpet was fine, except for some stains. *Why do I even care? It's not my house.*

"I can show you my birds if you want!"

Ray started down a long hallway. The two followed behind her as she walked behind a staircase. There was a small storage room behind it. There, she grabbed the bird cage and valiantly showed them to Cali and Harlow. One of the birds was white and stood boldly like the fluorescent purple on its chest and tail.

The other was white with yellow on its chest and tail. This one was standing more cowardly, it was the furthest down the cage, supposedly trying to hide from the world.

"This is Ace!" She pointed to the purple one. It had its head tilted to look at them. Cali thought it was hilarious that they had to do that. "And this," Ray pointed to the yellow one, it jumped and screeched and feathers went everywhere, "this is Jett."

"Are they yours?" Harlow asked. She got closer to the cage to look, which scared Jett.

Ray opened the cage to grab Ace who, without hesitation, jumped right onto Ray's finger. "They're my dad's. But since he's never home, I kind of got stuck taking care of them." Ray pet Ace with her other index finger. "I don't mind at all though, I love these guys."

"Your parents are never home, either?" Cali bit her tongue, regretting revealing that. *It was a horrible question to ask. Why did I do that?*

Ray cocked her head. "Well, parent. I don't have a mother, *hah*."

Cali felt horrible and looked down.

"Oh, don't worry, Cali, I've gotten over it." The pain in Ray's eyes said otherwise.

Harlow interrupted, "How did you get them to behave so properly?"

"Well—" Ray was cut off by loud police sirens. Harlow and Ray looked at each other, petrified and frozen with concern and fear. Cali looked at both of them, *weren't those just police sirens? It surely wasn't anything bad.*

Ray put Ace back in his cage, quickly slammed it shut, and ran to the front door. Harlow followed behind. Cali looked at the parakeets. They were concerned too, even Ace. Something was wrong.

Cali turned and joined Harlow and Ray at the front door. Ray was hanging out the door and staring at the far East side of the city. She had her hand on her forehead, as if that would help her see through the dark night sky. Harlow was on the porch, squinting and looking out as far as she could. Cali stood beside Ray, wanting to ask what was happening, but feeling too awkward to do so. The eerie, distant howl of police sirens didn't sit well in her stomach. A slight breeze slapped Cali in the face, and it was cold. Super cold. Cali could see Harlow was shaken by it, but not Ray.

"Cali, I need you to get my binoculars. They're in my room upstairs. Go down the hall and it's the one by the window on the left. We'll be on the roof."

Ray walked down the stairs and jutted her head towards a shed with a ladder by it. Cali nodded and walked back inside. She did what Ray told her to do without hesitation.

Ray's room was small, smaller than Cali's at least. There was a small blue area rug on the floor. Just like the whole house, her room was clean, only she hadn't made the bed in the morning. Her bed was barely an inch off the floor. *There was that cold breeze again.* Cali looked around and noticed the open window, so she looked out of the window. She could see Ray on the roof of the shed and Harlow stumbling on the ladder. Ray looked up at Cali.

"It's in my desk," she called.

Cali nodded, closed the window, and spotted Ray's desk. It was almost like Cali's desk, except it was brown and didn't have a ton of art supplies. There were mostly notebooks and schoolbooks piled onto the desk. She looked through the drawers and found the binoculars. She grabbed them and went back to the window, opened it, and called out to Ray. She then pointed at the binoculars. Ray held up a thumbs up and went back to helping Harlow.

Cali went back downstairs and outside. Harlow was very scared of heights; she was clinging onto the shed. Ray looked down at Cali and waved her up. Once she was on the shed, Ray kicked Harlow to get her to toughen up.

"C'mon, we aren't even on the roof yet."

Harlow looked like she would cry but nodded. Ray got up and walked over to a spot where the roof was about three and a half feet off of the ground. Ray lifted herself up and peered down at Cali. "Do you need help?"

Cali shook her head and lifted herself up. Ray looked at Harlow, who still clung to the ground.

"Harlow."

Harlow looked up and crawled. It was a few seconds before they finally got Harlow on the roof.

"Okay, now to the top."

STOLEN

Cali followed Ray as she made her way up to the highest point of the roof. Cali looked beyond the houses to realize Ray did have the best house on this street. The tallest anyways. She could see the flashing lights of the police far in the distance. They couldn't hear the howl anymore. Ray held up her binoculars and scanned the area. She gasped. "They're at the Fox Den!" Ray seemed to choke on anxiety as she quickly looked to the side. "Goddamnit! I knew they were up to something!"

She threw the binoculars off the roof and slammed her head into her hands. She swore to herself as Harlow tried to calm her down, even though it looked as if Harlow was just as nervous. The binoculars collided with the ground and broke with a small shattering noise. A car whizzed down the street; it was a white news car. *Of course.* Ray stared it down.

"We have to go back there." She choked as she started crying. "We have to. Let's go. Now." Ray quickly scaled down the roof, the shed, and down to the ground. Cali followed more slowly, Harlow was the slowest, undoubtedly.

"C'mon hurry up!" Ray shouted to Harlow just as Cali's feet hit the ground. Harlow nodded and quickly got down the ladder. Ray huffed, turned, and started sprinting.

Before Cali got any further, Harlow stopped her. "It's too dangerous for us."

Cali stared at Harlow in confusion. "I thought you cared for those people?"

The three sat on that rugged couch from before, their eyes glued to the TV. "C'mon, it'll be here somewhere," Ray muttered through gritted teeth.

From Swallowsville news station in Central North Dakota, this is 10:00 p.m. news with Clarissa Holte.

There it was.

Tonight at 8:00 p.m., there was a shooting at the Fox Den. Two are dead, five are injured. We are still getting the story currently, but it seems that Frankie Boone protected most of their workers without a scratch. We'll go to Quinn on the scene.

Before the scene changed to Quinn, Ray turned off the TV and threw the remote to Harlow. It bounced around in Harlow's hands before she caught it.

"Now we know for sure that Frankie is safe, why don't we just watch something else?" Harlow said, relieved.

She turned the TV back on and switched the channel to something more . . . interesting. It was a woman giving the history on Swallowsville's welcome sign. "It was, *er, uh,* manufactured not too long ago, *uh,* well more than one hundred years, but you get the point."

Welcome to Swallowsville!

This was Swallowsville? Shootings? Death? This was nothing like her old town.

This was Hell.

This would be Hell.

CHAPTER 5

Cali woke up instantly to the screeching of her alarm clock. She slammed her hand down onto the off button, stared for a few seconds, then groaned and rolled over.

She didn't want to go to school today. The news never mentioned if the shooters were caught. They could be at the school. It was Monday now and the principal had cancelled school for a few days. God, she hated Swallowsville, she hadn't even been there that long, but she already saw the horrors of it.

Xife was awakened by the alarm as well, and stood at attention, knowing Cali had to get up for school. Cali sighed and sat up, still hesitating. Xife jumped off the bed and walked out of her room. Cali slid off her bed and walked over to her dream journal.

She had no dreams last night, thankfully not like the one before. She reread the dream from before. The silhouettes dying, fighting, and in pain. Then it finally hit Cali. The dream must have signified what she would go through in her time at Swallowsville. *But what about the gym stadium?*

She wrote her ideas down with a blue gel pen, circling things, underlining, but left the part about the stadium ignored. She would most likely find out later. There was something other than the stadium that confused her—the two main silhouettes who dug their stares into her. Again, she would probably find out. She'd just have to keep her eyes open.

She got ready, ate, and other stuff she usually did before school, and walked out the door.

Cali walked, waiting for Ray to come by and walk with her, but there was no sign of her. Maybe Ray was just late. She yawned, thinking to herself, *those two silhouettes . . . one had a ponytail, right? Could that be Harlow? No, the journal said it almost hit the ground. Harlow's was way shorter. What about the one with curly hair? She didn't know anyone with curly hair. Weird.* Cali walked by the bus stop, still lost in thought. Suddenly, someone grabbed her leg.

"RAH!"

Cali jumped and kicked the hand away. The person came out of the bushes, laughing. It was Ray. "Dang, you're ten minutes late, dude."

Cali glared at Ray. "I thought I was about to be killed."

"For thinking you were about to be killed, you were awfully calm," Ray chuckled, wrapping her arm around Cali.

Cali pushed her away and continued to walk. "Do you *not* remember Wednesday?"

Ray's laughing stopped. She turned. Ray's eyes showed many emotions—pain, confusion, betrayal, defeat, anger, sorrow. How could someone feel so many emotions at once? Cali stared in curiosity, analyzing

Ray. Ray's eyes slowly stopped showing any emotion, she seemed too mentally numb. "Cali, I know you didn't mean that," she laughed.

Cali nodded. Ray walked beside her. Ray was eerily quiet, but she was smiling, the only emotion in her eyes was . . . *nothing*. There was nothing going on inside her head by the looks of it.

"Are you okay?" Cali asked. Cali was genuinely curious. Not concerned, but simply curious. She did this to Ray. Not Ray, it was Cali's fault, and that's how Ray reacted.

Ray nodded, smiling. "To answer your question, yes. I do remember what happened, Cali. In fact, I was up almost all-night last night. They never found the shooters, by the way."

Cali raised her eyebrows. "What? How?"

"They fled the scene," Ray said, "but they got descriptions. They are high school students."

Cali felt her heart drop and stopped in her tracks. "High school students? So they go to our high school?"

Ray nodded, frowning, then teared up. "I'm kind of afraid, honestly." She crossed and rubbed her arms.

Cali nodded in agreement. "I'm sure it will be fine."

By the time they got to school, everyone was already at their homeroom classes, despite it being pretty early.

"No one's out here."

The places where kids would usually hang out were completely deserted like, the trees, picnic tables, the rocks, and the statues.

"Let's just get to Mr. Array's class," Cali muttered and started speed-walking.

Once they got to class, everyone was already seated, and Mr. Array was trying to calm everybody down. But to no avail, the poor guy couldn't. He greeted Ray and Cali as they sat down.

"Sheesh. Clearly everyone heard about it," Ray complained.

"Guys, class, guys," Mr. Array still desperately tried to get the class under control and, failing, tried his only other option: slamming a book on the floor. That made everybody jump, including Cali, who already saw it was going to happen. *Perhaps that wasn't the best choice.*

"Okay, now that I have your attention, Mr. Overs wants to have a school assembly about . . . well you all can guess what about." He looked down sadly, then brought his head back up. "Once I take attendance, you all can head to the top gym." He smiled and gave a thumbs-up. "Now, when I call your name, I'll need you to say your name, please."

Cali looked over at Ray. Ray shrugged.

After Mr. Array was finished taking attendance, he got up from his desk and allowed kids to leave, row by row. Once he got to Ray and Cali's row, which was the last one, they followed each other closely.

"Where is the 'top' gym?" Cali looked over at Ray, who was trying to see through the taller people.

"The top floor, I thought I told you where the gyms were," Ray muttered, annoyed.

She wasn't annoyed with Cali, just the fact she was under average height in the school. But Cali didn't realize that and looked away, angry and then sighed.

Ray looked at Cali. "Are you mad at me?" Ray raised her eyebrows. "Did I say something wrong?"

"You're annoyed with me, I can see." Cali cocked her head, squinting.

"*Eh*? What? No, I'm just mad that I can't SEE THROUGH ANYONE!" She shoved a kid aside, grabbed Cali's arm, and advanced through the crowd.

Whoa. Those are some anger issues.

Cali glanced around nervously as Ray pulled her upstairs and through some hallways. They finally got to the gym. It was the largest school gym Cali had ever seen. It was like the size of her entire "old" school.

"Let's sit there." Ray pointed to an empty spot. She yanked Cali's arm and ran over. They sat down and peered at the desolate microphone in the middle. More kids started to pile into the gym, and the empty area around Ray and Cali filled, getting more cramped and claustrophobic.

"So," Ray turned to Cali. "What's your favorite color?"

Cali blinked, thinking Ray was joking. Ray raised her eyebrows, waiting for a response.

"Purple."

"Cool. I like red and black."

"Why do you ask?"

"I'm bad at starting conversations."

"What? Bad?" Cali snorted. "You're the one who always starts them."

"*Hm.*" Ray chuckled.

The ear-piercing screech of the microphone and speakers caught Cali and Ray's attention. A tall, athletic guy with sharp, slicked-back hair scanned the crowd with an icy glare. "I'm sure you all know what this assembly is about." He cleared his throat. "It's about what happened at the Fox Den last Wednesday. I want you all to feel safe in this school, that is my utmost priority. I would feel absolutely horrible if something were to happen to a student."

Ray nudged Cali. "That's the principal. He's really intimidating. I've been in his office a couple of times, *hah.*"

Cali nodded and looked back at him.

"THE SHOOTERS ARE IN THE BUILDING RIGHT NOW!" A kid yelled.

Everyone looked around but couldn't exactly find the person who yelled.

The principal sighed, "Yes, sadly, they are. We are trying our best to match the descriptions to people, but almost everyone in this school looks like the description—average height, white male with little facial hair and brown hair. Look around. How many people do you see that fit that description? A lot. So please, if you know anything, tell us. We want everyone to be safe in this school. Oh, by the way, we are defunding the drama club. The room will be made into something else."

A roar of disapproval came from a ton of kids. The principal wasn't fazed.

"I know, I know. A lot of you will be mad about it, but look on the bright side; you will now have another useful room."

Another roar came from the crowd. "What do you mean *useful*? Was it not useful before?" Someone yelled.

Ray turned to the person. "I feel you. The 'C team' doesn't get that much respect either. I hope you guys can find somewhere else."

The person glared at Ray with the dirtiest, angriest look Cali had ever seen. "At least you stupid jocks get to go somewhere! Honestly, drama is more important than athletics! What do you watch on TV? *Hm*?"

"I was just trying to say that I feel bad and that I understand. Sorry," Ray scoffed. "That's right." Ray rolled her eyes. "Maybe they should have the room taken away."

"You just said you understood them, Ray."

"Whatever. If they're going to be like that I don't care." Ray leaned forward and rested her arms on her legs.

"How badly does the 'C team' get disrespected?" Cali asked, cocking her head.

"Well, you saw our locker rooms." Ray looked at Cali. "It gets way worse, though. I don't know why they think they're so high and mighty. All they can do different is dribble a ball in different ways," she laughed.

Cali nodded, now entertained by Ray's little rant.

"Mostly, if Talivikki likes you, you're on the team. She plays to win and to get kids to higher places, like college basketball."

"Doesn't every coach do that?" Cali scoffed. *Who's Talivikki?* Cali wondered. *Most likely the coach. Hmm.*

"You'd be surprised. See, I *do* want to play college basketball, but the way it's looking currently, I may not get the chance, *hah*." Ray looked down. "Cola Woman really doesn't coach for anyone but herself. The school pays her well."

"Who's Talivikki?"

"*Eh*, she's this . . . intimidating, 6'5", blonde, Norwegian woman. She's the varsity coach. She hates me, *hah*. Everyone is scared of her. I don't know if varsity is scared of her, you know, since they know her personally. I'd be scared of her as a coach, though. She works them super hard."

Cali nodded.

"We will be changing the drama room into a meeting room. You guys can either use the bottom gym or go somewhere else," the principal announced over the shouting.

The gym went silent for a few seconds. Ray was the one to break the silence.

"WHAT?" Ray seemed to be the only one angry about it. Where were the other basketball players?

The person that Ray had fought before laughed. "See?"

"Oh, shut up. You'll have to fight for it over our dead bodies," Ray grumbled.

"Sure." The person laughed.

"We have the advantage."

"I do martial arts."

"Shoot."

This casual interaction was . . . strange. They weren't angry. It seemed like they were just joking around. *Were they friends? No, they would be calling each other by names. How did Ray talk to random people like that? Well, they were mad a few seconds a go, but that anger seemed to die out.*

This person was smaller, maybe 4'10", shorter than Cali at least. They had blonde hair with blue highlights. Their hair was straight. Dang, not what Cali was looking for. The hair needed to be curly or have a super long ponytail. Cali paid no attention to Ray and the person's "argument" anymore, she didn't need to, she had no reason.

Cali was very analytical; she had no true friends, so she didn't know how to care for others. She had to read the emotions of others around her to know when she was about to get insults—or punches—thrown at her. She knew what body language was aggressive and what body language was neutral. But Ray was different. Ray had so many emotions going on in her head at once that Cali couldn't tell what she was feeling. The only emotion Cali could identify was Ray's pain. That was the strongest one, at least, next to her energy. *Weird.* She looked over at Ray. Ray was still speaking to that person, seemingly happy. But there was just a weird look in her eyes that Cali couldn't shake. They were so . . . distant.

"That's really all I have to say. Have a good day, students." The principal turned off the microphone and walked off the gym floor.

"Is that all he ended with?" Ray asked, holding out her hand. She looked over at Cali. "He's just going to ignore it?"

Cali shrugged.

"*Ah*." Ray nodded. She turned to the person again. "I'll see you at the duel," Ray chuckled.

The person nodded, got up, and walked away. Ray and Cali got up and tried to leave along with them, but they got stuck in the crowd of kids.

"Again?" Ray muttered, gritting her teeth.

"Don't think about pushing anyone down the bleachers," Cali said, concern hanging in her voice.

"I might have to if no one moves."

"Don't."

After a while, they finally made their way to the gym floor. Ray looked at her phone. "It's 9:30. I'd say we'd just skip the rest of Mr. Array's class since we are already put in as 'there.'"

"That's not very *good*, Ray," Cali said.

"So?"

Cali rolled her eyes.

"Okay, goody two-shoes. *You* can go to class, but *I'll* be hanging out in the bathrooms."

Cali sighed. "Fine, I'll go with you."
"Great." Ray smiled.

Cali looked around the bathroom. It was empty except for Ray and Cali. Ray sat on the sinks and rested her back on the wall behind her.

"Dang. We have practice today. I wanted to go home and rest." Ray looked at Cali. "What do you think about basketball so far?"

"You've asked me this so many times," Cali replied, leaning on the sinks.

"Yeah, but you only answer, 'I don't know.'" Ray chuckled.

"Well, I *don't* know. I've only had one practice."

"True, but you're really good at basketball for a 'first-timer.'" Ray looked down at Cali.

"So, was that actually your first time or did someone teach you?"

My brother. That's what Cali wanted to say, but what if Ray used it against her later? She didn't trust the strange look in Ray's eyes. She trusted Ray not to hurt her physically, the notebook in her brain had checked off Ray's "physical threats," but not the "emotional threats." Ray was none of those traits that were check marked, but neither was she any of the "good" ones either. Ray wasn't normal in Cali's eyes.

"*Uh*, are you just going to stand there and stare?" Ray snapped her fingers and waved.

"I guess I'm just a natural."

"No natural I've ever been around has been that good without help. There's limits, Cali, limits." Ray squinted. "Is there something you are not telling me?"

"I guess I'm different."

"Cali," Ray laughed, "I know you're lying, and I'll get the truth out of you one way or another."

Cali stared back blankly.

"Don't look at me like that," Ray nervously chuckled. "Okay, maybe you're not lying. Sorry. It's just, I'm . . ." Ray looked for the right word, "impressed."

"Oh," Cali muttered.

"Flattered?"

Cali glared. "No, I really don't care. You can believe what you want to believe."

Ray rolled her eyes. "You were taught. Why don't you want to tell me?" Ray looked up as the bell rang. "Shoot. You'll tell me at practice, okay?" She hopped off the sink and walked out.

"No, I won't!" Cali said in an annoyed, sing-song-y voice.

Ray scoffed as she walked out. "See you at practice, and in English and Geography!"

Cali looked into the mirror. Ray would never know that Cali's brother existed. She would never be hurt again. Her cold, dead heart would never be harmed again. She knew what Ray would do. Get the information and then spread it around like wildfire. She slammed her hands onto the sink in frustration. *Why did the world treat her like this? Ray was trying to gain her trust to hurt her. But was Ray really trying to do that?* In Cali's mental notebook, Ray was *technically* innocent. She would just be excessively cautious.

Ray and Cali were supposed to meet up at the fountain in the middle of the school, the one between the two main staircases. They'd planned to do that in geography. Cali was there, Ray wasn't. Ray was probably talking to random people again. Cali sighed and sat on the fountain, going on her phone. She put one earbud in and waited for Ray to arrive. Cali then heard heavy footsteps. They were definitely not Ray's. She took the one earbud out and looked around.

Out of a hallway came a tall, blonde woman wearing a thick winter coat over sweatpants. Her clunky boots were making the heavy footsteps. Her blonde hair was up in a tight bun. She was clearly not a student, and looked to be about forty-five years old. Her eyes were glued to the ground. They were cold and serious. She was thinking. She walked past Cali on her way to the stairs when she stopped and looked at Cali.

"Who are you?" She had a very monotone voice, the scary kind of monotone. Her icy blue eyes drilled into Cali, threatening. They had a sinister background that Cali really didn't want to know. *Who knows what she could have been thinking about? Did she kill someone?*

"Cali," Cali said, nervously shifting herself. She put down her phone.

"*Hm.* Cali who?"

"Horn. Cali Horn."

"I've never heard of you before." She walked over to Cali and looked down. "Do you play basketball?"

"Yeah." Cali anxiously glanced away. "I'm on the 'C team'." This woman was checking off every red flag in her head. *And why was the air so cold around her?*

"Awesome. Maybe I'll see you in a few years," she laughed, before walking away, with her hands behind her back.

Cali watched her leave. She walked slowly, with a slight limp. *What happened to her ankle?* She was hurt.

Once the woman was out of sight, Ray, who had appeared silently and out of nowhere, grabbed Cali's arms and shook her. "Did you just talk to that woman?"

Cali nodded as Ray continued to shake her.

"*HAH?* WHAT?" Ray seemed either excited, scared, or concerned.

"Yes, I spoke to her!"

Cali grabbed Ray's wrists.

"And stop shaking me."

"You did?" Ray chuckled in an excited-nervous tone. "Do you know who that woman is?"

"No?"

"That was Talivikki!" Ray got right in Cali's face. "You know, the scary varsity coach I told you about!"

"Oh," Cali said, remembering.

"*Haha*! That's great!" Ray let go of Cali and stepped back a bit. "You should be glad she talked to you! That's so cool! She never talks to people!"

"Well, I was the only one out here." Cali got up, putting her phone in her pocket.

"No, you don't understand, dude!" Ray sighed. "Whatever, you will." Ray started walking. "Let's get to practice. The team will have to hear about this."

They walked down the hall under the stairs. It was the hallway most filled with posters, art, and other things.

Ray was overjoyed, she was speed-walking, ready to tell the first person she saw about what happened. *Just like she would do if she found out about my brother,* Cali thought. She sighed.

Once they got to the locker rooms, Ray slammed open the door, scaring everyone inside.

"Why?" Piper grumbled.

"Someone had a bad day." Ray laughed as she poked Piper in the arm. "*Hm*?"

Piper slapped her hand away. "Stop."

"So, you did?" Ray laughed.

"Ray, I'd leave Piper alone. She had a rough day. Her sister kept getting college scholarships," Sienna mumbled as she put her shirt on.

Piper punched her locker. "She said we would go to varsity together! She's a little, betraying, backstabbing baby!"

Ray blinked. "Well, anyway . . ." She looked around at everyone in the locker room. "Guess what happened to Cali." Ray wrapped her arm around her, even after the many warnings Cali had given her. Everyone raised their eyebrows.

"What happened?" Eliza asked, looking at the two through the mirror.

"Talivikki spoke to her." Ray smiled.

Everyone was dead silent. They all looked at each other, not knowing what to say.

"YOU'RE TELLING *ME* THAT THIS LOWLIFE WAS SPOKEN TO BUT NOT *ME*?" Piper pulled her braids in anger as hard as she could. "NO ONE EVEN KNOWS WHO YOU ARE!"

"Piper, chill," Ray said, amused.

"*GAH!*" Piper suddenly flung herself at Cali as hard as she could, her arms out and everything. Cali's quick reactions kicked in. Cali stepped to the side, grabbed Piper's left arm, spun, and sent her flying into the lockers. She was so small and light! Piper hit the lockers hard and hit the ground even harder. Cali stood there, staring, wondering what even happened. She could feel everyone staring at her.

"*Whoa!* New girl got some *fight* in her," Justice remarked, entertained.

Piper helped herself up using the bench. As she lifted her head, she gave Cali a death glare. Piper hauled herself up off the bench, looking down at Cali. She was mad, she evidently would not stop until she hurt Cali.

Again, Piper flung herself at Cali. This time, Cali let Piper slam into her. They fought on the ground, Cali was bombarded with many punches, which she took like a warrior. Cali let Piper get her frustration out before Cali kicked her off into the bench. Piper got up again, but Sienna grabbed her.

"Are you two done?" she asked, sitting Piper on the bench.

"*Sheesh*. We need to stop fighting!"

"Yeah, we sure do." Justice turned to look at Mel while she pulled on her injured ear.

Mel just rolled her eyes.

"I still don't understand what I'm doing wrong, especially when this *nobody* comes out of nowhere and starts getting credit for things!" Piper whined.

"Who said she was getting credit for stuff?" Ray asked.

Piper got up and pointed at Cali. "Usually, when Talivikki talks to someone, they're practicing on varsity the next day!"

"Not true, Piper." Sienna sighed. "Keep your story straight. I understand you're mad but get *over* it already."

Piper scoffed, not daring to talk back to Sienna. Cali walked over to Ray while Piper continued to find something to complain about, and Sienna continued to shut her up. Ray and Cali spoke at last practice, and Cali claimed the locker next to Ray's. She opened the locker to find her stuff all surprisingly still there. She got ready with all the rest, and when Ray was ready, went out to the court with her.

"*Hm.* Cola Woman isn't here yet." Ray spun in a circle, scanning the court.

"*Eh*, probably getting a Cola," Eliza piped up from behind the two.

"Yeah," Ray laughed.

"What do we do while we're waiting?" Eliza asked.

Ray shrugged. "Well, I know you'll do whatever I do, so . . ." Ray muttered.

Eliza jokingly gasped. "No, really?"

Ray laughed, patting Eliza's shoulder. "So, *stop*."

Eliza frowned. The rest of the team came out onto the court.

"Dang. It usually doesn't take Coach this long to get out here," Sienna mumbled.

"Yeah, as many years as I've been here, she's never taken this long," Piper grumbled.

"Piper, literally no one cares."

Piper glared at Ray while Ray smiled smugly. "Why you little—" Piper's power-steps were interrupted by a call.

"Hey, guys." Everyone looked over to see Coach Milan with some random, tall girl . . . a girl with a profoundly long ponytail. *That was her. That was the silhouette.* The girl looked overly sad and was almost in tears. She had a triangular-shaped face with a skinny, slightly athletic build. That long ponytail was jet black and was brushed neatly. The girl also had freckles all over her pale face. In place of normal fingernails, she had sharp, black, menacing nails. They looked like they could cut through anything. Cali then noticed that she had small scars all over her arms, she must've been actively picking at her skin.

"ARE YOU KIDDING ME?" Piper screeched. Sienna slapped Piper over the head.

"This is Ruby Aurthur," Coach Milan said, gesturing to Ruby. "She was . . . kicked off varsity."

Cali looked at Ray. Ray's mouth was open in shock. Everyone was shocked.

"This was really unexpected . . . so, be nice to her."

"So, *why* were you kicked off varsity?" Eliza asked.

Ruby looked up, glaring at Eliza. Ruby had grey, cold, dead eyes. She was angry and looked as if she would pick Eliza off the Earth right there and then.

"*Eh hah* . . . never mind then, your majesty." Eliza backed up beside Ray.

Ruby raised an eyebrow.

Coach Milan looked disappointed. "C'mon, guys, she's human."

Ruby looked down again.

"Let's just start with layups right away."

Ruby nodded and went to grab a basketball. Everyone watched her like hungry hawks. Ruby turned and stared everyone down, confused. Ray shook her head and grabbed a ball.

"Sorry, Ruby, they're acting like they've never been around a varsity player."

"Because we haven't!" Piper yelled.

Ruby raised her eyebrows and slowly walked away to the basketball hoops.

"What about your sister, you nitwit?" Sienna said.

"You know what, I don't even care. Don't say anything."

"Guys. Practice," Coach Milan held up her Cola-Red, pointing it toward the baskets before taking a sip.

Ruby looked baffled.

Ray walked up to her. "I'm guessing this isn't as 'hard core' as your old practice, huh?"

Ruby glanced away and shot her basketball at the backboard. "I'm guessing you don't want to talk," Ray chuckled uncomfortably.

Ruby didn't look at her, she just continued shooting.

Cali walked up beside Ray. "Why are you trying to befriend her?"

"Well, she got kicked off the varsity and instantly got put to the stupid 'C team'. Who *wouldn't* feel bad?" Ray shook her head.

Ruby looked down at them and shrugged. She gave a slight thumbs up and shot a layup. Ruby clearly wanted to be left alone.

Cali leaned sideways to Ray, "She wants to be left alone."

Ray looked at Cali. "But I feel bad." Ray looked back at Ruby, who was trying to ignore them both.

"Ruby." Ruby looked at Ray. "You don't mind if we stick around you, right?"

Ruby shrugged.

Coach Milan finally walked onto the court, surprisingly not holding her soda. "Okay, we better get working. By the way, Ruby, we don't exactly take ourselves seriously here. I only care if we lost by like . . . twenty."

"It's only happened three times!" Piper chimed in, crossing her arms and smiling smugly.

"Yeah. Those three were in a row. At the end of the season, too," Coach Milan muttered. "Anyway, let's start with layups."

During practice, Cali couldn't help but notice that Ruby was always pushing herself to the limit, even though she really didn't have too. Coach Milan tried to tell her she didn't have to work that hard, since she was now on the 'C team', but Ruby insisted that she would do what she wanted to do. Ruby stayed quiet the whole time while everyone else was having fun and messing around together. Ray tried to talk to her a couple of times but to no avail. Ruby didn't say a word. Ray, though, hung in there.

In the locker rooms after practice, Ray offered Ruby the locker next to Cali. Although Ruby already had her eyes set on that locker without even asking if someone was using it. She was lucky that it was an empty locker. Actually, Cali knew that the locker was *not* empty. Ruby already had her stuff in there—she must have been in there before practice started. Ruby looked around the locker room, obviously surprised that it was as disgusting as it was.

"Hey, Ruby," Ray said, looking right through Cali and at Ruby. Ruby was looking really annoyed with Ray. "Would you want to go to my house with Cali and me?"

Ruby shook her head.

Ray glanced away for a second. "You're kind of like Cali but way more independent." Ray nodded at Cali. "It didn't take me that long to get Cali to stick with me. She was dependent on me because I knew the layout of the school."

Ruby didn't care. She was independent and didn't need Ray to tell her. Cali didn't even understand what Ray's point was. She was just spewing nonsense.

"I'm trying to offer you some friends, so you don't feel lonely, Ruby."

Oh, Cali thought, *that's what she was getting at.*

Ruby shrugged and went back to her locker.

"Please, Ruby. Can you give us a chance?" Ray begged, her eyes glistening.

Ruby sighed and banged her head on her locker door. She seemed to understand that Ray would not stop. So she agreed.

Ray smiled. "See? You can befriend anyone if you annoy them enough! Just follow us to my house. It'll be fun, trust me."

Sienna walked up to Ruby. "I may as well introduce myself." *There went Sienna, trying to establish her dominance.* "I'm the main man here. You can just call me Sienna or, what they like to call me, Mama."

Ruby raised an eyebrow. Cali could see what she was wondering why she should even listen to Sienna.

Sienna's stare was intimidating, *always* intimidating, but it didn't seem to faze Ruby. She shrugged.

"What?" Sienna glanced around at the team.

Ruby stared blankly.

"I'm not going to be playing Charades."

Ruby held up a thumbs-up and left. Cali and Ray followed her out. Once they got out of the gym, Ruby gestured for Ray to lead the way.

"Do you ever speak?"

Ruby nodded and scratched her chin.

"Why don't you speak right now?"

Ruby shrugged and looked incredibly nervous. Cali looked at her arms again. They were scarred, picked over, all scabby. Some scabs were bleeding.

Cali pointed at Ruby's arms. "What happened to your arms?"

Ruby quickly untied the hoodie from around her waist and put it on. She held her hand up, as if to say "no" or "don't ask."

Cali nodded.

"Yeah, what's up with your arms? That's the first thing I noticed, other than your long ponytail," Ray asked innocently.

Ruby looked down sadly and sighed. She shook her head, looking at Cali.

"Don't ask about it, Ray," Cali said.

"Oh. Sorry about that, Ruby."

"Not the best first impression. I'm trying to be as respectful as I can."

Ruby nodded in understanding.

"Plus, once we get to my house, I have something to show you!"

"Is it your parakeets?" Cali asked.

"Well, don't ruin the surprise!"

CHAPTER 6

They all sat around the living room, each on different furniture. Ray laid back in an old recliner. Ruby rested her head on her hand while her elbow kept her up, Cali sat up straight on the couch, away from Ruby. They all were watching the news; it was Ray's choice. She still had not gotten over the Fox Den incident, and she didn't have to, but Ruby looked bothered and uneasy.

"So, Ruby," Ray sat up in her recliner, the back of it slowly rising behind her with that annoying buzzing noise. Ruby looked over at her, glancing at both the recliner and Ray. "Why were you truly kicked down from varsity?"

Ruby looked away for a second, slightly biting her knuckles. For the first time, Cali and Ray heard her speak. "I was replaced." Her voice was quiet but high-pitched, it was higher than Cali's voice, and Cali's voice was exceptionally high. Not the highest, though. Her voice had regret and sorrow hanging on each of those three words. Each one heavier than the next.

"Replaced?" Ray leaned forward. Cali stared in shock. "Well, what did you do?"

"I didn't do anything. I believe that I was a really good player, but there is someone who is always better than you."

"Who replaced you?"

Ruby put her hands behind her head and sighed, sinking into the couch. "Some girl named Keagan Perry." Ruby threw her hands out. "No one seems to know who she is! I get called to the office, and next thing I know, I'm face-to-face with my replacement!"

"Who's that?"

"Exactly!" Ruby let her hands go limp and slammed them into her knees.

"*Hm*. I can tell you don't want to be on the 'C team'," Ray said, getting up. "What if we helped you get back onto varsity?"

"How would you even do that?" Ruby sat up, interested.

"Well, we could take her down." Ray laughed.

Cali raised her eyebrows. *Were they about to plan a murder right in front of her?*

"It could work." Ruby smiled. "Thanks."

"Wait, wait. You're not doing this alone, Cali and I are going to help you. Mostly because I need something to do, *hah*." Ray walked in front of the coffee table, looking down at the two.

"Ray, you're going to help a complete stranger? Really?" Cali muttered, getting up. "You need to stop trusting random people!"

"I trusted you, Cali. Why can't I trust Ruby?" Ray crossed her arms.

Cali hated that Ray was right, and it looked like she couldn't back out. She would have to suffer through this, even though this was strange and uncomfortable for her. Ruby was a stranger, but so was Ray.

Cali looked over at Ruby; she was more excited than a child on Christmas. Cali was suspicious of Ruby, the vibes she got from her were weird and strange. *Did Ray really compare her to Cali in her own head? Is this what Ray thought of Cali?*

"I'll show you what she looks like tomorrow, at lunch." Ruby got up, excited. "Here, we can plan at my house. It's actually not too far from here. Only a couple of blocks."

Ray nodded. "Of course!"

Cali took Ray aside. "Ray. I get bad vibes from her. We shouldn't go to her house. You have not even gone to mine yet," Cali yell-whispered, gripping Ray's shoulders.

"Cali. It's fine! You get bad vibes from literally *everything*. Plus, even if she was bad, everyone saw how you threw Piper. You're more than capable of defending yourself." Ray grabbed Cali's wrists and held them.

"Ray, please—" Cali pleaded as Ray walked right past her.

"Let's go!" Ray smiled.

"Great!" Ruby opened the door for Ray, who walked out eagerly. Ruby then looked down at Cali, her face suddenly serious. "I know you don't trust me, and that's fine. But we won't get along well if you suspect me all the time."

Cali sighed. "I don't care. I really don't; I just don't want to go into a random person's home and get killed."

Ruby squinted. "Maybe I *will* kill you."

Cali blinked in concern, shaking her head. "Excuse me?"

"Plus, I guess since I'm just like you. I could easily replace you then, right?" Ruby smiled and snickered. "I work quickly, and fast. I'm actually already doing my fast work. Ray is the perfect, gullible person to manipulate." Her grip tightened on the door handle. "So what I'm saying is, if you just trust me and help me, I won't do anything. Got it?"

Cali shook her head again. "No, that's not how it goes with me."

"Then how does it go? You know what I'll do and it's easy, honestly."

Cali hated that Ruby was right. She *did* need Ray. If she didn't, she would have no one, just like the past.

Cali sighed and nodded.

Ruby held the door wide open and held her hand out, gesturing her to go out. "Great!" She smiled.

Cali looked at Ruby nervously as they walked out together down the street. Cali was on the outside, almost stepping onto the street. She didn't listen to their conversation because she was too busy wondering if they both were about to be slaughtered. She had her arms crossed and her head down.

"Hey, Cali," Ray said. "What's your idea for Keagan?"

"I really don't know; we'll have to see," Cali muttered sarcastically, as she smiled at Ruby. Ruby stared at Cali with a cold, dead stare.

"*Hm.*"

"This is my house, guys." Ruby pointed at a big maroon house made out of brick. It had many windows, all with black shutters. The front door was made of bright wood with multicolored windows all over the top half of the door. There was a brick porch leading to the door with stairs protruding away from it. On the porch, three white pillars held up part of the roof. Coming from the porch was a brick walkway that stretched to the sidewalk. Ruby's house was on a corner, and the garage was on the right side of the house, though Cali couldn't see it that well; she could only see the front at the moment.

"*Whoa*," Ray uttered. "Your house is super nice!"

"Thank you." Ruby chuckled. "It's even nicer on the inside."

They walked up the sidewalk.

"There are some weird rules I have to tell you about. My dad is extremely strict about who I have over, so I'll have to sneak you guys in through the window."

Cali looked at Ray nervously, however, Ray was hungry for an adventure.

"Alright!" Ray laughed.

Cali had lost hope in Ray's intelligence at this point. Ruby led them through the yard, sneaking around the bushes to avoid the abundance of security cameras. "He's always watching them," Ruby informed.

They arrived at a window that was open a little. "This one doesn't have any alarms on it. He said he was sure that he put alarms on all of them, but I figured this one out pretty quickly. I'll climb in first."

Ruby opened the window fully and snuck inside. She then looked down at Ray and held out her hand. Ray grabbed it and was pulled up as easily as if she was a feather. Ruby then went back for Cali, but she ignored Ruby's help and got in by herself. Ruby gave a quick warning glance as Cali planted her feet.

"He's not home yet, so we don't have to be that careful. Just don't touch *anything*. He'll notice if something is out of place and check for fingerprints," Ruby uttered as she scaled the angled white stairs.

"Why is your dad so strict?" Ray asked.

"Well, long story. A gang of kids broke into our house years ago and beat my grandfather to death. We keep his ashes in his own bedroom, *hah*."

Ray blinked. "Oh."

"Yeah, that's the response I usually get." Ruby snickered.

"If you don't mind me asking, is there an exact reason why they killed your grandpa?" Ray asked hesitantly.

"He was at the wrong place at the wrong time. A group of kids saw him, saw that he looked a bit wealthy, and killed him. I've always wanted to get revenge on those people, but they're probably adults now."

"Oh, so you were young when this happened?"

Ruby opened her bedroom door. "No, actually, this was two years ago. I was your age. I'm guessing you two are freshmen. Fourteen, right?"

STOLEN

Cali and Ray nodded. "Yeah."

Ruby's room was ruby-themed. The walls were painted a soft red color, the desk was made of a reddish wood and had a black office chair. The rug was black and super fluffy. It looked like the same type that Cali had in her own room. The bed was centered in the middle of the wall on the north side and was red with black blankets.

"You seem to like red." Ray put her hands in her sweatpants pockets.

"Yeah. I do, I thought it went well with my name." Ruby walked over next to her desk and slammed her hand into a bulletin board. "Okay, let's get to work."

"Well, the only thing I can really think of is framing her for stuff. There's that Halloween dance, right? And the fall and winter festivals. We could do something then."

"I wonder if we could see what her grades are?"

"Oh, I have a friend who can probably get us in," Ray offered.

"No, that would be suspicious." Ruby leaned on her desk. "What if we stole a master key from a janitor? Oh, the fall festival is coming up! I have the *best* ideas ever!" Ruby put her hand on her face and smiled an evil grin.

Cali looked at Ray nervously, but Ray's eyes sparkled. Ray was taking all of this in. Cali sighed and crossed her arms.

"We could get into her grades, I could hook my laptop onto whatever there is, and we'll have it. I'll project it from my laptop!" Ruby laughed. "We just have to make sure it works. So, tomorrow after school, you two will steal a master key from one of the janitors!" Ruby pointed at them; her smile stretched the farthest it could go.

"Us?" Ray cocked her head. "How do you even do that?"

Ruby shrugged. "I mean, it's easy, we can go downtown, and I can show you."

"Excuse me," Cali butted in. "I'm not going to jail, Ruby."

"You won't get caught." Ruby glared. "Just trust me. I'll only steal from like two people."

Ray looked uneasy. "You really shouldn't, Ruby."

"Well, you want to help me take down Keagan, right?"

"Oh, of course, I do!" Ray nodded. "But, *stealing*?"

Ruby walked up to Ray, put both of her hands on her face and forced Ray to look up at her. "Then how will you know to steal that key?" Ruby stepped towards the door. "C'mon, let's go."

Ruby pulled her car onto a side street in downtown, right next to the children's toy store. Ruby scanned the area for a bit, looking for the perfect person to steal from. Ruby slowly opened the center console and pulled out a black mask. "*Hmm*" she purred, putting on the mask.

"What's that for?" Ray turned sideways and looked at Ruby in the mirror. Ruby was in the middle of stuffing her ponytail into the back of her shirt.

"People can't see you that well with a mask." Ruby looked back. "It works. Trust me." She smiled and pulled up her mask. "C'mon."

Ruby unlocked the doors and got out of the car, with Ray and Cali following. Ruby was already advancing toward a tall, older man. He was looking at some items on display in the toy store. Ruby just walked past him. That's what it looked like to Cali at least. Then she held out her left hand, showing a black, diamond raven brooch.

Ray smiled and pulled Cali close to her. "Whoa, it looked like she just walked past him," she yell-whispered.

Ruby waved them over.

Ray walked up to her. "How did you do that?"

"If you see if something is sticking out of their pocket, get as close as possible, and *bingo!*" Ruby flipped the raven and caught it mid-air. "You get cool things like this!"

Cali looked back at the man; he was frantically searching for what Cali assumed was the raven brooch. He looked at the ground, in a nearby metal trash can, on the counter, everywhere he could, but Cali knew he would never find it.

"Remember you have to do it right, or else you get caught. Since this is your first time, you *will* most definitely be caught. I'll give you guys my masks. It'll all be good. I have a fox mask and a butterfly. I have a sheep one that only I can use."

"I'll take the butterfly!" Ray shot her hand up quickly.

Ruby looked down at Cali. "Looks like you're wearing the fox mask, Cali." Ruby reached down and ruffled her hair. Cali pushed her away. "Now let's get going." Ruby pushed through them both, pushing Cali farther away and harder than Ray.

They walked back to her small, blue, *stupid* car. As Cali opened the car door, she turned. She saw someone all too familiar, but she couldn't put her finger on who they were. Her hair was styled in one big bun: the ponytail holder almost breaking. She had darker skin and was shorter, but taller than Cali. This person stood with one hand on her hip and the other on the back of their head; She looked nervous, concerned even.

"Cali, hurry up," Ruby growled.

Cali finally got into the car. Ruby was still admiring the raven, twisting it around to look at all of it. "This could be worth a lot of money. I doubt it's real, but . . ."

"How do you even sell it?" Ray asked.

Ruby pulled down her mask. "Just online. People love things like this. Shiny. People love shiny, children, especially. I once sold something for $2,000. It was great!"

"Why do you steal in the first place? It seems like you're pretty stable," Cali muttered.

"Well, it's fun and gets you hyped up on adrenaline." Ruby laughed. "Anyway, let's get going."

CHAPTER 7

Cali had no nightmares again, but she opened her dream journal and studied it. She wrote that she found Ruby, but not the curly-haired girl. Cali could guess it was Keagan, but she couldn't be sure. She wrote down *"Keagan Perry"* and circled it.

Cali laid back in her chair, putting her legs on her desk and crossing her arms. She was forced to help Ruby or else she would lose Ray. Ruby already had Ray wrapped around her little finger, and there was no way Cali could pry Ray away. She had to do this. Then maybe, Ruby would leave, forever. Or at least not be a part of their lives anymore. Cali didn't want to be around a criminal.

Keagan Perry.

How long had Ruby been on varsity? Did she even work hard or play well? Cali looked up at the ceiling. *Did Keagan actually deserve that spot? Maybe Harlow knew something.*

Cali wrote down another thing: *personalities*. Then she underlined it.

She started with Ruby, *a narcissistic, selfish, long ponytail wearing*—her pen ran out of ink. She sighed. *Maybe there was more to Ruby's personality? No. She was just a criminal. Nothing more.*

What about Ray?

Ray was energetic and friendly . . . *too* friendly really. She had horrible anger issues, but they didn't seem harmful in any way. What about the uneasy feeling Cali got when she looked in Ray's eyes? Cali was smart enough to know there was definitely something else going on with Ray. There had to be. Why else would she have a gut feeling? Cali knew to always trust her gut. She would be more careful around Ray.

Cali looked down at her pen. *"Who are YOU?"* She hated that question. People always asked her. Cali's answer was always, "Cali Horn." No one ever thought anything of this, she stopped thinking anything about it. She was right; she was Cali. She was a ticking time bomb of revenge, anger, and frustration. Everyone only thought of her as a moody teen. Sure, she *was*, but her hormones weren't the *only* thing guiding her anger. No one believed her, but she was fine with that.

Cali hated all that sappy, sad stuff. She hated to think about herself in such a horrible, demeaning way, so she pushed the thoughts away.

Cali looked at her alarm resting on the table next to her bed. It was time to get ready for school. She took one last look at the journal then got up to start the day.

The air felt cold. Something was different today. Like something had changed. *Oh, what did I get into?* The raven. *Ravens meant something, right?*

Cali looked to her left. Her brother's door was slightly ajar. Her mother must have been in there. Cali had not seen her mom for another night; she was working. She worked all day and came home late. Cali always refused to go into her brother's room, but the door was cracked open, inviting her in.

She opened the door slightly. Her mother must have sprayed his cologne; it was hanging heavily in the air. It almost stung Cali's nose, but she didn't mind; it reminded her of him, anyway. She was always surprised that the room had not been cleared since her father and Louie always fought over the most stupid things. Cali guessed that her father had regretted the fights. He would never admit the fights were wrong, but they hurt him. That's only what Cali thought; she had not seen her father in ages. She didn't even remember what he looked like.

I don't remember what my father looks like! Pathetic. That's pathetic! Her inner monologue seemed to yell at her. Cali covered her ears, somehow believing that doing so would quiet her mind.

She glanced around hopelessly as her mind insulted her more. She couldn't seem to stop it, no matter what she did. Cali sat on the floor and leaned against the wall. She stared down at her socks, zoning out completely and leaving the world around her. She was shutting down mentally. That's why she had not come into this room since December of last year. She would give anything for this room to be replaced. *Forgotten.*

Just like Ruby.

Ruby.

Cali laughed. Ruby had been replaced and longed for revenge. Now, Cali didn't entirely believe in ghosts, but the revenge of her brother seemed to linger in her. Before Louie passed, he was fighting with someone. Cali never knew who he was fighting with, but it was obvious. He also never told their parents, either. That's why Cali believed his death was murder. She would *always* believe it was a murder. Although that was the only thing to go off of—a fight.

What if she took her anger out on Keagan?

No, that's not what Cali wanted; she only wanted Ruby gone. After what seemed like hours, Cali stood up. She looked around the room. The walls had been freshly painted last month, and there were his favorite artists' new posters still all over the walls. Cali continued to look around, observing everything that was new. She looked over at the clock above Louie's bed and knew she would be late to school if she didn't get going.

Cali spun and ran out of the room, slamming the door behind her. She knew Ray would be waiting for her, and she was right. As she ran, she could see Ray and Ruby up ahead.

Cali stopped and stared. Ray was laughing as Ruby cracked jokes. It looked as if Ruby had some new necklaces, meaning she had been hard at work last night. Cali guessed she had sold the raven.

Ray waved her over, and Cali hesitated. Then she remembered she *had* to help Ruby for her to leave. Everything could then go back to normal. She approached them.

"Ray tells me that you always seem to be late, I didn't believe her at first. You seemed like the responsible one," Ruby sneered.

"I *am* responsible," Cali muttered. "You're the one who steals."

"I steal for a good reason, Cali." Ruby put her hand on Cali's right shoulder, then dug her nails into her skin. Cali winced.

"Then what's the reason?" Cali stepped on Ruby's foot, but Ruby didn't even react.

"I help others in need by stealing, but right now, I need the help of others. That's where you come in."

"Your answers don't even make sense," Cali yelled. "You can't justify it, so *stop!*"

Ruby laughed and looked at Ray. "Then why are you helping me?"

Ray cocked her head. "Yeah, you don't *absolutely* have to help Ruby, Cali."

Cali glanced at Ray. Ruby raised an eyebrow, amused. Cali was quite sure her shoulder was bleeding by now.

"You can't answer. You can't seem to figure out a reason to *not* help me, so stop complaining." Ruby released her grip on Cali's shoulder. As she pulled away, Cali saw that Ruby's sharp black nails were coated with a deep red. Ray grabbed Ruby's wrist and inspected her hand.

"Did you hurt Cali?"

Ruby immediately turned into a five-star actor.

"It was an accident! Are you okay, Cali?" Ruby looked at Cali's bleeding shoulder. She quickly gave her another scratch.

Cali winced again. "Yes, I'm okay."

"Then let's get going. We're going to be late," Ruby said in a matter-of-fact voice.

Ray was already turned away and walking ahead.

Ruby walked beside Cali. "Cali, look. I'm impressed by you, really. You really don't want to give in. I used to be like that."

Cali glanced away, trying to ignore her.

"Although I know that *you* know that you cannot win against me."

Cali sighed.

"Is that true?" Ruby smiled.

"Yes. I want to get rid of you."

"Harsh." Ruby patted Cali on the shoulder. "But you won't get rid of me. After I'm done, I'll be a part of your high school life for a while. I may not be your friend, but I will be there."

"So, you admit you're just using us."

"I thought that was obvious."

Cali stayed silent.

They caught up to Ray. "Dang, you guys are slow-pokes! We're going to be late!"

"Since when did you care about being on time?" Ruby chuckled.

Ruby slammed her hand down on the lunch table. "Keagan has been flaunting her 'victory' in my face this whole day!" Ruby slumped down into her seat.

"What did she do?" Ray bit her spoon.

"My friends from varsity said that she's been really cocky," she sighed.

"Well, we're going to get you back on varsity. You said you were going to show us what Keagan looked like; can you show us now, or . . .?"

Ruby got up. "Yes. Now."

Cali looked up. This was the first time she realized the cafeteria ceiling was two stories high; a second floor had railing on the outskirts of it.

"We're going to go up there."

Ray cringed. "I've never been up there before."

Ruby pulled her forcefully from her seat. "We're going up there."

Ray nodded and Ruby let her go.

"How do we even get up there?" Cali asked.

Ruby raised her eyebrow, surprised that Cali was doing what she wanted for once. "The stairs, then you take a turn down a hallway and *blah, blah, blah*, you're there."

Ruby turned and waved them to come with her. They walked through a single, bigger hallway. It was pure white with a tinge of yellow. There were glass-covered display cases on either side encasing many trophies, jerseys, and posters from over the years. Cali noticed the posters were about people. She stopped to read some. Ray did as well.

"So, this hall is basically a hall of fame?" Ray put both of her hands on the window.

"Not exactly." Ruby stopped and turned. "If you want to see the *real* hall of fame, you go to the third floor, and it's right in front of you. How did you *not* know that?"

"I don't have any classes on the third floor, so I never go up there, not even to see the varsity's gym," Ray said.

Cali turned. "Wait, so you've never seen the varsity's gym?"

Ray nodded. "This is my first year in this school, just like you. I've never seen the gym."

"Oh." Cali looked back at the poster. Boone. She did a double take. "Charles Boone."

Ray perked up and walked over. "Boone? I didn't know the family played sports."

Cali heard Ruby's feet tapping nervously, but ignored them. "How big is the family?"

"I thought all of the children were only-children." Ray scratched her chin.

"That's what I just assumed. This poster is pretty ripped. I'm surprised you even got 'Boone' out of it."

Ray was right. The poster was half ripped. You could only see half of the man's face, and some of the letters atop of Boone were ripped.

"Can we get going? We don't have all day." Ruby grabbed the two away from the glass. "This is called The Balcony, by the way."

Cali looked around. The fence had sharp, gold points glaring up at the ceiling. As Ruby said, it was like a royal balcony and stretched around the cafeteria. There was one other hallway on the left side; assumingly identical to the hallway the three just visited. Ruby leaned over the fence, with one hand on the flat part of the fence with the other over her forehead. Cali stood next to Ray and looked down over the sea of kids.

"So, what does she look like?" Ray asked.

"Tall, strawberry blonde, curly hair, white, glasses, freckles. She wears jean jackets a lot."

"Do you have this all written down?" Ray chuckled.

"Yes."

"Oh."

"There she is!" Ruby pointed at the crowd. "See her?"

Cali squinted. "Where?"

"The fifth table up, third table in. You should be able to figure out who it is based on the description I *just* gave you."

Cali looked down again, trying harder to find Keagan. Then she saw her. She was talking to some other girls, who Cali assumed were the varsity girls.

"The girls she is with are Olive and Erie. The most short-tempered girls on the team." Ruby slammed her hands down on the fence.

Cali couldn't see Keagan very well, but she at least had the idea in her head.

Ruby turned back to the two. "Remember, after practice, come to my car and I'll give you the masks. I left them at home since I didn't want them to sit in my cold car all day. I'll go home now to get them. I hope you remember how to get back to the main floor," Ruby scoffed and left.

Ray looked at Cali, who was still staring down at Keagan. "How are we going to break into the school?"

Cali shrugged. "Break a window?"

"No, that is too 'illegal,'" Ray chuckled.

"We're breaking into a school. It's illegal any way." Cali laid her head in her hand and rested her elbow on the fence.

"They won't close the school that quickly. The varsity will still probably be getting out of practice when we're there," Ray huffed.

"So, people other than the janitors will be there?"

Ray nodded. "Yeah, we have to be more careful then. Also, there are cameras." Ray pointed to a white camera staring down at them. A blinking red light let them know that they were being recorded.

"Talivikki is always in the office chatting with the principal. I guess their parents were friends. That's what I heard, at least."

"Did Talivikki even go to this school?"

"Oh, yes, she did. She did live in Norway until she was like five, probably. I have no clue. All I know is that she hurt her ankle and couldn't get into the WNBA. She became a high school coach and only got angrier." Ray snapped her fingers sarcastically.

"Oh, so is that why she has a limp?"

"Yeah." Ray messed with her ponytail. "You know those Norwegian Forest cats? She reminds me of those."

"What does that have to do with anything?" Cali shook her head.

"Absolutely nothing." Ray smiled.

The bell rang and all the students in the cafeteria returned to class. It looked almost suffocating from above.

Cali looked back at the camera. The red dot still lingered, and the black glass reflected a small version of Ray and Cali.

In the office, three people sat around a triangular desk.

"So, why did you pull me in here?" Ruby asked. She was annoyed and angry that she had been interrupted. She was putting on an act. The same one she had used to draw Ray and Cali closer.

"What are you planning this time?" Talivikki countered.

"What do you mean? What, I can't make friends now? *You* kicked me off varsity and then expect me not to talk to any of the team members? What am I supposed to do? Stay quiet?" Ruby sulked.

"It's your nature to be timid and shy, then use people for whatever you so desire." Talivikki pinched her nose bridge. "Just like you did with Harlow, and with whatever you're doing now."

"*Ah*, shoot, the jig is up," Ruby laughed sadly. "Plus, she did that to herself. She willingly gave me the money."

"Whatever you are planning, don't do it." The principal pointed at her, shifting it with every word.

"This one will bring attention to the school, I'm sure." Ruby grinned.

"Ruby—" the principal was cut off by Talivikki's *shushing*.

"No, attention? This school hasn't had any attention since I had my injury. That was about thirty years ago. This school needs attention."

The principal looked at Talivikki like she was crazy, and she was. "The Fox Den?"

"Seems like Talivikki is on my side!" Ruby snickered again.

"People have already moved on from the Fox Den." Talivikki nodded.

"So, we're going to let her do whatever she wants, just for a bit of *attention*?" The principal rubbed his eyes.

"We could use it. We could try." Talivikki looked back at Ruby.

"If you pull this off, I will let you back on the varsity. I will also put Ray and the other freshman on the 'B team'."

"REALLY? You're going to let me back on the varsity?" Ruby jumped from her seat.

"Yes."

"SWEET." Ruby quickly ran out of the office.

"Why were you being so hypocritical?" The principal rubbed his face.

"I don't entirely want her to know the plan. It seems like it's working well, though."

"Harlow?" Cali faced an enraged Harlow, who had dragged her aside on her way to class.

Cali winced as Harlow gripped her shoulders with great strength.

"Why are you hanging out with Ruby?" Harlow yell-whispered.

"I can't exactly say." Cali tried to hide her feelings of guilt.

Cali couldn't help but look down; Harlow's eyes flamed with anger. Harlow lowered her head closer to Cali's face. "You shouldn't be around someone like her. She's a horrible person!"

"I know, Harlow. I can see how horrible she is." Cali looked up and met Harlow's gaze. "I know what I'm doing. I'm going to help her so that she leaves us alone."

"No! You don't know what you're messing with, Cali! You're fourteen dealing with an almost eighteen-year-old! She already has you tied around her finger. She won't leave after you help her; she'll leech off you. You aren't as mature as you think you are, Cali."

Cali glared. "I've been through Hell and back."

"That doesn't make you mature. It just seemed to make you cold. You can't even take my criticism. Please listen to me! You're going to regret everything."

At Harlow's criticism, Cali tuned out. She knew fully what she was doing; Harlow didn't know what she had gone through. She *was* mature, more mature than Harlow, it seemed.

"Cali! Listen!" Harlow said, resigned and hopeless at Cali's brick wall of a personality. "You don't know what you're doing! She's a dangerous person! You can't change her!"

"I don't want to change her. I want her to leave us alone," Cali snorted.

"She won't leave you. Like I said, she will leech off you as much as she can, Cali," Harlow laughed, knowing she couldn't get through to Cali. "Don't come running to me for answers when you get yourself into legal trouble."

"Why didn't you talk to Ray first? You know her better!"

"I know Ray would just disagree with me the whole time, but I will talk to her," Harlow sighed. "She would disagree with me about Ruby being a horrible person. I thought you would agree with me because you don't know what you're getting into. I thought you were more emotionally intelligent. I guess not. You'll learn." Harlow let go of Cali and stood up, staring down at her. "Hopefully."

Harlow left, leaving Cali to drown in her own frustration and denial. Cali knew what she was doing. She was emotionally intelligent. She was Cali Horn. The girl that never spoke at the back of class, the girl who was always last to present, the one who was never applauded, the girl who lost her brother.

Practice was relatively uneventful. Ruby pushed herself to her full capacity. Ray and Eliza caused issues with Coach Milan. Piper, Mel, Justice, and Sienna bickered. Hayden, River, Cali, and Kimberly just *existed* in the background. Situation normal.

The team was trying to work on a play in preparation for their first game the following Thursday. Cali most likely wouldn't play, since she didn't have that many practices in. Ray told her it would be fine since "no one actually cares about the 'C team'."

Cali was leaning on the purple mat when Eliza came up to her. Eliza wore one of the red practice jerseys over her head. She pulled it down and put hands on her hips.

"So, Cali." She leaned against the mat. "Why were you with Ruby yesterday? You looked right at me."

"That was you?" Cali raised an eyebrow. "I couldn't tell."

"That sucks." She sighed. "Anyway, answer my question."

"We were out eating; Ray was with us as well." Cali glanced away.

"What? Eating from the dumpsters? I saw you guys coming from the alleyway!" Eliza dragged her hand down her face. "*Sheesh*, you're a bad liar."

"I'm not lying. We took a shortcut."

Eliza laughed, "The alleyways go from down the street to some apartments."

Cali stayed silent.

"Look, just tell me what you were doing. It's not that hard."

Cali looked behind Eliza to see Ruby staring directly at her. "It's really none of your business."

Eliza sighed, "I'll find out." Then she walked away.

Ruby came up to Cali and patted her on the head.

"Will you *not* do that?" Cali pushed Ruby's hand away.

"I'll do what I want," Ruby snickered. "I have the masks, by the way."

Cali and Ray stepped out into the parking lot. It was cold, and it was time for them to get the masks. Ray led the way, knowing where Ruby's car was.

"She said to me that she always parks in the same spot every day. The back-parking lot in the eighty-third row, third car in."

"How do you remember that?" Cali asked while pulling her beanie on.

"I have a pretty sharp memory," Ray chuckled and pointed ahead. Cali could see Ruby's car, although Cali could only see the front due to the fog.

"It looks like it might snow. It's cold! Hurry up!"

Finally, they got to Ruby's car. Ruby was sitting in the driver's seat on her phone. Ray slammed her hand down on the windshield. Ruby jumped and flipped off Ray.

"We don't have all day; it's cold," Ray yelled at Ruby.

"Yeah, I hear you. I have the masks here."

She pulled out the butterfly and fox masks. The butterfly was a bright red and the fox mask was made of red fox fur. "Don't wreck these. They're expensive."

Ray grabbed the red butterfly. "So, you didn't steal them?"

"I had to buy them first to steal something else. Then I moved to actual masks," Ruby muttered.

Cali put on the fox mask and noticed Ray struggling to put her hood on.

"Here." Ruby yanked on Ray's hood. "There, it wasn't that hard." She glanced over to Cali. "You don't look like you need help."

"I don't." Cali pulled her hood over her head and pulled the strings.

"Okay, I'll be out here waiting for you guys. Don't take too long. I've got to feed my goldfish."

"You have a goldfish?" Ray asked, cocking her head.

"Yes, so hurry up," Ruby said. "I'll be leaving after forty minutes. I hope you planned this."

"We didn't, but I'm sure it shouldn't take that long." Ray walked away and Cali followed.

"Remember, forty minutes, tops. Remember the security cameras. They'll be watching." Ruby closed the car door.

"Yeah, yeah, yeah." Ray cracked her neck.

"Can we start running? It's cold."

Ray then dashed off. Cali tried to catch up as much as she could. They stopped in front of the door. Cali glanced up nervously, having second thoughts about the whole thing. Ray seemed to have second thoughts as well.

Ray sheepishly opened the door, letting Cali go in first. The hallway was just as cold inside as the outside chill. Cali thought they would at least have the air conditioning on for the janitors and the varsity, but was wrong. The lights were off and the white light creeping in from the doors was the only light source they had.

Cali could see that the main room was far up ahead due to the light from the great windows that replaced the ceiling. The hallway had posters stuck everywhere along the walls, identical to any other hallway in the school.

"So, where to first?" Ray whispered.

"Why are you asking me?"

"Sorry, I'm freaked out." Ray glanced around. "After school has a weird, freakish vibe to it. It doesn't help that the lights are off!" Ray stuck her hand out.

"Then let's turn the lights on."

"You go first!"

Cali nodded and put one foot forward, then stopped.

"We don't have all day." Ray grabbed Cali's wrist and off they went.

"Where are we even going first?" Cali asked as Ray stopped and let go of her wrist.

"Well, the janitors probably finished our gym already. They probably haven't gotten to the 'B team's' gym." Ray scratched her neck. "I barely know the layout of this school and neither do you. They're also going to have to clean classrooms."

"How many janitors are there?" Cali asked while basking in the warm, blue sunlight from above.

"I have no clue. Maybe five?"

Something dropped on the other side of the staircase and the girls looked over.

"Someone's here," Cali hissed.

As they stood frozen, not knowing what to do next, the janitor grumbled as he picked up whatever he dropped.

"Up the stairs," Ray hissed back.

"Our footsteps!"

"Just run like you're running for your life!"

Ray shoved Cali forward and then took off. Cali chased after her, scaling the stairs faster than lightning. Ray practically threw herself at the floor at the top of the staircase. She looked back at Cali.

"We have to hide and think about this."

"But where?"

"Mr. Array's classroom." Ray nodded and waved her over. They anxiously walked down the hallway to Mr. Array's classroom. Ray stopped by the door and slowly opened it. "No one is here."

Cali followed Ray in. It was dark; it was *always* dark, but this time it was almost pitch-black, saved only by one small lamp in the corner that projected orange light. Cali felt comforted by it.

"I think we are safe here." Ray sat on the desk. "It looks like they already cleaned this place."

Cali sat next to her. "So, what's our plan?"

"I was hoping you would come up with it," Ray chuckled. "Maybe we could lead a janitor somewhere, throw something, then hide?"

Cali blinked. "I'm horrible at explaining," She sighed. "You know how the doors kind of dip, you know?"

"Yeah."

Cali pulled her mask off and put it on her lap. "We could hide in a 'dip,' throw something as a distraction, sneak up behind the janitor, and steal the key!"

"I'm kind of afraid, so you can steal the key."

Cali shook her head. "You're more nimble than I am. You could get away much faster."

"Ah, true. But remember how you threw Piper? You can throw whatever we choose." Ray took off her mask. "Let's just wing it. I want to sit in here for a second, though."

Cali nodded in agreement. She could hear the vents start and shut off; she could also hear the varsity in the distance. Cali turned to Ray. "We've only seen one janitor. There's probably one up here."

Ray nodded. "Oh, of course, there is. I'm ready now, let's go." Ray put her mask back on and grabbed a stapler off Mr. Array's desk. "This should do it."

"Ray, can we explore the third floor before we actually do this?" Cali peered up at Ray.

"Yeah, of course, that's where I was going to lead us to." She chuckled. "Put your mask on and let's go."

Ray poked her head through the door as Cali put her mask back on. "It's clear. Follow me."

Cali nodded at Ray and did as she was told.

They scaled the stairs, each being as quiet but quick as they could to not alert anyone.

"*Whoa,*" Ray stopped. "Cali, look at this!"

Cali stopped beside Ray and rested her eyes on the grandest Hall of Fame in the school. It was white with one big portrait in the middle flanked by two medium-size portraits, and other smaller ones following along the wall. The lights were still on and lit up the main portrait with a mighty, holy white light. On the outskirts were green plants that looked as if they had just been watered. Small pink and white flowers poked out from the leafy green plant.

"Who's the main one?"

Ray and Cali stepped forward.

"Jeffery Ajorne." Cali's eyes skimmed across the golden plaque. "The founder of this school, it looks like."

"I think I've heard the name before. The family now owns a huge business or something. I don't know. Nothing too important to us." Ray looked at the person on the right. "There's Talivikki when she was younger, the person on the left was her coach. He died a few years ago in a car accident. It was really strange, I heard. They say he was spectacular at driving buses. One story I heard is that he drove Talivikki and her old team through a blizzard."

Cali looked down at the mention of a car accident.

"They say you wouldn't expect someone like him to crash." Ray glanced over at Cali and did a double take; she removed her hands from her pockets. "You good?"

"Oh, yes." Cali looked at the other portraits. "I don't think we have time to look at the others. They don't seem to be as important."

"Right." Ray glimpsed around. "I don't see any janitors . . . oh no!" Ray gripped Cali's shoulder. "The cameras are *on*," she hissed fearfully.

Cali felt her heart drop. The red light was on as well. Just before Ray pulled her into a hallway, she could've sworn she saw the camera swivel, tracking them.

"I hear basketballs down here." Cali could see Ray smile behind her mask. "The varsity must be down this hall!"

Up ahead, there was a large dip, and the sound of basketballs got louder. The doors were just like the 'C team' doors, although the varsity doors were cared for. It seemed as if they had been changed not too long ago. That was most likely going to be the only similarity to them, the doors to the gym.

Ray looked through the square window. "They're conditioning, it looks like." Ray nodded her head at Cali. "Come here and look. I think I can see Keagan, and dang she is fast."

Cali stood on her toes and peered in. They were all tall, all seven of them. Cali saw Keagan at a good angle for the first time. She was taller than Ruby by a couple of inches, but still under 6'0". She had a short golden, strawberry blonde ponytail that flowed gracefully as she ran. She seemed so perfect; no wonder Ruby had been replaced.

"That redhead there is Delilah." Ray put her finger on the glass for emphasis, as if it would help. "That is Piper's sister, her twin. The one she always complains about."

Cali nodded. Delilah looked almost just like Piper, except she seemed to be able to keep her composure. She was tall, but the shortest girl on the team at the same time.

Talivikki stood up tall like a bold statue. She was leaning to the left like always. She had on a white tank top with her big grey coat acting like some kind of cape.

"Talivikki just gives me shivers," Ray commented.

"Same." Cali stopped looking. "We should probably plan where we are going to go."

"Well, it seems like there is a classroom over there." Ray pointed to a door. "We could hide in the classroom, wait for the varsity to get out, camp in the dip, and do our plan." Ray held up the stapler. "I got this puppy right here." She smiled through her mask.

The door suddenly burst open, forcing Cali to smack into Ray. A tall girl with smooth, dark skin, navy blue hair, and glasses stood in front of them. She turned, showing her bull-like nose ring that was very fitting for her mood. Cali recalled seeing her by Keagan in the lunchroom.

The girl frowned upon seeing two. She snorted, "Drama kids."

Ray laughed and stepped forward. "We ain't no drama kids, and even if we were, I love the drama kids and there isn't anythin' wrong with that." Ray's country accent showed.

"I don't have time for this," she uttered and walked on proudly.

"Something tells me she isn't too happy, *hm*?" Ray chuckled. "If she came out, that means there's more coming," she said, prodding Cali to move. "Go! Go!"

Cali opened the classroom. Her eyes rested on a table in the middle that emitted a dim light. Cali could see desks forming a semi-circle around the table.

"I don't like this place," Ray muttered. "Look atop the cabinets."

The cabinets had little lights beneath that only showed terrifying, preserved faces. They looked like household pets, some were marine animals, some were weird birds Cali couldn't name. There was one that wasn't on a cabinet but was in the corner. It looked to be a great grey wolf. Its sharp fangs threatened Cali even in its afterlife.

Cali turned her head at the sound of Ray gasping. She was looking down at the table. Cali stopped beside her. Inside, there was a human skeleton resting on a giant light. "This isn't real, Ray."

"Of course, it isn't!" Ray turned. "I hope I don't take this class next year or something."

"I think it's a science class. AP Science?" Cali shrugged.

"Oh, I'm not doing AP Science, *hah.*" Ray stepped toward the door. "We should start listening." Ray put her head on the door, only the mask got in the way. "Goddamnit." She tore the mask off and threw it onto the floor.

Cali waited patiently for Ray to say something. She looked around again. *Would she be in this classroom? What would happen after they helped Ruby out? Would life go back to normal and be boring?*

"I don't hear anyone." Ray turned, picking up her mask. "They must be done." She cracked open the door and peeked outside. "Lights are off. Time to wait in the dip."

Ray and Cali hid on the left side of the dip, partially hidden by the door; Ray was more hidden than Cali, however. Cali was on the right side of Ray, ready to throw the stapler.

"I just didn't want to be in this room, I don't know if there's more," Ray whispered.

Cali rested her head against the wall. "Well, a janitor should be here soon."

Soon was not the way to put it. Cali was sure Ruby was gone by now. They had been sitting there for far too long. "Ray, I don't think any janitor is coming. Ruby has probably left by now."

"I doubt she actually left," Ray chuckled.

Ray was probably right. *Why would Ruby care about her goldfish?* A smirk crept across Cali's face. Ruby was a presumably heartless person; Cali thought about Ruby too much. She was already down the rabbit hole. Maybe now was the time to confront Ray about Harlow. "Did Harlow ever talk to you?"

Ray cocked her head. "No." Ray's head perked up. "I hear someone," she whispered.

Not now.

Cali listened as hard as she could. There were indeed heavy footsteps coming their way; with the rolling of the janitor cart following.

Cali looked at Ray, looking for a signal to throw the stapler. Ray gave a thumbs-up.

Cali threw the stapler; it was close by, but just far enough away. The sound of footsteps and rolling of wheels stopped briefly, then picked back up, coming closer.

A man passed by them. He was younger than Cali thought he would be, which means he was probably in shape and fast. He was tall also, which meant a longer stride. Cali could feel Ray tense beside her; Ray also knew that this was one of the worst scenarios—a fit, young janitor.

He stopped and looked down at the stapler. The master key gleamed on his keyring. Cali crept over like a cat stalking its prey. Her breath caught in her throat; her hand hovered over the key. She finally snatched the key, but caught his belt because she didn't use the right technique.

The janitor turned and looked down at Cali. Cali heard the door behind her creak and Ray's footsteps.

Cali hopped up and ran as well, trailing behind Ray. The janitor yelled something, but all Cali could hear was her heartbeat.

"We have to go out the front door," Ray yelled.

They ran down the stairs as fast as they possibly could. Cali and Ray almost tripped down them multiple times while trying to skip some. The front door was in sight, except there were people waiting. They were older. They were the other janitors the two had not seen.

Cali guessed the younger janitor used his radio to warn them. Cali didn't focus on their age, but she tried to focus on the fastest way to get out. Knowing Ray would not listen, Cali followed her, hoping Ray had some brain cells left.

As their feet hit the bottom deck, Ray raced toward the carts. Jumping on one, she looked back and laughed at them. Cali did the same and jumped on a cart. She was surprised by the momentum she had built up. The trip was short as Ray and Cali jumped off, sending the carts flying to the side. They opened both doors and ran out.

"We have to run to your house. We can't run to the back; they'll catch us there," Ray said through breaths.

Cali nodded and took the lead.

The snow fell faster and heavier as they neared Cali's house. Cali could barely see anything ahead of her. After getting pelted by snowflakes and sleet, they finally got to Cali's house. Cali opened the door, let Ray in, and slammed the door behind them. They both collapsed in front of the door side-by-side.

Ray tore off her mask. "Oh my god, that was great!" Ray laughed. "You got the key!"

Cali held up the key with her thumb and index finger. "Yep."

"I wonder how long it's going to take for Ruby to realize we're gone," Ray said. "You going to take off your mask now?"

Cali nodded and tore off her mask.

A *bang* on the door jolted Ray and Cali. Cali opened the door.

It was Ruby. She was annoyed but smirking. A thunderclap rang out. *Ironic,* Cali thought.

"Thundersnow." Ruby stepped inside; Cali closed the door behind her. "I see you got the key." Ruby held out her hand and Cali handed it over. "Did you see if you could get in?"

"It's a master's key, isn't it?" Ray chuckled nervously. "We got the right one, right?"

"Oh, yes, you did. But does it let you in the office?"

Cali shook her head. "We got chased. We didn't get the time to see at all."

"You could've made time!" Ruby snorted.

Ray glanced away for a second. "No, we really couldn't have."

Ruby rolled her eyes and threw the key back to Cali. "You outran the janitor; you could've made a turn to the office."

"The cameras were on. There were people in the office," Ray spat out, frustrated.

"I won't argue," Ruby sighed. "You can try tomorrow."

"Absolutely not," Ray grumbled.

"Fine, winging it then?"

"That's what we always do," Ray chuckled.

Ruby looked down at Cali. "It looks like there is going to be a blizzard. Would you mind if I stayed over tonight?"

Cali glanced to the side. "You can; just don't go to my room."

"Why's that?" Ruby raised an eyebrow. "Is your room messy?"

Cali rolled her eyes. "Yes."

"*Hm*." Ruby shrugged. "You don't seem like the type of person to have a messy room. Guess I'm wrong."

"Do you guys want to watch a movie or something?" Ray asked, excited. "I'm going to assume you have some movies."

Cali shrugged. "I could probably find some."

Ray looked into the living room. "Seems like you have a nicer, comfier couch than I do." Ray chuckled sadly and walked in, followed by Ruby and Cali.

Cali grabbed the remote and turned on the TV.

"I see you have a different TV service too, strange," Ray commented.

Cali inhaled, annoyed, but let it go this time.

"I like horror," Ruby said.

"No surprise," Cali muttered.

After hours of watching movies, Ruby and Ray would still not call it quits. "It's two in the morning guys, can we please go to bed?"

Ruby snickered. "It's going to be a late start tomorrow anyway."

Cali sighed, knowing Ruby was probably right. "I'm going to go to my room; I'll be back."

"Alright." Ruby nodded.

Cali speed-walked down the hall to her room, quickly and nervously glancing at her brother's door. She sat down at her desk and looked down at her dream journal. She sighed and opened it.

She skimmed over the dream; she had found Ruby and Keagan. She knew the shooting was about the Fox Den. *What about the yelling? The random death? The groups fighting? What about the stadium?*

There was so much that had yet to be revealed. Perhaps there was even stuff she missed in the dream. She didn't like that. *What did she miss?* She thought she wrote everything down. Now she was all worried about what she could have missed.

Cali heard a door open, but it wasn't her door—it was Louie's.

Cali threw her own door open. It slammed into the wall, scaring Ruby and Ray.

"I told you guys *not* to come back here," Cali hissed.

"I-it was Ruby's idea," Ruby stuttered, pointing back at Ruby.

Ruby snorted. "Who is Louie? I thought you were an only child."

Cali stood there, staring.

"*Hm?*"

"It's no one."

"No, it's someone." Ruby cocked her head. "I'd like to know."

"So would I." Ray glanced into the room.

Cali shoved Ray and Ruby away and slammed the door shut. "It's no one. Go back to the living room."

"Who is Louie?" Ruby pressed on.

"He's my dead brother," Cali screeched. "Are you happy that I told you?"

Ray put her hand over her mouth, knowing she had messed up. Ruby's eyes sparkled with empathy and regret, something Ruby had never shown or perhaps even felt in a while.

Cali stood up. Her breath was shaking. She was struggling to keep herself together. She had let her guard down. She would be hurt again.

"Promise me," Cali started, "You will never say anything about him. Ever."

Ray nodded. "I'm so sorry, Cali; I was curious, and I didn't know! I promise I won't say anything!"

Cali didn't listen to Ray; it was Ruby whom she wanted the apology and promise from.

Ruby nodded. "I promise. I know what's it's like to feel left behind. I've experienced so much death in my life. I've been left behind by those I needed the most. I know."

Cali was confused by Ruby's sudden empathy. Maybe this was a sob story to make Cali believe that she wouldn't say a word. "I know you'll say something to your friends."

"My friends don't care about a word I say, Cali. You may not know them; they are not on the varsity."

"Why are you being so formal! Just . . . stop!" Cali pleaded.

"Cali, listen." Ruby grabbed her shoulders. "I won't say a word. You can trust me." She smirked.

Cali was uneasy. "You make it so hard for me to trust you. You're a criminal!"

"Cali . . ." Ruby's eyes sparkled with possibly fake empathy. "I have no one to spread it to. Why are you so worried about this? Who would be so horrible to make fun of you because of your dead brother?"

"Stop trying to act good." Cali sniffled.

"I know what you're feeling." Ruby looked down. "I know exactly how you feel," she muttered under her breath.

"You don't." Cali pushed her away. "Stop trying to act like you do, you're just like Harlow," she growled. "Go back to the living room and do not come near his room again!"

Cali slammed the door behind her.

STOLEN

Ruby looked at Ray. Ray put her hand on Ruby's shoulder. "That was good for a first try at comforting someone."

"It wasn't." Ruby squinted. "She really doesn't trust me, *hm?*"

Ray and Ruby walked back to the living room. "I can see why she doesn't trust you. You do steal, you know. That's a pretty valid point in my eyes."

"*Ah*, I understand that. But I have an addiction to stealing, I told you this." Ruby looked at Ray.

"Yeah, true. She didn't trust me at first, but it seems like she warmed up to me." Ray sat down on the couch, and Ruby sat down next to her. "It seemed like she was warming up to you, too. You kind of messed that up, man."

"I know." Ruby looked downcast. "I think all she sees me as is a criminal . . . which I am. But she doesn't know the reason. She wouldn't accept the reason. I don't have the personality that makes people stick around, so I threatened people or 'acted' timid."

"And I'm completely willing to help you. Plus, that's Cali Horn for you. A cold, stone wall for a brain and heart." Ray sighed. "Maybe if you didn't threaten her at first, then maybe she would have trusted you more?"

"That was a mess-up as well. Like I've already told you, I didn't know how else to get her to help me."

Ray shrugged. "I mean, at least you know now."

Ruby nodded. "I like the kid, she's smart. Not emotionally. She's not mature at all." Ruby turned to Ray. "Does she believe she is mature?"

"I would think so." Ray shrugged. "I won't speak for her, though."

"She really needs to stop believing she's the only one with problems." Ruby leaned back. "She's very self-centered. Have you noticed that?"

"I really hate to talk behind her back, Ruby."

"Makes sense. Well, hopefully, she learns."

"You know, Ruby, you may seem cold on the outside, but you're so nice on the inside. I don't know how some people fail to see that." Ray nudged her.

"*Heh*, I honestly thought at first that I could use you at first. But now I think I found an actual friend," Ruby chuckled.

"I really like Cali, and I hope she changes," Ray muttered.

"Look at me, people change, surely she will too." Ruby looked down.

"At the moment, though, it looks like she won't be changing any time soon. You have to wait it out. You probably have to 'tame' her like a wild cat, *huh*?"

Ray chuckled, "Probably."

"I know I've told you this before, and when we met, you even made that comparison. Cali reminds me of a younger me. That's why I want to stick around her for her to change," Ruby snickered. "She definitely went through something; usually no one is born as cold as she is."

Ray nodded in agreement. "I wish she would tell us. I mean, we can try to ask her, but she'll probably think we'd try to spread it 'around.'"

"Do you think she experienced bullying?"

"Maybe." Ray shrugged. "She did tell me she went to a smaller school. So who knows? She won't tell us, anyway."

"*Hm*, are we going to keep repeating the same stuff over and over or are we going to keep watching this movie?"

Ray laughed.

CHAPTER 8

Ruby and Ray were right, school did start late. Ruby was in the kitchen trying to work Cali's stove. Ray had to step in and show her. "You don't know how to operate a stove?"

"I don't have to cook for myself," Ruby said, looking away, embarrassed.

Ray sighed. "Here, I'll teach you."

Cali scrunched her nose in disgust. *I should just kick Ruby out already. She was a rotten thief, and a horrible person.*

Ray glanced over at Cali; she jutted her head toward her to tell Ruby she was being judged. "Is there a problem, Cali?"

Cali looked down. She hated Ray's "random passive-aggressiveness." Cali didn't even like when Ray was energetic. *What did she even like about Ray?* Cali refused to say that the two were friends, of course, she couldn't figure out what she liked about her. "No." *Why didn't she say what was on her mind?* Cali laid her head on the table. Ray was no different than anyone else.

Ruby opened the fridge. "Do we have any eggs?"

"*We?*" Cali rolled her eyes. "This is *my* house."

Ray inhaled angrily and Cali shot her a look. "Cali, please, Ruby is trying to be nice to you. She may be a criminal, but she is trying to get better. She is trying to change. You should try to change your own attitude! I talked to you about this before. Did you suddenly forget?" Ray was fed up. "Cali, you know you need me. I'm willing to help you change, just like I'm willing to help Ruby. The only difference is that Ruby wants to change, and you don't! You're hurting others!"

Cali glanced away. She didn't need to change; she was perfectly fine. She had her reasons for the way she acted. Ray and Ruby just wouldn't understand.

"Criminals are horrible people," Cali muttered. "You're lucky I haven't turned you in yet!"

"She may be a criminal, but don't you realize how much you guys have in common?" Ray hissed.

"I refuse to be friends with a criminal!"

Ray slammed a plate on the floor and jumped at Cali. Cali was taken off-guard for once and forced to the floor. Ray hovered over Cali, pinning her down by her shoulders. Ray looked like she could kill. However, Cali didn't fight back. Ray calmed down after a few seconds.

"Why didn't you fight back?"

"Was I supposed to?" Cali cocked her head.

"Well, I thought I would get a reaction out of you." Ray smiled. "You *do* care about me, don't you?"

Ruby stood in the corner, confused behind the logic in Ray attacking Cali. *Didn't Ray want Cali to trust her?*

Cali said nothing.

"So, you aren't going to say you don't care about me? So, you must care some?"

Cali sighed in annoyance. *Why couldn't she say she didn't care about Ray?* "Get off," she muttered.

Ray nodded and did as told. Ray held her hand out to help Cali up, but Cali refused it.

Ray chuckled, "I'm getting through to you. This can work." She smiled.

"Keep dreaming," Cali said under her breath.

"Ray, can I talk to you for a second?" Ruby asked, pointing into the living room.

"Of course."

They left Cali in the kitchen. The pan on the stove was sizzling, and it was annoying her.

In the living room, Ruby and Ray were already talking. "Why did you attack Cali? Do you not want her to trust you?"

"What would you have done?" Ray asked.

Ruby pondered for a few seconds.

"That's what I thought. How else was I supposed to prove she cared? We can't drop her. Ruby, I'm on to something here!"

Ruby laughed and smiled. "You're right, but how did you know to attack her?"

"A guess." Ray smiled cockily.

Back in the kitchen, Cali thought about the situation. Ray, the one person she felt semi-safe around, attacked her. She wasn't safe. She had to leave. She was trapped here, cornered . . . what were they talking about?

A cold breeze hit Cali from the side. She looked over at the open window. *Why was that open?* It didn't matter now. She had to get out. So Cali jumped out the window. She was only in her sweater and shorts, and it was below freezing outside.

Ruby and Ray walked into the kitchen to find Cali gone and no other clue than an open window.

"Where did she go?" Ray looked around frantically. "She can't be outside; she'll die within an hour in the clothes she was wearing!"

Ruby was just as panicked but kept herself together. "Where would she even know to go? We know she wouldn't go to either of our houses."

"She's either at the Fox Den or downtown," Ray said. "Get your keys."

"The roads will be closed down."

"We'll get through them!"

Cali sat behind the now-abandoned Fox Den. She was shivering and it hurt to breathe in the air; it was so cold. *I'm going to die out here.* Cali laid her head on a cold dumpster. She scanned the frozen landscape. She smiled. *No more suffering.* As Cali passed out, she could hear a muffled, fuzzy voice in the distance.

"CALI!"

Cali slowly started to awaken. Her hearing was the first thing to come in. She could hear the slow beeping of a heart monitor. Next, it was her sight. She was staring up at a white ceiling. She looked to her right to see that heart monitor. Was she in a hospital? She sat up quickly.

"Cali." Ray stopped crying. "Cali, you're alive!"

Ruby was smiling. "You're lucky we found you."

"Why didn't you let me die? You clearly hate me," Cali scoffed.

Ray sniffed, still trying not to cry. "Cali. We care. Why don't you see that? How much more will it take for you to realize?"

Cali looked down at the floor beside her bed. "You attacked me."

Ray chuckled with slight annoyance. "I was trying to figure out if you cared about me. You do because you didn't attack me."

Cali stayed silent.

"I know that you know when to fight back. You had your guard down around me and that's why I could actually attack you."

Cali hated that Ray was right. She did have her guard down; she shouldn't have. She only had her guard down around her brother. She only cared about her brother . . . her parents, not so much. They probably wouldn't even know this happened. Cali teared up. *I do care about her, damnit.*

"Cali, look at me, please." Ray chuckled. "You are cared for, you're safe. I won't attack you ever again."

Cali felt relieved at the mention she was safe. However, her brain was telling her differently. Her instincts told her she needed to run again. *This was just them trying to build up trust with her, right?* Her brother. Louie Horn. She had trusted him, always. *Why didn't she trust her parents?* Louie had to build up trust with Cali. *Why couldn't Ray and Ruby?*

"You . . . care?" The words sounded alien to Cali, like they weren't her own.

Ray lit up. "Ruby, we did it."

Cali glanced from both of them. "Did what?"

"Cali, we're trying to be friends with you."

"*Hm.*" Cali glanced down.

"Cali, you're safe now." Ray messed with her ponytail nervously. "Whatever you went through is over now. This is a new era."

Cali felt comforted yet felt so misled. "Ruby," Ruby perked up. "Are you still going to steal?"

"I haven't stolen in a bit. One day."

It suddenly hit Cali she only had known of Ruby's existence for a about a week. That wasn't enough time for Ray to have Ruby's personality change. *Ruby was faking.* "We've only known Ruby for a day, and I've only known you, Ray, for a week! How is that enough time for me to trust you and for you to completely change Ruby?"

Ray's eyes glimmered; she looked at Ruby. "I spent the night at Ruby's house the first day we met. We talked the whole time. She spilled her whole life story. She said that she felt like she found someone who cared about her and was willing to change for me. She wanted this because she needed me, I cared for her. Ruby's 'friends' don't care for her." Ray was getting angrier with every word. "I don't care if it's only been a short time Cali. She's already trying to improve, and she has. She made a promise to me not to steal, and that I could leave her if she did steal. She cares enough to give up stealing for me."

Cali blinked. "What if she's acting?"

Ray slammed her hand down onto Cali's ankle, hurting Cali once again. Ray realized what she did and apologized profusely. "God, I can't with you, Cali." Ray got up and stormed out of the room, leaving Ruby and Cali stuck together.

"Cali," Ruby said softly. "I'm not putting on an act, I swear. I didn't know how else to get you to help me."

"You said you work fast, and you've already got Ray around your finger."

"I said I work fast so that you would possibly help me faster. You did." Ruby snickered in a sadder tone, "I know I made myself seem like a horrible person; I am a horrible person."

"Yes, you are, Ruby."

"I'm trying to improve Cali. Give me time. If you genuinely want, after you help me with Keagan, I will leave you alone forever."

Cali nodded. "That's what I wanted in the first place."

Ruby smiled kindly. "Cali, you'll learn."

Cali rolled her eyes. *What was there to learn?* She knew Ruby was a bad person and that she only wanted to use her.

"Cali, I really did want a friendship with you. You remind me of my younger self." Ruby glanced away. "I was tormented by the loss of my grandfather. I had someone taken away from me, just like you did. I grew cold, the older varsity players were harsh to me about it. They taunted me, always. You and I have so much in common; you just won't see that for a while. I only started to see and regret my actions after I met Ray. She was the person I needed in my life, she refilled my grandfather's spot, and I began to get over his death."

"Are you saying I should get over the death of my brother?" Cali mumbled angrily.

"Kind of, but not in the way you're taking it," Ruby scoffed. "What I'm saying is, I believe you need to find the person that 'refills' your brother's position. I'm not saying to replace him exactly, but you should find someone that makes you whole again."

Cali thought for a second, neither Ray nor Ruby resembled her brother. *Who would she find?*

"It took me a while to find my other half, and it may take you a while too. I promise you this, life will be a lot better once you find this person." Ruby sighed. "Don't take up an addiction like I did. Don't go into stealing. If I could go back and say to my younger self that I only needed to find someone who cared, I wouldn't be the person I am now. Change takes time, and people change at different rates, Cali."

Cali never thought that her thievery was an addiction. "Why did you start stealing?"

"Ray said it was my attempt at filling the pain. I believe she's right. Ray's a smart kid, *hah*, because she *was* right. I only started stealing after my grandfather died and I got into my bad group of friends. They showed me how to cover up my pain in one of the worst ways possible."

Cali stared at Ruby, not batting an eye in understanding.

"I may not be your 'whole,' but I will stick with you and do everything I can for you to trust me. I have an idea to show that I'm changing as well, hah."

"What is it?"

"It's a surprise," Ruby said. "I'm going to be an adult here in a year. It's about time I started to get my life around, *hm*?"

Cali rolled her eyes.

"You really don't know me all that well. Like you said, we've only known me for a short time, I realize now how badly I set myself up. You had every right to think badly about me. I notice that you are wary around Ray, but you still care about her. Why don't you care about me? Is it because you know what I'm capable of, and you have no clue what Ray is capable of?"

"I don't like the look in her eyes."

Ruby cocked her head. "What's wrong with the look in her eyes?"

"They seem so distant, there's so many emotions going on, I can never tell what she is truly feeling," Cali said.

"I noticed that too, but I didn't think anything of it." Ruby shrugged. "I don't think it's anything."

"I have a question; do you still want to take down Keagan?"

"Oh, absolutely. She doesn't deserve her place." Ruby glared, but she wasn't glaring at Cali. "We're still going to take her down."

"Will there be any benefit for Ray and me?"

"You're thinking of Ray too." Ruby snickered. "But yes, there will definitely be rewards for you guys, don't worry. It's going to be awesome."

Cali nodded.

"Cali, we are the same. You're just like me. You need to stop putting me down."

Cali rolled her eyes again and looked away.

CHAPTER 9

It was Wednesday now, and because of Cali, they got to skip the school day yesterday. The three sat around their lunch table. "Today has been boring. Keagan isn't at school today," Ruby said.

"She's sick?" Ray glanced around.

"I haven't seen her all day, so I guess." Ruby picked at her food.

Cali was looking around along with Ray. Ruby was right. Keagan wasn't at her usual table.

"We don't have practice tonight. We should go out somewhere," Ruby suggested.

"Like where?"

"Well, they reopened the theatre, its renovations are finished now." Ruby shrugged. "I thought it would be good for us. You know, to get along, hang out, enjoy something."

Ray smiled. "Hey, you're thinking of other people now."

Ruby nodded. "Trying to." She looked at Cali. "Do you think you could go today?"

Cali glanced down. "I guess."

"Alright." Ruby took a bite out of an apple. "I do have somewhere to go before we meet up. We'll meet inside the theater."

Cali remembered what Ruby said about her surprise. That's probably what she was planning.

"Alright, sounds good," Ray said, giving a thumbs-up. "What movie?"

"I don't know, whatever there is."

"What time?" Cali asked.

"Probably 4:15." Ruby shrugged. "Rough estimate, I don't really know. At least be there by 4:00, I guess."

"Alright, I forgot to feed Xife today," Cali said. "It'll be a quick second before I can be there."

"Well, Cali. You don't know where the theatre is, so I'll come with you, if that's okay," Ray asked.

Cali hesitated, remembering a few days ago. "Sure."

"Alright."

Cali ripped open a new bag of cat food and let it flood into Xife's bowl.

"You seem to be getting along with Ruby better." Ray rested her head in her hands. "You seem willing to go with us more." Ray chuckled, "What did she tell you in that hospital room?"

Cali sighed in annoyance. "Nothing, really. We aren't getting along any better. She's still a criminal, and you still attacked me."

"It was for an actual reason. Anyway, I'm guessing she told you exactly what I told you. That you guys are about the same? *Hm*," Ray said with amusement.

Cali stayed silent.

"Fair enough." Ray chuckled.

"Are you ready?"

"I was waiting for you. Let's go then," Ray walked past Cali.

Cali put the cat food on the counter, grabbed her coat, and left with Ray. It was strangely nice out. The sun was shining through the clouds, melting the snow.

"It's a nice day out. I wonder what Ruby could be doing," Ray muttered.

"She mentioned to me that she had a surprise to show that she was changing."

"Oh. She never mentioned that to me. *Hm.*"

"Does that bother you?"

"Oh, not at all," Ray chuckled. "She probably told you that so that you would trust her more."

"Is that bad?" Cali cocked her head.

"No, it's good, actually. I thought you would hate that." Ray shrugged. "I like to see you two starting to get along." Ray looked down at Cali. "You don't have to tell me, but I'd like to know. What did you go through?"

Cali stayed quiet.

"Sorry."

Cali nodded.

"The theatre is up ahead." Ray's phone went off randomly. "Oh. Ruby says there's a change of plans and we're now going to meet at Archie's Place."

"What is that?"

"It's a small restaurant in downtown. It's a bakery but has other food. It also has some arcade games that I hold the records on," Ray laughed cockily. "It's been gaining popularity ever since the Fox Den shut down. It's sad honestly, people loved the Fox Den but they're already replacing it. It isn't right."

"I thought you told Ruby that replacing something was the right way to go?"

"What? That's not what I meant at least."

"She told me that you were the person that was her 'whole,' replacing her grandfather." Cali raised an eyebrow. "That's what she told me. She told me I needed to find someone to . . . replace my brother."

"Shoot. I came off wrong." Ray stared down angrily at the ground. "Don't listen to her."

"But I thought you wanted me—"

"Don't. Listen. To. Her," Ray hissed.

Cali backed away as Ray was mere inches away from her. Ray's eyes widened with guilt. "I apologize. Listen to her sometimes. Just not this time. Don't replace your brother, ever." Ray looked down. "I mean, that's not my place to tell you that; you're your own person."

Cali was completely confused.

"Look, forget I ever said anything. Let's get going, it's 4:00." Ray grabbed Cali's arm and walked faster.

After awhile, they reached Archie's Place. Ray was right, it was small. The red brick exterior looked like it hadn't been cleaned in a quick second. The windows were shined up so much you could go blind from looking at them. The sign was hung off the side of the building, hanging down from a fancy-looking pole. The sign was green with some red swirls around bold, yellow letters that spelled out the place's name.

As Ray opened the door, a bell rang, letting the people know there was new customers. Ray saw the first open spot and took it.

Ray sighed, "I wish the Fox Den could stay open. It's too bad they buckled under the pressure and quit. *Ah, I shouldn't say they were quitting, probably taking a break.*"

Ray's indecisiveness did confuse Cali. It was something Cali was not used to at all.

"It's 4:10. Ruby will be here soon." Ray nodded at the door. "So Cali, we have our first game soon. Saturday, in fact. We'll be getting our jerseys and warmups. What number are you going to choose? You can't choose eleven. That's my number."

"What about fourteen?" Cali asked.

"That's cool." Ray chuckled. "Eleven and fourteen, a duo. Going to play college basketball together."

"You think I'm going to try and play college basketball?"

"You never know, things change. You could want to in the future." Ray rested her head in her hand.

The bell rang. There Ruby stood. She had cut her hair shorter. She had dyed one strand of her hair a bright red. She had a small bit of her hair in a ponytail while the rest hung down just below her neck. It was strange seeing Ruby with short hair; her ponytail was her signature.

Ray slightly gasped, "Oh, that idiot."

Cali raised her eyebrows.

Ruby sat down next to Cali; she was smiling the most Cali had ever seen her smile. "I mentioned to Cali that I had a surprise and well," she pointed to her hair. "I cut my hair."

Ray stared silently.

"It looks great," Cali said, forcing a smile. Cali wasn't forcing the smile because her hair looked *bad*, it looked *great*; but Cali didn't expect Ray to act like this. Ray would usually be super supportive, *why wasn't she being supportive now?*

Ruby slowly frowned as she realized Ray didn't approve. "You don't like it do you?"

"Why would you cut your signature hair? Didn't you take some type of pride in it? It was *you*." Ray glared.

Ruby was somewhat confused, just like Cali.

"I wanted to distance myself from what I was, and my hair was a part of that."

Ray rolled her eyes. "Hair is important, it's your pride."

"Not to me."

"*Hm*." Ray sat back and crossed her arms. "I still don't believe you should have cut it."

Ruby got defensive. "You can't change the past, Ray, that's what you told me. You can't change the fact that I cut my hair."

STOLEN

Cali got stressed watching the two.

"Hair is a big aspect of who people are."

"THAT'S WHY I CUT MY HAIR," Ruby yelled.

Everyone in the restaurant looked at them. The two were almost like angry barn cats. Cali never thought the two would ever fight, they seemed so close already, and she knew that the weird look in Ray's eyes meant something bad.

"I'm going to go check if my high scores are still held up. I swear if they aren't." Ray left the table and went to the arcades. Cali and Ruby sat awkwardly, staring ahead and trying to comprehend what happened.

"She has anger issues," Cali hesitated. "I wouldn't take it to heart." Cali felt weird having to comfort someone for once.

Ruby raised her eyebrows and looked down at her. "You're trying to comfort me?"

"Not really."

"*Hm*, but thank you." Ruby looked over at Ray.

Ray screeched and slammed her hands down on the arcade machine. The presumable owner of Archie's Place came out of the kitchen and threw a hat at Ray.

"GET OUT!" he yelled.

Ray's face lit up with embarrassment and guilt as she backed away towards the door. Ruby and Cali stared in disbelief as Ray suddenly dashed out of the restaurant.

"Should we follow her?" Cali asked.

Ruby nodded and slid out of the booth with Cali following behind. The two walked out of the restaurant;

Ruby held the door open for Cali as she walked out. Cali looked around the area, but Ray was nowhere in sight.

"I forgot she's fast," Ruby muttered.

Cali stayed quiet.

"Here, I'll text her." Ruby began to walk. "Let's walk to the theatre. By the way, the movie we're watching doesn't show until 7:00."

"Wait, so what do we do until then?"

"Well," Ruby snickered, "the theatre is *huge*, so we can explore around. It'll be a good thrill, fun. Memories."

"It won't be trespassing in any way, right?" Cali asked, catching eye contact with Ruby with a serious glare.

"I mean, I can't promise anything. I'll try to not get us into any legal trouble, I promise." She smiled.

Ruby finally got the text from Ray. "Yeah, she's on her way to the theater. It won't take us that long; it's only a few blocks down."

"She ran how many blocks in how many seconds?"

"A *lot*."

They continued to walk toward the theatre; Cali took in the sights of downtown Swallowsville.

"It's almost time for the fall festival," Ruby commented. "September 13."

"That's Friday the 13th."

"It works perfectly," Ruby snickered. "This Friday too. I already told Ray what we were doing. I should probably tell *you* exactly what we're doing."

Cali nodded.

STOLEN

"I never truly told you why we were getting the key. Well, Keagan is going to be speaking at the festival because she's just such a Goody Two-Shoes." Ruby scoffed. "She's speaking because she's the most likely to get to the WNBA. All of us on varsity have that goal. We're the ones Talivikki *wanted*. She basically handpicked us, really."

"So, you want to play in the WNBA?" Cali asked, curious.

"Well, yes, but they don't get as much attention. I got on varsity my freshman year because it was what I always wanted. I caught wind from the older varsity players of what we were really here for. Then, I didn't want to play in the WBNA, but now it seems like my only escape. I doubt that was Talivikki's purpose, but whatever."

"Isn't it unrealistic that any of the varsity players will go to the WNBA?"

"Sadly, yeah, it looked like that. I may hate Keagan with a burning passion, but she made me realize that it's possible. But *she'll* be the one going, not me. I want to go. She has many different options but not me . . ." Ruby was getting angry. "That's the same time when my grandfather died, one of my best friends, killed by a ruthless bunch of kids. I had nowhere to go; I didn't trust my parents no matter how protective they became of the family. That's when I met," she said looking away, snickering nervously, ". . . my group of friends. That's when I started to steal. I wanted to leave them, but basketball and stealing became my only escape. Now, when you take away stealing, basketball becomes my only escape."

"You went very off-topic."

"Oh, sorry. Did you catch what I was saying?"

Cali nodded.

"On the day of the festival, we won't have practice, we never do on that day. We'll meet at my car, and we'll go to the festival early to hide and get set up."

"Sounds like a plan," Cali muttered.

"Cali, I have a question."

"Hm?"

"What do you want to do when you're older?" Ruby cocked her head.

"Now, I know you're only fourteen but, genuine question."

Cali looked down at her feet to think. She liked art, but never wanted to pursue it. It was just a hobby, but if it came down to absolutely needing a job, she would probably pick an art major. "Something with art."

"You're an artist? Man, I wish I could be an artist."

"It's only if I absolutely needed a job."

"Well, you're going to need a job." Ruby laughed. "You're in high school. You're going to need to start thinking about stuff."

Cali shook her head. "I have time."

"That time passes." Ruby pointed ahead. "There's the theater."

STOLEN

Cali looked up. The theater was an ordinary, 1960s theater. It had a large, lighted, jet-black square sign that hovered over the sidewalk. Cali could see the venue's name, Swallowsville Theater, lit up on all sides of the square. The titles of current movies in paper letters appeared right under the name.

As they drew closer, Cali could see the movie posters more clearly, some were horror, comedy, drama, everything. On the inside, the walls were slanted toward the doors and ticket vendor. The walls and floor were the darkest black Cali could've ever imagined. The ticket booth was also the same black. The window was polished and you could see the worker inside, talking on the phone and paying no attention to anything outside.

"Hey, can we buy some tickets?" Ruby asked in an intimidating tone. It even scared Cali a bit.

The ticket clerk jumped up, looking annoyed. "What movie?" he asked, putting down his phone and resting his head in his hands.

"Uh, *Planet of Tomorrow* at 7:00 p.m."

"Aren't you a bit early, shorty?"

Ruby inhaled in annoyance. She got closer to the booth and lowered her head. "I'm 5'9" almost 5'10"."

"You look 5'8" Are you lying?"

"And why are you insulting a customer?" Ruby hissed.

"It was just a name. A nickname."

He stood up straight, matching Ruby's aggression.

Ruby stepped back from the booth, raised her head, and scanned the ceiling for cameras. Cali wondered what Ruby was about to do. Ruby stared at the ground for a few seconds before looking up again with a mischievous smile.

"I'll take those tickets myself if YOU WANT TO BE RUDE!" Then, she punched through the glass, which shattered upon impact.

The ticket clerk apologized profusely while Ruby fought through the glass, but then took some paper and sliced Ruby's knuckles. Ruby's face lit up with pain and she pulled her hand back through, slicing her arm more.

"Take your damn tickets!" the clerk said as he threw the tickets at Ruby. "Be lucky I'm too scared of you to alert security!"

Ruby scoffed. "I'll be back," she said, lowering her head to emphasize the crazed look in her eyes.

Cali felt uneasy.

Ruby snatched the tickets off the ground and headed into the theater. Cali quickly followed behind, hiding her face.

As the door closed behind the two, Cali uncovered her face and stepped toward Ruby. "Why would you do that?"

Ruby sighed. "He made me mad, okay? Now we have to find Ray."

Cali scoffed. "You shouldn't have gotten angry!"

Ruby looked down at Cali. "He called me short, now let's go."

Ruby was still very much a delinquent.

Cali stood there, taking in the theatre. It was one of the biggest theatres she had ever seen. The walls were jet-black, just like the outside. The only difference from the outside is that the floor had all sorts of neon shapes that glowed in the dark.

Ahead, there were many different hallways that went to different theaters. In the middle, there was a snack bar with food and snacks. Only one person worked in it, and he had strawberry blonde hair that was long and spiky.

Cali looked back down at the ground and stared at the neon shapes. One now stood out to her. It had blood on it. Ruby's blood. Cali's eyes scanned Ruby's arm, which was dripping blood. "Your arm." Cali pointed.

"Oh, yeah. I'll get that fixed. Let's just find Ray. I believe she's probably by the arcade or laser gun area."

"There's a laser gun area?" Cali asked, glancing again at her arm.

"Yep, let's go." Ruby grabbed Cali's arm and walked toward a hallway, passing the one worker. Cali looked at him again. He looked so familiar to her. Cali noticed that Ruby, too, was glancing at him.

The hallway was the same jet-black with the shapes. Movie posters lining the walls. They were the same posters as the ones on the outside, although there were some posters for the laser gun and arcade area.

"Do you really think Ray is playing in the arcade area?"

Cali couldn't help but stare at Ruby's arm. It was still bleeding, and Ruby wasn't paying any attention to it.

"Absolutely. She must have lost her high score at the restaurant. She'll move here." Ruby snickered and scratched her bleeding arm. "She's really controlling, if you haven't already noticed."

Ruby was right, Ray *was* controlling.

Cali could see the arcade's neon sign as they reached the end of the hallway.

"This is the arcade area," Ruby said as the two-stepped into a huge, neon-lit room.

The lighting strained Cali's eyes at first, but she quickly got used to it. There were rows of arcade games that stretched so far that Cali could not see the end.

Ruby stopped and put her hands on her hips. "Ah. It's going to take a bit to find her." She cupped her hands to her face to call for Ray. "RAY?"

Cali elbowed Ruby. "Don't yell, it echoes."

How else will we find her?" Ruby asked, smiling and stepping away.

Cali stood back and admired the mismatched neon colors. It was mesmerizing. As she observed the area, she noticed a tiny balcony that stuck out. *Maybe they could go up there and then look for Ray?* It might be more difficult to get there, but it would be faster to look for Ray.

She ran up to Ruby and accidentally yanked her injured arm.

"There's a balcony that we could go to." Cali realized she couldn't see over the arcade machines. "Here." Cali dragged Ruby out of the row and pointed towards the balcony.

Ruby raised an eyebrow. "It will take us longer. I think it's best if we just go through every row. She can't be too hidden. In fact, I bet if you listen close enough, you can hear her crying," she snickered and shook off Cali. "Now let's get going."

Cali rolled her eyes. "You can look for her. I'm going to go up to the balcony."

"Whatever."

Cali backed away until she was sure Ruby couldn't see her anymore, then she turned around. She went back to thinking why the snack bar clerk looked so familiar. Cali assumed she may have seen him at school. Maybe they had the same class together or something.

Cali approached a black door camouflaged by the wall. The only thing giving it away was the steel door knob. As she opened the door only to have it close behind her with a spring mechanism, Cali was left in a pitch-black room. There were no neon glow-in-the-dark shapes to guide her, so she pulled out her phone and turned the flashlight on to its brightest. The room turned out to be another hallway just like the rest, with jet-black walls. She started to second-guess herself as she went on through the hallway. It didn't seem to have an end until Cali came across some stairs.

Cali looked behind again, contemplating her decision, then took the first step up. Cali got more confident as she got further up the stairs. At the top, she shined her flashlight around, trying to find a door. Cali took another step forward, but was cut short as she tripped on what seemed like air. She slammed into a metal box on the wall beside her. Cali winced in pain and pushed herself slowly away from the wall. She instantly looked at the box with her flashlight. *Why was there a random breaker box right here?* Curious, she opened it and looked at all the switches. If Cali wanted to, she could shut down the theater and ruin many people's evenings. She fought the urge but couldn't help but stare at one switch . . . the one for the security cameras.

She looked around, even though she could see nothing. Her hand hovered over the security switch. Cali couldn't help but feel like it would help them later on. *They were just watching a movie; why would they need it?* Ruby and Ray were unpredictable people, so she flipped the switch. Cali's Goody Two-Shoes heart raced as she realized what she did. She didn't care about the balcony anymore, and bolted back down the stairs.

Once Cali reached the door, she almost kicked it off its hinges. She heaved and stared down with her hands on her knees.

"Someone in there?" Ruby snickered.

Cali rose and saw Ruby and Ray just arriving at the door. "Well, I turned off the security cameras."

Ray raised an eyebrow. "Why? We won't need them."

"That's what I thought," Cali said, still panting slightly. "Maybe someone saw me enter," she offered as a quick excuse.

"*Ah.* Smart." Ruby patted her on the head.

"Please don't." Cali threw Ruby's hand off her head. "Well, what now?"

"Ray and I are going to go get some snacks from the snack bar if you're interested."

"Sure."

Ray and Ruby seemed more tense than before. Cali didn't bother to ask why.

"Ruby, your arm?" Ray pointed at it, concerned. "What happened?" she asked, glancing back at Cali.

"Oh, I just scratched it while I was looking for you."

Ray didn't buy it. She rested her elbow on Cali's shoulder and turned to her. "Is that really what happened?"

Cali shrugged. "Don't know."

Cali could see Ruby hold a thumbs-up over Ray's head.

"*Hm.* Alright." Ray dropped her arm and looked ahead. "Ruby, you have money, right? I would assume the one taking us out would pay. If you have that moral at least."

Ruby didn't react to Ray's jab. "Yes, I have money."

The trio stepped up to the snack bar. The worker turned to help them. "What can I get you?"

Ruby stared down at him with fiery anger in her eyes. This differed from what she dished out to Ray and the clerk outside. Cali looked down at the worker's name tag, Nick Perry. *Oh, that's why he looked familiar.*

Ruby snickered and raised her head, "Do you happen to be related to Keagan Perry?"

Nick glanced to the side. "Yeah, I'm her brother."

"Do you not know who I am?"

"No clue," he muttered.

"Do you not know how your sister replaced me? She got me kicked down to the 'C team'!"

"Did you deserve it?" Nick bit his lip.

Ray backed Cali away from Ruby. "Maybe it was a good idea you turned off the cameras," Ray whispered.

Ruby stood there, blankly staring at Nick. "I did not deserve it at all. I worked so much my whole life to get to varsity my freshman year. Your sister came out of nowhere and ruined it for me! Basketball is my only hope! I can't lose it now!" Ruby slammed both hands on the counter and lowered her head.

Nick didn't seem affected. "Look, I hate her too. Now what do you want?"

Ruby scoffed, not knowing what to say.

Nick raised an eyebrow. "Were you expecting to get something from me? I mean, I don't hate her in 'sibling way.' I hate her. Just plain hate."

Ruby jumped at him and dragged him away. Cali tried to stop Ruby, but Ray put her arm out in front of her.

Cali turned. "Are we just going to let her kill this kid?"

"She's a powerhouse. What else are we supposed to do?"

Cali sighed and followed Ruby. They ended up in some storage closet far away from the snack bar. Ruby was struggling to put an extension cord around Nick's wrists. Eventually he gave in and let it happen. "So, you know you could've just blackmailed me instead of this."

Ruby scoffed, "Will you tell me some anyway?"

"Oh absolutely." Nick smiled. "Keagan doesn't even want to play basketball. She wants to be in track. Our parents won't let her run track because they see it as 'inferior.'"

"How is one sport more inferior than another?" Cali chimed in.

Nick laughed. "You live in Swallowsville, baby! It's basketball athlete central! How did you not know that?"

Cali glanced at Ray and Ruby. "I never realized that."

"By the stories I told you I thought you'd realize that," Ruby muttered. "So, you're telling me she doesn't even *want* to play basketball and she took the place away from someone who really needed it?"

Nick nodded.

"Do you have any information that can ruin her life?"

"Nope. All I have is that she doesn't want to play basketball. I would tell you more if I could. We don't talk much." Nick leaned his head against the wall. "Now can you let me go? I won't tell anyone anyway, I can't. But you will have to repay me."

"With what?"

"Get her taken down. Please." Nick laughed.

"Why do you hate her?" Ray asked.

"Our parents prefer her over me. I wouldn't be working here if they liked me the same." Nick laughed then frowned. "I'm sick of it. She's going to be more successful than I ever will be."

"Just like Piper and Delilah," Ray muttered. Piper seemed way more aggressive than Nick; however, Cali barely knew the guy.

"Anyway. Can you let me go? I work here every day, I'm also homeschooled, so I have time to talk. Just let me know, I'd love to see how this plays out."

Ruby ripped the extension cord away, threw it to the side, then held out her hand. Nick accepted the help, then quickly walked out.

"Nick," Ruby said, turning.

"*Hm*?"

"Was Keagan homeschooled?"

"Oh, yeah. I thought you'd know that?" He laughed.

"Did you just think she just showed up?"

"So, nothing big, like a bribe?" Ruby stepped forward.

"Our folks wanted to use her for the fame since she's always been good." He shrugged. "I don't know if there was any bribery, but I wouldn't be surprised. Just get her taken down. I feel like it would be a sigh of relief for us all."

"Could I get your socials?"

"I don't give out socials. Sorry. Like I said, I'll be here, though."

Ruby nodded.

Ray nudged Ruby. "You trust this dude?"

Nick raised an eyebrow. "You see my nametag?"

"No, I mean, what if you're going to tell Keagan about us," Ray stepped forward.

"Nah, I'm not like that."

Ruby bit her lip, realizing Ray had a point. "If you do, I'll be sure to put a damn bullet in your head."

"You ain't gonna be putting a bullet in anybody's head, Ruby!" Ray shook her head and threw her arms out. "You aren't starting a new thing!"

"It might be needed," Ruby glared.

"Ruby, you're not going to cover up one crime with another!" Ray chuckled with annoyance.

"I was changing before you came around!"

Cali glanced at Nick, who stood amused. Ray's shoulders and arms went limp, followed by an expression of disbelief.

"Oh really?" Ray shook her head in shock. "Without me, you would never have changed."

"I thought about what Cali said." Ruby jutted her head back at Cali. "We only knew each other for about a day; that is not enough to change someone. I was changing."

Ray looked at Cali with that strange look. She was shutting down mentally. "I was your last and final push! At least thank me for that!"

"Do they always act like this?" Nick whispered to Cali.

"No, they were getting along earlier," Cali muttered.

"*Hm.*" Nick crossed his arms. "It seems like Ray has some anger issues."

"She's controlling."

Cali stared at Ray's dead eyes.

"Every time she loses control in something, she freaks out." Cali stopped herself before she spilled her heart out to him. *Why was she speaking to him anyway? He was a stranger.* Nick was already sneaking away.

"I do thank you for it. But sometimes you're so controlling! It makes it hard for you to be around! It's always your rules! Like my hair." Ruby pulled her hair a bit, showing it off to Ray with pride. "Stop being so controlling! For our friendship's sake! You told me to think of others while you're only thinking about yourself."

"I do think of others! Why do you think I helped you?"

"Because you wanted control of something else, didn't you?" Ruby said in a monotone voice, much like a parent disciplining a child. Ruby stared at her shaking hands. "Say it, just admit it."

Ray stood silent.

Nick yawned, coming back over with popcorn. "Want some?"

Cali raised her eyebrows. She held up a hand and shook her head.

"Sorry." Ray put her hand through her hair.

Ruby sighed, "Sorry as well."

"I'll try to not be so angry."

"Man, this is pretty cheesy, *huh*? Right Cali?" Nick commented, trying to act like her friend.

Ray turned to Nick and laughed. Ray was acting weirdly, something was off-putting. Cali could see Ruby was concerned too.

"Are you sure?" Ruby stepped forward to put her hand on Ray's shoulder. Ray stepped back.

"Let's just go play some laser tag and forget all of this!" She chuckled.

Nick was already back at the snack bar eating his popcorn.

"Ray, you don't seem well." Ray shrugged and smiled. "Nah, I'm good." Ray held up Ruby's arm. "She's hurt, do you have any bandages?"

Nick shook his head. "No, sorry."

The door opened and the ticket clerk walked over. He laid his elbow on the desk and glared at Ruby. "She's hurt from trying to kill me."

"Well, what'd she try to do, Reg?" Nick flicked Reg's arm.

"You've never been around a girl anyway. Probably exciting for you." Reg slammed his hand down on the counter. "They're older."

"Actually, these two," Ruby pointed to Ray and Cali, "are fourteen. I'm seventeen, almost eighteen."

"But you are still older," Reg snorted.

"This is Reg. He's got a short temper. Almost like your friend Ray over there. He has an 'off' switch, but it seems like he doesn't. Malfunctioning," Nick laughed.

"He's nice once you get to know him. He's my best buddy. He tries to act mature, but he's only fifteen, so what would he know?"

"You're seventeen." Reg rolled his eyes and ran his hand through his curly black hair.

"Only two more years of life experience."

"You'd be surprised."

"You're seventeen?" Ruby cocked her head. "You look twenty-five."

Nick laughed, "Thanks for calling me old."

"I do have an 'off' switch," Ray hissed. "I know when my anger is needed and it's unneeded."

Nick nodded, although disagreeing. "*Ah*, you're fourteen, you'll learn."

Ray rolled her eyes. "I'm so sick of people thinking I'm so dumb!"

"Then don't act dumb."

Ray tried to fire back but couldn't find the right words.

Reg looked at Ruby's arm. "I'll forgive you this time. Let's get you something." Ruby hesitated. Reg shook his head. "What do you think I'm going to do? I'm half your size."

Ruby nodded and they left. Cali and Ray took a step, but Nick stopped them.

"No point in going with them. It's nothing."

Nick looked at the counter and raised an eyebrow. "Hey, Reg, who's on ticket duty right now?"

"Aller," he called.

Nick bobbed his head side to side. "Oh." He looked up at Cali and Ray. "Ray." He jutted his head toward her. "I hope you don't take offense in anything I say. I'm just trying to help in the only way I know."

Cali couldn't help but think that Nick was the bad guy, going against his sister, thought he seemed nice enough.

Ray nodded. "I understand."

Nick looked down.

"Nick, would you truly go against your sister?"

"Oh, absolutely, I don't see how people like her. She's so obviously fake in a way. I don't mean fake in a bad way. I just mean that she's making friends with the wrong people. I know how varsity can be. It drove my ex-girlfriend so insane that she quit. It isn't for everyone, and it sure isn't for someone who doesn't want to do it." Nick seemed to take some of his words back, "I don't exactly go against her in the way that harms her. I mean to take her down so that I can get some attention from my parents. You know. I'm bad at explaining, so I'm sorry if it doesn't make sense."

"So, you want her to move down to track so your family can be equal?" Ray asked.

"Well, it took a toll on her mental health. I want the old Keagan back. I don't want this burnt-out, angry Keagan. I want the happy-go-lucky, sweet Keagan."

"You seem very undecided," Ray sneered.

Nick grinned. "Yeah. I love her, but I hate her at the same time. I want attention. We all do."

Cali nodded, somewhat understanding his feelings.

Reg and Ruby came back, arguing about something. "Well, you wrapped it wrong too many times and now my arm is going to be hurting for days." Ruby glared.

Reg snorted, "Stop complaining! You want to bleed all over?"

Nick rubbed his forehead. "Will you guys cut it out?"

Reg rolled his eyes and nodded.

"Ray, Cali, we're going to play laser tag." Ruby took their arms and dragged them away.

"Have fun," Nick called.

"Yeah, have fun, loser," Reg shouted.

As the three disappeared into the darkness, Reg and Nick stood staring. "So, what happened between Ruby and your sister?"

"She said she got replaced. I feel bad. She seems like she really needs it. I can kind of see her in me. You said she tried to kill you, right?"

"Yes."

"She seems like a delinquent. Remember how I used to be when I came here?"

"You were horrible."

"Yeah. I feel that she's like me, or what I used to be."

Nick laughed.

Reg rested his arm on the counter. "Yeah, I can agree with that."

Nick nodded.

"Do you plan on helping her with that?"

"Yeah, I told her that Keagan doesn't want to play basketball. Hopefully, she does something. I said some harsh things while they had me cornered, though. I hope they don't get the wrong idea; I tried explaining."

"I'm sure it's going to be fine, Nick." Reg shrugged. "I didn't hear one peep out of the shorter one. I feel like she'd be the one to make sense of all of it."

Nick nodded. "I don't know. She's pretty young."

"I'm young too. I'm pretty responsible, mature."

"Dream on."

Ruby and Cali had to practically drag Ray out of the laser tag area so they wouldn't be late for their movie. More people showed up; mostly kids and some middle schoolers plagued the laser tag area. Ruby had Ray by the hoodie, and Ray was trying to push her away.

"You can go without me."

"It's 6:45!" Ruby let her go. "You won't have time!"

"That's why I said go without me!" Ray chuckled. "See you there!"

She waved, turned, and dashed into the darkness.

Ruby sighed in annoyance. "Let's get going to our movie then."

Cali looked at Ruby's arm. The bandage slipped again. "Do you need your arm to be wrapped again?"

"Nope. I loosened it a bit while in hiding," Ruby snickered. "I thought Ray would recognize some of those kids. Maybe she does."

Cali shrugged.

"I've probably already said this, but it seems like you're becoming more comfortable with me." Ruby messed with her bandage. "Is that true?"

Cali shrugged again.

"So, not a 'yes' or a 'no'?"

"No."

"Sure." Ruby nudged her. "You didn't attack Ray when she attacked you. You had your guard down. You at least care about her."

Cali stayed silent.

"Fair enough," Ruby mumbled.

They walked past the snack bar; Ruby waved at Nick. The theater was fuller now that more people were off work. "I think Nick's a pretty cool dude."

Cali shrugged. "He's okay."

"You already know what I'm about to say, Cali," Ruby said.

Cali rolled her eyes. She wanted to speak her mind, but she could only speak her mind during times of anger or fear.

"Our theater is A12 B6. I hope you know your numbers and alphabet," Ruby sneered.

"There it is."

Ruby stepped ahead and opened the door for Cali. The inside of the theater was an average theater room, all black with white lights lighting the way. You could only see a sliver of the movie screen due to the small hallway that blocked off the rest. "You're going to like the seats."

The hallway ended and the full theatre could be seen.

"The seats are amazing, comfortable, soft. If you fall asleep, I am not waking you up."

"I don't fall asleep during movies," Cali said.

"Good," Ruby muttered and went to choose seats for the three of them.

They were far in the back, against the wall. "Why are we so far back?"

"So, we can talk and no one would really hear us. Besides, I don't think anyone is going to be in here."

Ruby held her hand out, showing Cali that the theatre was empty. They sat down, and Cali instantly went on her phone to ignore the opening teasers. Ruby eventually did as well.

It was well into the movie before Ray walked in and sat down next to them. "It's empty in here," she said, out of breath.

"The movie is about over." Ruby snickered.

"I'm going to guess laser tag is more interesting than this movie. Cali looks half asleep, and no one is here."

Ruby shrugged. "I didn't pay, anyway."

Ray cocked her head. "What do you mean you didn't pay?"

"Cali paid."

Cali lifted her head off the seat and looked over. "What?"

"You paid," Ruby said through her teeth.

Cali squinted. Ruby was lying right to Ray's face just so she didn't have to deal with Ray. "Sure."

Ruby breathed a sigh of relief. "Should we leave? I've been on my phone the whole movie."

Ray nodded. Ruby and Ray got up, and Ruby had to drag Cali out of her seat. Cali never had any theater seat this comfortable. The theater in her old town had old, uncomfortable seats that interrupted any possible enjoyment of the movie. Other than that, the town of Yarmen was just an average rural town.

Cali was starting to enjoy Swallowsville's luxuries, just not its people. It was a beautiful town with horrible people. As Cali and the others walked out, she couldn't help but think back to the Fox Den incident. "Did they ever find the culprits for the Fox Den thing?"

Ruby looked down at Cali. She seemed uneasy. "No, they never did. Let's not talk about it. It will never be solved anyway."

Cali glanced over at Ray, looking for some other answer. Ray shrugged it off.

"You're just trying to forget about it?"

Ruby grabbed Cali's shoulders unexpectedly. "You wouldn't understand. You come from a small rural town; this is normal."

"Since when are shootings normal?"

Ruby laughed. "You'll learn when you're my age. I've seen violence in Swallowsville more times than you have."

Ray stepped in. "I'm on Cali's side. This isn't normal."

Ruby looked down. "I know it's not normal, but . . ." Ruby sighed, trying to find words to say, "You'll learn."

Ray snorted, "Well, we'll try to do anything we can to stop this violence. I helped you stop stealing. Why can't I stop violence?"

"That sounds like something Harlow would say," Ruby snickered.

Ray's eyes widened, realizing her hypocrisy.

"Ray, you did criticize Harlow for wanting to save those in the shooting," Cali commented.

Ray's eyes flared with intense anger. "Forget about that," she growled.

Cali nodded. Ray definitely couldn't take any criticism whatsoever.

"I think we should all just go home," Ruby offered. "Tonight hasn't been the greatest. I have one more thing to get before I go home. I'll show you tomorrow."

Ray nodded and stormed out.

Ruby and Cali stared at the doorway. "She can't take any criticism." Ruby sighed. "Trust me about the violence, you cannot stop it. Don't even try."

Cali shrugged. "School will be different when I'm left to deal with Ray."

Ruby snickered, "Cali, Ray doesn't want to deal with you, either. She wants you to change your stubborn ways."

Cali raised an eyebrow. "I don't see a problem with me. I have my reasons."

"She needs someone who isn't distant like you. She's becoming angry with me because I wasn't in her image.

How I cut my hair wasn't how she originally saw me, so she sees that as delinquency towards her. Distance."

Cali had a hard time understanding.

"You understand in your own way, I think."

The two continued to talk about Ray in the hallway while Ray sat right outside the door, listening to it all. She grew angrier and angrier just being there. She knew how right they were, but that's what she hated—*how right they were*. Ray speed-walked away, stopping just before the end of the hallway to punch the wall.

CHAPTER 10

Ray walked into her room and landed face down on her bed. She felt empty and defeated, knowing what the two thought of her. The door opened and a tall man stood staring at Ray from the hallway. He had a black beard and spiky hair.

"Ray, you have to make dinner." He turned to leave.

He had distant, green eyes, much like Ray's. Their eyes were the only trait that proved they were related. This was her father. Usually, he was home late, but there were these rare times where he would be home early.

Ray nodded and followed him downstairs. She stayed quiet the whole time, too angry to talk to him.

Ray's mother left Ray behind with her father while Ray was in Kindergarten. Her father didn't truly have custody of Ray. Her mother just didn't want her at all. Ray never knew why, but there had to be a reason.

It seemed as if no one wanted her. Her father sat down at the small wooden table in the kitchen.

"What do you want, Henry?" Ray asked.

"Ray, I've said this before. Address me by 'dad' or something."

Henry stroked his beard. He didn't speak like a professional at all, like a "normal guy," but he wanted respect. He stopped trying to "talk professional" to Ray years ago as he realized it wouldn't help.

"What do you want?" Ray muttered, turning away from him.

"Whatever we have."

Cali stepped into the hallway after waking up in a classroom. She was dreaming. Another nightmare. She was in her old school. Frustration rested deep inside of Cali. She was trying to forget this all, that's why she moved away. She didn't move from town to town just to have nightmares about the place.

She knew exactly what the nightmare was about. It was after the winter concert. Cali's mom would be late because of work and leave Cali alone in school. Three kids ran past Cali: one was her younger self and the other two were old classmates. Cali ran after them. The three ran until the younger Cali ran into and locked herself inside the unisex bathroom. Younger Cali hopped onto the sink and waited for the two to leave.

The two girls were Avery and Itzel, Cali's worst bullies. This incident was Cali's mother's last straw.

Itzel had a high black ponytail, that was styled fancier than normal because of the concert. Usually, it was fluffier. It was adorned on the top of her head with small reindeer antlers that stuck out. Itzel almost looked like a younger Ruby, although she wasn't tall and didn't have freckles, plus she had olive skin tone. Itzel's right eye was a bright, icy blue, but a brown contact lens covered it up.

Avery was the polar opposite of Itzel appearance-wise. She was blonde with pale skin and green eyes. She had freckles and was only about two inches taller. Her blonde hair was very curly, and some of it wrapped around her glasses.

Itzel wore a red sweater and Avery wore a green one.

Younger Cali felt like throwing up with the anxiety that pelted her. It felt like her lungs were shrinking and her body was going numb. Cali wanted to save herself so badly, especially since she knew what would happen.

Itzel stopped banging on the door and listened. She nodded for Avery to step back. Avery did so. Younger Cali wasn't buying this and didn't move an inch. She remained perched on the sink, and waited for them to break in. Itzel sighed in annoyance.

"The door has a malfunctioning lock, Avery. If you throw yourself into the door, eventually it will break."

"Why didn't you say that the first time?" Avery muttered. She threw herself into the door. After a few hits, the lock gave out as predicted. Cali was now staring down at the two, who were grinning in the most evil way. Cali propelled her power forward and jumped.

Itzel brought out a switchblade and flicked it open with a sickening *click*.

Cali froze and her jump failed. She crashed into the ground and scampered to get up. Avery slammed her foot down onto Cali's head, sending her back down to the ground. Cali gritted her teeth, trying to numb the pain somehow.

"Hey, Cali," Itzel laughed.

Cali could feel the blade on the back of her neck and the pain getting sharper and sharper.

"How's your day going?" Avery snickered.

Cali stayed quiet and Avery stomped on her again. She felt like she would black out. This was her end. She could feel her body slowly shutting itself down. Itzel nudged Avery.

"Don't kill her, you idiot." Itzel grabbed the back of Cali's sweater and pulled her up, choking her. She propped Cali against the wall and inspected her.

"She's fine," Avery said frantically.

"You gave her a concussion," Itzel growled and brought the knife up to Avery's throat. Avery backed off quickly.

As the two fought it out, Cali felt a cold breeze. She looked over at the sink to see the open window. Cali must have been too focused to even feel the breeze before.

She dove for the window. Itzel grabbed Cali's ankle at the last possible second, and instead grabbed only her shoe. Cali landed headfirst in a snowbank, and got up and stumbled to the sidewalk that led to her house.

Itzel and Avery didn't chase after her. They picked their battles. Well, Itzel picked their battles.

The present Cali followed younger Cali the whole way. Cali's mother's car eventually approached her. Instead of wheels screeching, it was the shrill shattering of a plate. Cali awoke in her bed, suddenly feeling sick.

Back at Ray's house, Ray and Henry got into an argument. Henry threw a plate at Ray, and Ray held a shard out to Henry. Henry stepped forward, Ray backed against the wall and poked her throat with the tip of the broken plate.

"Ray, calm down," he said sternly.

"NOBODY SEEMS TO WANT ME ANYWHERE," she yelled as her voice broke.

Henry felt defeated but showed no emotion.

Ray's face twisted with anger after failing to get a response from Henry. She threw the plate down and ran for the front door. Henry tried to grab her but fell. Ray eventually ran to school.

Cali got up and looked at her phone.
Something felt off.
Really off.

CHAPTER 11

Cali and Ruby walked into the locker room looking for Ray, who was nowhere in sight. Cali knew that it was unlike Ray to miss school, let alone practice. Nothing had happened during the day; it was just a school day, but something felt off.

"I'm getting worried about Ray," Ruby muttered. "Her step-dad isn't the nicest person. I wonder if something happened?"

Cali bit her knuckle in worry.

Ruby looked down at Cali. "I really appreciate that you're worried."

"Not now," Cali muttered.

"Ray's gone missing." Piper nudged past Cali. "Great!" She laughed.

Cali glared. Piper, knowing Cali could tear her apart in seconds, laughed more but backed off. "She's not missing, by the way." Piper shrugged. "She's walking with Sienna, Ray looked sick."

"Why are you talking about me?" Ray muttered, shoving Cali a bit to get past her.

Ruby and Cali let out a sigh of relief. "Thank God, we thought something happened to you," Ruby said.

"I had a doctor's appointment," Ray said, turning her back to them. "I don't feel good."

Mel and Justice walked in.

"The festival is tomorrow," Justice shouted. "You know what the seniors gotta do!"

Sienna rolled her eyes. "You guys gotta decorate and stuff, *blah, blah, blah*, we know."

Justice frowned.

"Cali," Ruby whispered. "Does Ray have the key to the office?"

Cali nodded.

Ruby tried to talk to Ray, but Ray didn't seem to budge at first. She became more hostile, so Ruby hugged her. Ray stopped instantly and it seemed like her anger drained out completely right on the spot. Ray quickly pushed her away.

Cali walked over.

"I'll give you the key. I'll meet you guys wherever you go."

Ruby nodded.

Piper got on top of the bench. "We're getting our jerseys today!" Piper pointed at herself. "I call number thirteen and no one else can have it!"

"No one wants a bad number," Sienna mumbled.

"I'll take twenty-four," Mel mumbled.

"I'll take twenty-five then." Justice nudged Mel.

"I'm taking eleven," Ray called out.

"Hey." Eliza stepped up. "I want eleven."

Ray blinked. "Are you kidding me?"

Eliza laughed. "Race?"

Ray stared at her for a few seconds, then bolted over the bench for the door. The rest all walked out together, all excited for "jersey day". Coach Milan was already in the center of the gym, laying out the jerseys and shorts accordingly, while Eliza and Ray shoved each other out of the way. They formed a circle, staring down Coach Milan like vultures that hadn't eaten for a while. The jerseys and shorts were white, with three purple stripes running up the sides. The letters and numbers were purple as well.

Cali, for once, felt excited.

"Okay, I'm going to let Ruby pick first." Coach Milan nodded at Ruby. "Ruby, step up."

"One." Ruby pointed down at number one. Ruby picked up her jersey, wrapped it around her arm, and stepped back.

"Now, the seniors. Mel, Justice, whoever else."

It took a quick second before everyone finally got the jersey they wanted. Now, it was down to Eliza, Ray, and Cali.

Ray was the first to step up.

"I want eleven," she said while pushing Eliza back.

Coach Milan handed Ray eleven and she jumped in excitement.

Eliza scoffed, "Fine, I'll take fourteen."

"*Huh?* That's what Cali wanted!"

"And I wanted eleven; I don't see the problem."

Coach Milan handed Eliza number fourteen.

"Cali, you should go for nineteen, there's just something about that number that fits you," Sienna whispered to Cali.

Cali squinted. "I'll take twenty."

Sienna laughed. "I knew you would do that."

"Twenty it is then," Coach Milan said, handing the jersey to Cali. She put the rest of the jerseys away. They were ordered to put their jerseys away in their lockers and come back for practice.

The first thing the team practiced were plays. Cali was on the side as usual. She noticed something strange while watching the others. Ray usually stuck right with the play, never deviating from the path even when there could've been an open shot. She also got mad at others when they got the play wrong and tried to explain the play in her own, broken way.

Ruby deviated from the path whenever, either from her years on varsity or because it was in her nature. *Perhaps both?* Ruby didn't help the others at all while at least Ray tried to explain a smidge. Ruby wasn't put high up on Coach Milan's standards and was treated almost like the others, although Milan pitied her. Ruby was worked like the others, but she always worked herself harder.

Ray didn't seem to work herself to her fullest. She was at the exact same pace as everyone else. Cali felt like this made sense. Ray was controlling and Ruby was independent. Cali thought of this often, and it seemed true. It was interesting to Cali to see how their personalities mixed in with the way they played basketball.

Cali wondered if anyone else thought the way she did. Perhaps Ruby or Sienna did. She eventually decided to ask Ruby.

Cali sat in Ruby's car while Ruby got the key from Ray. Ray stayed home; she never specified why and would not tell Ruby.

Ruby slid into the driver's seat, twirling the master key. "I should probably tell you where we are going," Ruby snickered. "We're going to pick up some earpieces so we can talk while we're onstage. Then, later tonight, Ray and I are going to take a look at the festival."

Cali stared at her. "Why can't I go with you guys to the festival tonight?" Cali cocked her head.

"It will be your first time seeing it, we don't want to ruin the surprise for you." Ruby shrugged. "You don't know how excited I am for next year! My class gets to decorate the festival!"

Cali smiled at Ruby.

"In four years, you and Ray's class will get to do it. I'll be almost done with college and looking into the WNBA. *Sheesh*, five more years."

"Ruby, I have a question."

"*Hm?*"

"What do I act like during the plays? Do I deviate from the path like you do, or am I like Ray and stick to the path?"

"Oh, you're like Ray." Ruby raised an eyebrow. "Why?"

It wasn't the answer Cali wanted, and actually she was slightly offended by it. "It's weird seeing how personalities merge with how people play basketball. You change your path so it benefits all, though it confuses others sometimes. I think Ray sticks to the path because she doesn't like change. Remember how she didn't like your haircut and how you said that was because she was controlling?" Cali was getting awfully wordy; Ruby tried her best to keep up. Cali took notice. "Ray also gets mad at others for deviating when it isn't really necessary."

"I don't mean that you hate deviation. I mean that you're very insecure on the court. You don't like to take risks." Ruby was messing with the keys and had her eyes glued to them. "You agree, right?"

Cali hesitated, thinking before she spoke, "I can see that. I guess I don't notice the openings when they're there."

"You do."

"What?"

"You do, Cali. You don't want to take the risk in case you mess someone else up."

Cali cocked her head, still not grasping an understanding.

"Oh, by the way." Ruby pulled a *Hoopsters* book from 2015. I'm not sure if you know this, this book is just a basketball book. Cali bit her lip. "I did some research on your brother."

Cali went to open the car door to run, but Ruby quickly locked the doors.

"Cali. You can't keep running from this. Please, let me speak," Ruby pleaded.

Cali crossed her arms and sunk into her seat.

"You are a great basketball player. Ray and I talked about this when we first met. I was wondering where you got it from, but when I figured out that you had a brother, it all started to come together." Ruby sighed in annoyance, "Cali. Look at me."

Cali looked over.

"You can't fight genetics."

Ruby opened the book to Yarmen's page. She pointed to Cali's brother. *Louis Horn. Born to Naja and Joel Horn.* She brought the book down to read his report:

> *"Standing at a height of 6'3", Louis averages fourteen points a game, ten rebounds, five steals, and three assists per game. He has been playing on Yarmen's varsity since he was a freshman. Louis is committed to playing with UCLA."*

Cali stared down at the dashboard.

> *"Then he was found with drugs and kicked out of UCLA in 2013, two years into his career. Louis died in a car accident in 2014."*

"What? Drugs? I thought he just dropped out! That's what my parents told me. He's not a criminal. You have the wrong Louis Horn," Cali said frantically.

"You didn't know he was a criminal?" Ruby slowly put her hand over her mouth, realizing her mistake.

"He is *not* a criminal. Criminals are horrible people; my brother is *not* a horrible person!"

Ruby slammed her hand down on her horn, alerting Ray from inside her house. "Cali, your brother is *dead*," she yelled. "He was losing it all, so he became a criminal like me."

"How do you know?"

"Why else would someone become a criminal? I didn't go out and decide to become one. I joined my group of friends and they got me to steal. It then became an addiction." Ruby rested her head on the wheel.

Cali's throat burned with tears. She turned away and let tears flow freely.

"Cali, I'm sorry," Ruby sighed. "I'm sorry that your life isn't as perfect as you want it to be."

"My life is *far* from perfect! Quit acting like you know me!" Cali growled. "I . . . my parents lied to me."

Ruby stayed quiet while she listened to Cali cry softly. She looked out of her window. "Right, sorry. I went too far."

"You just want to protect your ego."

Ruby nodded. She disagreed, but was trying to calm Cali down. "Let's go get those earpieces." She started the car. "It's getting dark and cold, so we better be fast."

Cali couldn't believe Louis was a criminal. It seemed like her truth had been turned upside down, so she ignored it completely.

"Ruby." Cali continued to stare out the window, down at the moving stripes of the road. "Why did you threaten me at first? Why did you hate me at first?"

"I was selfish, I wanted Keagan taken down, and I knew you were going to get in the way. I realized that you liked Ray too much, and I relaxed. Ray really wants you to change to fit her world. I think you're fine, you're fourteen. I was like you, cold-hearted." Ruby fleshed out the question. "Ray is controlling, remember, she wants people to fit her world."

Cali nodded. "Ray hates me?"

"She doesn't hate you, she's just mad that you don't fit her vision. She wants everyone to be nice, funny, and comfortable. That's not what life is, and she is going to realize that," Ruby snickered. "Let Ray change on her own and don't listen to her. Don't change right now Cali, you will on your own." Ruby ran her hands through her hair. "Cali when you're playing basketball, who can you control?"

Cali paused. "Me?"

"Yes, thanks for actually knowing," Ruby snickered. "Although communication makes it way easier to play as a team."

"What are you trying to tell me?"

"I don't really know I'm just rambling."

Cali felt her shoulder, remembering how Ruby dug her sharp nails into it and left five small now-healed scars. "Do you still wear your nails? You know that you left scars on me, right?"

Ruby raised her eyebrows. "Back then, that was my reason. I wanted to remind you that I would never leave, but now I will leave you alone. I truly care about you, so I stopped wearing them altogether. Though I will wear them when I believe I will need them." Ruby held up her hand, showing her normal fingernails.

"What would you need them for?"

"What I did to you. Put scars on you so you would remember me." Ruby laughed. "I may not be a thief anymore, but I still love being the bad guy."

CHAPTER 12

The three walked through the entrance of the fall festival. Cali instantly stopped to take in the overwhelming beauty of the place. White lights streamed over the booths, posts, and everything else, giving the place a dimly lit outside aesthetic. The festival was on a flat large plain outside of the city. The stage was the most decorated. The curtains were crimson red and neatly attended to. The rest of the stage was made from wood and steel.

Ruby pushed past Cali and Ray with a bag. "I see the seniors did better than last year."

"Yeah," Ray laughed.

"Let's go backstage."

The three hopped onto the stage. Ruby moved the curtains to the side and let Ray and Cali in. The stage was dimly lit and had a viewing screen attached.

Ruby waved them over behind towers of cardboard boxes. The backstage seemed like it wasn't cleaned out since last year, so there were many random things in the way.

Ruby opened her bag and brought out her laptop. "I'll do what I have to do. You guys will have to find somewhere to go in the meantime." Ruby held out the earpieces. "Take these and go have fun . . . and thank you guys for the help."

"Wait, so we did all of this work, and we don't get to do *anything*?" Ray scoffed.

"You'll be rewarded, trust me." Ruby looked down at her laptop. "This is the end."

Cali got up. "Ray, let's go."

Ray looked at Cali with defeat in her eyes. "Wait, this is actually it. This is the end of this all?" After this, she wouldn't have to deal with Ruby anymore.

"Yes."

"I really don't want this to end," Ray admitted. "As much as we've fought, I've had fun this week."

How was Ray so attached to Ruby after such a short time? "Ray, let's go."

Ray huffed and left with Cali.

Ray and Cali sat at a lunch table by the food booths. It was around 6:00 p.m. when people of all ages streamed into the festival.

Ray explained to Cali that each club from the school had their own booths. For every three people in the club, they got one booth. The Drama Club was the biggest club, but they didn't have a booth since they had nothing to sell. They were at the festival to advertise their next play with posters. The second biggest club was the cooking club with six booths and eighteen people in the club. The club leaders had the biggest booth with the oldest members.

Then Ray talked about how the festival started and how she knew *all* the history. It happened every fall to celebrate the first settlers of Swallowsville, and the winter festival celebrated the date when Swallowsville was officially made a town.

Ray perked up as she saw Piper and Sienna together and waved them over. Piper reluctantly sat down next to Cali, crossing her arms, and looking ahead.

Sienna sat next to Ray. "Hey, guys." She looked around. "Where is Ruby? I always see her at the festivals."

Ray and Cali looked at each other nervously. "She had a headache, so she didn't come," Ray blurted out.

Sienna squinted.

"For how 'tough' she is, wouldn't she just take some medicine, suck it up, and come to the festival?" Piper scoffed.

"If you think you're tougher, why aren't you on varsity?" Sienna rolled her eyes.

"Well, she did get moved down, so . . ." Piper grinned. "Clearly she wasn't that tough!"

Ray jumped over the table and grabbed Piper by the shirt. "SHE ONLY GOT MOVED DOWN BECAUSE SHE WAS THE LEAST LIKED!"

Piper stared blankly, unable to comprehend Ray's reaction.

"YOU'D END UP JUST LIKE HER!"

Sienna pulled Ray back.

"People are looking, you dumbass," Sienna mumbled. "But Piper, she's right. I'm starting to realize why

Talivikki didn't choose you. You and Delilah are both good at basketball."

Piper glared down at the ground.

"Delilah has a good heart with a diabolic body, while you have a violent heart but a small body," Sienna explained. "Do you get what I'm saying?"

"I didn't choose to be born the way I was born. I didn't want to be smaller than my sister. I want my sister's body if she won't use it to her full potential."

Sienna rolled her eyes.

"You don't need your sister's body, you just have to be a good teammate."

Ray looked down. "I'm a good teammate, right?"

"No."

Ray cocked her head. That clearly wasn't the answer she wanted. "What? How?"

"You yell at everyone, too." Sienna dragged her hand down her face in annoyance. "I only excuse you because you have Cali with you, she'll help you change, but Piper, on the other hand . . ."

"I don't need to change."

"You will have to if you want to get onto varsity. Trust me. Talivikki will bite your behavior right in the ass as soon as she can."

"Why do you have to swear so much?"

Piper rolled her eyes and rested her heads in her hands.

"I take care of six kids; don't you think I'm stressed a lot? It carries over." Sienna shrugged.

Piper's head perked up. "There's Keagan, and she's with Harlow..."

"Those two have been best buds since Keagan is the most likely to be famous. I mean I *think*." Sienna laid her arm on the table. "I hate Harlow."

Ray scoffed, "You seem to hate everyone."

"Harlow is a very fake person. She only acts nice to people because she wants a good reputation."

"I've been out with Harlow a few times, though!"

"Well, it seems like her tactics are working. I heard that she talked to Cali. Cali, did she speak to you?"

Cali thought about it for a second, that was the first day of school, where Ray left Cali alone.

"Yes."

Sienna laughed, "Did it make you feel comforted?"

Cali nodded.

"See? She read you, easily. Don't trust her, you guys, she and I have a long history," Sienna laughed.

"You used to be one of the top students in Swallowsville before Harlow came out, then you stopped trying," Piper spilled.

Sienna slammed her fist down on the table. "Yeah. Why do you think I smoke pot, you little—"

"Hey, guys." Harlow walked over with a smile. "I see Ruby isn't with you two." Harlow cocked her head. "That's good."

"She had a headache," Ray sighed.

"Oh. So, you're still talking to her even after I told you two to stop. She's a criminal."

Sienna glanced at the three, amused. "Look, Harlow, these kids can do what they want. Let them make mistakes and learn. Just because you're 'famous' doesn't mean you can push others around."

Cali was sick of Harlow's "criminal" excuse. Now that Cali knew that her own brother was one, she found it easier to sympathize with Ruby. She had already started to, but now it was much easier.

Harlow blinked. "I want them to have a normal high school life. If they're around a criminal, they won't."

"Look. Harlow. Just leave, alright?"

Harlow nodded and left in defeat.

Ray was saddened. Sienna nudged her. "Sorry for the bomb."

Ray shrugged and smiled. "It's fine."

This was obviously a lie, since Cali could see pain in Ray's eyes.

Cali rested her head on the table. She knew Harlow would be bad. Harlow had already yelled at Cali for being around Ruby *and* called her immature. Harlow wasn't the best person. *No* one was the best person. No one around her was perfect, not even Cali.

"You guys want to come with Piper and me to get some food from the cooking club?" Sienna asked.

Ray showed her the mini sugar donuts. "We already got food."

"You're coming anyway." Sienna got up. "Keagan's speaking in like, forty minutes. We have to get food while we can."

Those forty minutes seemed to pass in seconds.

"Attention, festival-goers," the mayor of Swallowsville, Griffin Antler, stood onstage next to Talivikki. "I would like you to focus your attention to the stage. For the first time in five years, a possible candidate will go on to play in the WNBA."

"God, this is so cheesy," Sienna mumbled.

"Agreed," Piper responded.

Keagan came out from behind the curtains clad in a teal dress that flowed nicely behind her. She waved to the people who crowded around the stage.

"This is Keagan Perry, a seventeen-year-old, straight-A student. She hasn't committed to any colleges yet, but plans to commit to UCLA."

The microphone was abruptly cut. A deeper, scratchier voice came over the speakers.

"Keagan Perry is not a straight-A student like they tell you. I have her grades here to prove that to you." The screen switched on, displaying Keagan's fake grades, Cs, and Ds. "Another thing is, she doesn't actually want to play basketball! She wants to be a track star," Ruby growled over the speakers.

Ruby had somehow figured out a way to change her voice, almost completely changing her plan from before. All Ruby was going to do was display her grades.

Keagan looked horrified, Talivikki was amused, and the mayor was extremely confused.

Sienna slammed her hands on the table and glared directly into Ray's eyes. "Ruby is doing this isn't she?"

Ray shook her head frantically. "I don't know!"

Piper laughed, enjoying the varsity player's suffering.

The speakers were quickly turned off and so was the screen. Nobody knew what to say, the air was filled with tension.

Talivikki laughed. "Seems like someone is jealous of Keagan!" She looked out into the crowd. "Now, none of this is true. Someone got into the office and changed her grades."

The mayor got his microphone turned back on. "Sorry for the inconvenience. Keagan, I will let you speak for yourself."

Cali realized this would be the first time she would hear Keagan speak, so she perked up.

"Yeah, none of that is true," Keagan spoke like more of an adult than anything. "I was here to give a speech about how you can be like me and get anywhere you want to." Keagan laughed. "I know this is all awkward after what happened, but I will now continue what I was here to speak about."

"She speaks really . . . professionally," Ray mumbled.

"Well, what else did you expect since she's so 'perfect.'" Piper rolled her eyes.

"She reminds me of Harlow in a way. She's really quiet though, as I've heard, unlike Harlow." Sienna messed with her braid.

"I think I'm going to go home," Cali announced, getting up from the table.

"What? Don't you want to listen to Keagan?" Ray grabbed Cali's arm.

"Not really." Cali moved Ray's hand. "I've heard enough."

"Let her go." Sienna nodded.

Cali left. She really didn't know why; it was more on impulse. She realized she didn't have a ride home, so she sat by Ruby's car.

A couple of minutes later, Ruby came running from the festival. "Cali?"

Cali looked up. "I see you changed plans at the last minute."

"Yeah, we got to go. I think someone saw me." Ruby shoved Cali up and got into the driver's seat. Cali slid into the passenger's seat and quickly put on her seatbelt. Ruby pulled the car out of the parking lot and left with a screech of the tires. "Oh, I think everyone heard that," Ruby mumbled.

Ruby sped down the roads to get Cali home as quickly as possible. Ruby had said before that the ride to the festival was usually ten minutes long. Cali got home in five minutes. Ruby left immediately as soon as Cali got out.

It was around 7:20 p.m. Cali opened the door and walked down the hall into her brother's room. She looked for any signs of her brother being a criminal, and lo and behold, buried deeply in his drawer she found a court order.

So, it was true. Louis was a criminal.

Cali sat down on his bed, staring at the court order. She felt guilty for ever hating Ruby for being a criminal. She was so hypocritical.

Cali thought back to Ray's hypocrisy, back when she repeated something that she had criticized Harlow for. She thought back farther than that when Ray used her father's credit card. Ray was also guilty for judging Ruby for stealing when she herself was stealing. Perhaps in Ray's eyes, it was justified. Or maybe it was because Ray, in her world, couldn't do any wrong. They all had a few things in common . . . they all lost someone . . . and basketball.

Cali laughed, realizing that everyone around her was imperfect, even herself, and that she never could be perfect, no matter how hard she tried.

CHAPTER 13

Cali stood in the Blackridge High School's locker room—an away game. She was holding a paper and crying softly.

The paper had Sienna's picture on it with bold, black letters underneath that read, "MISSING." Sienna had been missing since mid-September, a full two weeks. This was the official report of Sienna's disappearance. It hadn't been filed right away, since Sienna had a history of running away. Piper was the one to finally file it after coming to terms with her being missing.

Cali was in the showers, where no one could hear her crying. Ruby was the first to check on her.

"Hey, are you okay?"

Cali didn't look up.

The last time they had seen Sienna was two weeks and a day before, in practice.

"Ruby." Sienna pulled Ruby aside, away from the others. "You shouldn't have done anything to Keagan."

Ruby glared. "Who are you to lecture me? I'm older than you; you should have more respect."

"You're only older by a day, Ruby," Sienna mumbled.

Ruby continued to glare.

"I'm not going to say anything to anyone, I just want you to know I know what you did."

Ruby brought her voice down. "Talivikki and the principal already know that I did that."

Sienna laughed, "Of course, they do. That's them for you."

Nothing happened other than that since the festival. Cali began to distance herself from Ruby, but Ray and Ruby were still friends. There had been no reward like Ruby promised, and Keagan was still on varsity and Ruby was still on the 'C team'.

Everyone on the team was sad, but the one who was the most depressed was Piper. Piper had given up on almost everything and even stopped coming to practice. Though she wouldn't admit that she was sad, she did announce that she didn't care about Sienna. Everyone knew it wasn't true.

Piper came to games, and she was in the locker room, but legally Piper could not play. Ruby rudely grabbed Cali's arm and forced her to stay with the team. Everyone sat around on the benches, staring glumly at the ground.

Ruby got angry. "Guys, we have a game to play!"

Everyone glared up at Ruby, even the 'outcasts': Hayden, Kimberly, and River. Since no one in the group was truly a leader, no one there knew what to do to take the first steps. Justice took some responsibility as the oldest. Usually, Ray would try to act like a leader or hero, but when it came down to it, she couldn't do it. She wasn't emotionally ready.

Piper walked up to Cali and swiped the paper from her. "Have fun playing you guys."

"You aren't even going to sit on the bench? You aren't even dressed in your jersey," Justice commented.

"Oh, I am." Piper lifted up her hoodie. "Milan won't let me play."

Ever since Milan had practically insulted Sienna's disappearance, the team had stopped calling her Coach. She was just Milan.

"Guys, you need to stop moping over Sienna's disappearance. We didn't lose much at all." Milan threw her cola on the ground, losing her temper. "Especially you, Piper!"

Everyone looked at Milan in horror. The one coach they loved turned out to be a horrible person. Not surprising, considering what had happened in the past week.

"How can you say that?" Justice growled. Now that Sienna was gone, it was time for the older kids to show their maturity and responsibility.

Milan glanced away. "When you're here, you're *here*."

Everyone glanced at each other with anger in their eyes.

Life at school had gone downhill for the 'C team' ever since Sienna went missing. There were no suspects at all. Cali suspected Ruby at first, but that was quickly ruled out since Ruby was with Ray and Cali at the time of the disappearance. The culprit had to be among them.

Milan opened the door to the locker room angrily. "Guys. Our game starts in five minutes, and you haven't even warmed up!"

"We're getting there, Milan," Justice mumbled and got up.

"*Coach* Milan."

"Nope!" Piper got up and shoved Milan to the side. "Not after this season you won't be *Coach* Milan."

Ray got up and pushed Cali out. Blackridge's basketball court was almost the same size as Swallowsville's 'B team' court. The bleachers, benches, and logo were black. The mascot was a black lion with bright white eyes, which made Cali laugh because it reminded her of the silhouettes in her dreams. Blackridge was pretty far up North, closer to Canada.

Native American reservations made up most of Blackridge's population. Most of North Dakota's demographic was Caucasian, there usually wasn't much diversity in smaller schools. However, the closer into the cities you were, the more diversity existed.

Each team had their own themes, Cali noticed. Since they were a small farming town, they played country songs for the varsity game. Swallowsville had generic pop music. Since Blackridge was more rural, the team looked like and played like they were from the country.

The team didn't warm up at all since, as Milan said, they had only five minutes.

Cali was a starter on the 'C team' along with Ray, Piper, Justice, and Mel. Usually, Mel would switch with Sienna, but no one knew who she would be switching with now that Sienna was gone. Justice was the jumper, Mel was a post, Ray was a point guard—though she was bad at managing and leading. Piper was a shooting guard, and Cali was a wing player.

Ruby always complained to Milan that these weren't the correct terms, but Milan brushed her off.

Cali was guarding a girl who was about the same height as she was. As a wing, she was the smallest, meaning the players she had were also the smallest. That didn't mean they were the easiest to guard. Most of these wing players were really cocky. Ray said that she had it worse, but Cali had to disagree.

The girl had tan skin with some scars on her face. Her hair was jet black with a light blue streak in it and pulled into a low, spiky ponytail, kind of like Ray's.

"So, what do you order at Gale's Burgers?" Cali's defender asked, smiling smugly. Gale's was an international worldwide burger chain. Cali ignored her.

After an hour, their game was finished, and it was time for the 'B team' to play. Everyone knew what was coming, since they had lost badly. Milan would lecture them about how Sienna's absence shouldn't have brought them all down, and how they should have focused on the game and all that. The entire team had enough of it all and didn't even go back into the locker room. Instead, they all went to the concession stands to buy food.

In some way, Sienna's disappearance brought the team together. Everyone was nice to each other and comforted each other when needed. The only person who would accept none of this was Piper. Everyone could tell that she was hurting horribly. So, the team pitched in and bought her a kitten.

"We have something for you, Piper." Justice brought up a box from under the table.

"We know how much you've been hurting, so we all pitched in to get you something that we hope you'll like."

"It has holes in it. What kind of present has holes in—" Piper quickly tore it open, realizing what it was.

Out popped a small, fluffy, white, and gray kitten with darker gray stripes on its back. It wore a little red collar with a flat heart charm attached to the buckle.

"You can get anything etched into the collar when you name it. We have money for that too." Justice smiled.

Piper was moved to tears, but kept her composure. "I think I'll name it Mars."

"Why Mars?"

"Because that's the God of War."

"*Ah*. Makes perfect sense."

Piper was trying her hardest to be her normal, anger-driven self, but her efforts turned into something more horrible. Piper laid her head down on the lunch table.

Hayden patted her on the head, trying her hardest to comfort her. "Thanks, Hayden."

Hayden held a thumbs up.

Ruby sat at the other end of the table, anxiously picking at her arm. Cali nudged her. "Why are you so anxious?"

"I know one of us did it!"

Everyone turned their head toward her.

"You're saying one of us caused Sienna's disappearance?" Piper scoffed. "Well, we can cross off Hayden, River, and Kimberly. They're always at home. Mel, Justice, and Cali wouldn't have the heart to." Piper squinted and pointed at Ray. "She would. She's insane!"

Ray's eyes widened. She jumped over the table, just as she did at the festival, grabbed her by the hoodie and screamed, "YOU'RE ACCUSING ME WHILE YOU COULD ALSO BE THE CULPRIT!"

"This is only going to divide us if we accuse each other," Hayden said.

Everyone raised their eyebrows. Ray hesitated before letting Piper go.

"Hayden's right," Justice said. "We have to be, you know, *a team*."

Piper nodded.

"Hey, you." Cali was prodded in the shoulder. "My mom said I should apologize for taunting you."

Cali looked behind her to see the girl she was guarding earlier. "What?"

"You heard me."

"Why? What is your name even?" Cali asked.

"Alli." She turned to leave. "Now, I said that I was sorry. I'm going to leave now." Alli turned to leave but turned her head to see if Cali even cared.

Cali looked at Ruby, confused.

Alli ran back over and grabbed Cali's shoulders. "Please talk to me. You look so cool. What's your phone number!"

Cali pushed her away. "Sorry. I don't know you."

"You're the Horn girl. I heard your brother was a good basketball player." Alli took a step back.

Cali was caught by surprise.

"You also have Keagan going to your school. My sister is great friends with Keagan, actually."

Ruby jumped up. "Cali will take your number." She smiled back at Cali.

Cali shook her head. Her part was done. She didn't have to help with Keagan anymore.

"Cali, can I talk to you?" Ruby waved Ray over.

Cali sighed and nodded. Ray came over and they walked into an empty hallway.

"Keagan technically hasn't been taken down yet. Our deal was that we would get Keagan taken down from varsity."

"Ruby," Ray stopped her. "Can you lay off for a bit? Please?"

"No," Ruby shouted. "Please! I know I promised rewards and there will be if you just help me!" Ruby went into her little "poor me" act.

Ray sighed in annoyance. "Okay. What are the rewards?"

"I'm working with Talivikki. She wants us to gain attention for Swallowsville and then I will be put back onto varsity and you two will be put onto the 'B team'."

Ray and Cali looked at each other in shock. "Wait, Talivikki knows about us?"

"Yeah. I'm not sure if I was supposed to tell you or not, but yup." Ruby gave a thumbs-up.

"What kind of arc is this?" Ray chuckled. "Well, if this *is* true then I am in!"

Cali wasn't too sure. "I don't really want to move up on the list."

"Well, whether you do something or not you will be moved up. That's what Talivikki promised, and she is a woman of her word."

Cali groaned in annoyance and dragged her hand over her face. "Fine, I will help, but this is the last time. You know what else we need to do? Find the person behind Sienna's disappearance, and the people involved in the Fox Den shooting."

"Yeah!" Ray was super hyper now.

"You aren't heroes," Ruby mumbled.

"We can try," Cali said.

The next second, it seemed, they were interrogating Alli, a sixth grader, "What do you know about Keagan?"

"I mean, I know that she was really horrible to my sister. My sister plays on varsity," Alli said nervously.

"Who is your sister?" Ruby shook her.

"Roze." Alli shrugged. "It's weird, spelled with a 'z' instead of an 's.'"

"We should talk to the varsity right now," Ray piped up. "They aren't playing."

"Alli, can you come with us and point out your sister?"

Alli nodded and led the way.

Eliza stopped Cali. "Cali. Are you serious?"

Cali cocked her head. "What?"

"Exploiting a sixth grader?" Eliza put her hands on her hips, annoyed. "Cali, I thought you were better than that."

"It's for a reason that I can't get out of. Why do you care anyway?" Cali asked.

Eliza smirked for a second but soon became serious. "I know why you're doing what you're doing. I heard."

Cali glanced down. "You can't tell anyone."

"Oh, trust me, I won't." Eliza held up her hand. "I also know who the kidnapper is, but I won't tell you so that you can learn a lesson. You might need it later on."

Cali grabbed Eliza's shoulders. "You know who did it?"

"*Shhh!* Keep it down!" Eliza scanned around and leaned forward. "Yes, I know who did it."

"Then tell me!"

"Cali, no. Let me finish." Eliza pushed Cali's hands off. "You know who it is at heart. Use the brain that you were given and figure it out."

Cali glared. "Why don't you tell me who did it?"

Eliza ignored the question. "I'm always in the wrong places at the wrong time. I know too much, actually,"

Eliza's voice broke. "That's going to be the death of me, I'm sure! Just listen to your heart, but use your mind as well."

Cali nodded, but felt uneasy.

"Make the right choices too." Eliza sat down at the table next to them. "Sienna went missing, now you're taking on the big job of finding it out yourself instead of leaving it to the police, and of course, the police are not doing a thing about it. You got yourself pulled into a big thing that you don't want to get into. I've dealt with people like you before. I probably have never told you this, but I want to be a therapist. That's why I am the way I am," Eliza rambled. "I seem to have a curse that I am always in the wrong place at the wrong time. So, I'll use the curse to help people like you. Cali, I'd like you to come to my house sometimes just so I can talk to you. I don't want you to go down the wrong path. We may be the same age, but I definitely know more."

Cali nodded.

"No offense. Anyway, they're probably looking for you. See you later, Cali."

Cali watched Eliza go back to the team. She shook her head. "What in the world?" Cali said to the ground. *She knows who did it.* Cali looked back at her. "She did it. Eliza did it? *Eliza* did it!" she said under her breath.

Cali caught up to the three. Alli was searching the crowd looking for her sister while the two egged her on.

"Guys!" Cali tugged on Ruby's sleeve. "I have something important to tell you!"

"Not now, Cali," Ruby muttered.

Cali rolled her eyes and stepped away.

"There she is," Alli exclaimed.

Roze turned over to them and rolled her eyes. "It's that tall girl," Roze mouthed to her friends.

Alli walked them over to Roze. The varsity team went silent seeing the younger kids. They also seemed extremely annoyed.

"What do you want, Alli?"

"These guys want to know how you and Keagan were friends." Alli glanced back, looking for reassurance. Ruby gave a thumbs-up.

"I remember you," Roze mumbled. "You're on varsity."

"Yup." Ruby eyed Ruby and Cali to stay quiet, but Ray didn't get the message.

"No, you're not—"

Ruby clapped her hand over Ray's mouth, and muffled her words. Roze raised an eyebrow. Cali could guess that Roze was the leader, more like a tyrant of the varsity.

"You got moved down, didn't you?" Roze spoke and moved slowly ... like a dangerous snake.

"Are you a point guard?" Cali asked.

"Yes, why?"

"Makes sense," Cali sneered.

Ray elbowed her in the stomach.

Roze glared. "Anyway, what do you Swallowsville blowouts want?"

"They want to know how you know Keagan," Alli said.

"Look, I don't have time to talk to you about this. It's a long story." Roze shooed them off.

"We won't play against you guys until December. Please?" Ruby put her foot up onto the bleachers.

Roze shifted her weight from one leg to another. "Fine, I'll give you my phone number. Then, we can make arrangements."

"Who do you think you are, Roze? God?" Alli stepped forward.

Roze scoffed, "Do you think you're special for being used by these guys?"

Alli frowned.

"Hey, be nice to your sister," Cali spoke up. "Please."

Roze got down to Cali's height. "And who are *you* to say that?"

"Cali Horn. I'm on the 'C team'."

Roze laughed.

"A first-year telling a fourth-year what to do? *And* she's on the 'C team'!" Roze looked back at her team. They all laughed awkwardly. *Probably scared not to laugh.*

"Why should that matter?" Cali looked her dead in her, obviously fake purple contacts. "In the end, we'll all end up walking across the stage to get a piece of paper and a handshake."

Roze raised her eyebrows. "You're still younger. You're perfect for Swallowsville!"

Cali punched Roze in the side of the face, silencing her instantly. Cali could hear Ruby and Ray gasp in the background. Roze held the side of her face, shocked.

Cali stood with her arms crossed. "I might be small and younger than you, but you will *not* push me around," Cali growled.

Roze's team slowly all smiled. Some looked at each other in disbelief.

Ruby and Ray pulled Cali back.

"Why would you do that? She's a top player," Ruby hissed.

"I don't care," Cali whispered back.

Roze's face slowly turned from shock to impressed. "I want to talk to just you."

Roze got off of the bleachers and looked down at Cali, who now realized how tall Roze was; she had to be at least 6'3". Ruby and Ray were also taken aback. Cali nodded, knowing she couldn't decline.

The two walked into the hallway. Roze stayed silent until they reached a classroom where she shoved Cali into a desk and slammed the door shut.

Cali sighed, wondering what she got herself into now.

Roze stood over Cali, who knew she was about to have it handed to her. As soon as Roze went in for her hoodie, Cali ducked and went under the desk. Cali stared at her from the other side. Roze threw the desk over and ran at Cali. Cali tried her best to get away, but was scooped up and practically baseball pitched into a wall . . . a reminder that she wasn't indestructible.

Cali wheezed in pain as Roze stood in front of her.

"You will never be able to beat someone in a fight, no matter how fast you are. You will always have that height disadvantage."

The door opened and there was Eliza waving a red napkin. "*Olé*," Eliza smirked. "Are you done?"

Roze nodded. "Look, I was just trying to teach her a lesson."

"That's what I do, now back off." Eliza helped Cali up.

"What were you even trying to get across? Were you just trying to protect your pride?" Eliza had no fear of talking to Roze. "Your teammates seem to already hate you."

Roze snorted, "She's going to need my help anyway."

Eliza rolled her eyes and kicked Roze in the shin. "You may be a powerhouse, but your shins will always get you down." Eliza whispered to Cali, "Remember that."

Roze shook off the pain. "I bet I know what your weakness is."

Eliza turned to Cali, ignoring Roze. "Look, first you learned that no one is perfect, but now you need to learn what weaknesses people are born with and how to exploit them. You're going to need to."

Cali raised her eyebrow. "Why is that?"

Eliza tilted her head forward.

Cali realized what she was talking about. She was going to need it for whomever had Sienna, whomever caused the Fox Den shooting, and Keagan.

Roze ran her hand through her hair. "Sorry."

Eliza turned again. "Sure, you are." She smiled sarcastically.

Roze glared. "I look forward to working with you, Cali. See you later."

Roze waved and quickly left the room.

Eliza sighed. "Look, the Fox Den shooters are going to be strong. You are a small woman." Eliza poked her. "You will never win that battle face-to-face. That's why you'll need to learn weaknesses. Same with the person who caused Sienna's disappearance. Weaknesses. You're the type to fight, so I'm guessing that you will end up fighting. Probably even to the death."

"Look, Eliza. I don't want to be rude or anything, but I'm not here for a therapy session."

Eliza laughed. "No. Listen to me. You will need it. Like you just saw, you aren't invincible."

Cali nodded. "I'm *not* weak."

"God, I hate, but I love, your stubbornness."

Cali found Ruby and Ray talking to the varsity team, although Keagan was nowhere in sight. The players around the table were who she now knew to be Olive, Delilah, Connor, Joy, Erie, and Skye. These were the elite of the elite in North Dakota.

"Oh, so Keagan is better than I am?" Ruby growled.

"Why do you think you got put down to the 'C team'. Not even the 'B team', but the 'C team'." Erie rolled her eyes. Erie had seen Ray and Cali in animal masks.

"Why would you say that?" Delilah asked innocently.

"Shut up, Delilah. You're too innocent for a fight like this."

Delilah glanced away, confused, but quiet.

"Hey, can we not treat Delilah like that, she's the second best," Skye piped up.

Erie rolled her eyes. "Yeah, can we be nicer. We might end up hanging around each other for the rest of our lives."

Joy put on her warmup after giving Erie angry look.

"I don't really care, Joy," Erie said pettily. "Look, Ruby, we aren't buddy-buddy anymore. Get lost."

Ruby's mouth hung open. "So, it is just about how good someone is?" Ruby flung her arms and hands out.

"I've been with you guys since middle school! Were we never friends?"

The team stayed silent.

Ruby's voice broke, "We've been together since we were twelve. We went through everything together!"

They all glanced at each other. Delilah got up and hugged Ruby. "Look." Delilah had a soft voice that gave you a hug, the complete opposite to Piper's loud, childlike voice. "I know I only knew you for a year, but don't worry. Next year a couple of us will be gone and you will be on varsity again. There's no need to worry. It's all going to work out in the end."

"Are you sure you and Piper are related?" Ray asked.

Delilah nodded. If you had ever asked Piper if she and Delilah were related, Piper would deny it, always. Delilah was the complete opposite of Piper in every way. Delilah was tall (5'7'), muscular, menacing, but on the other hand, she was kind and nurturing, and gave back to the world. Piper was short (4'11), skinnier, fueled with rage and always took without ever giving back. Yet, they were twins. The only things they had in common were their blood, genes, and their hair. Piper's face was sharp, and Delilah's was rounder. Piper had two braids and Delilah had one.

"The only difference between Delilah and Piper is that Delilah is getting college offers at fifteen!" Olive slapped Delilah's back. Delilah looked uncomfortable.

"Is everything okay here?"

Cali looked up to see Keagan standing tall, not dropping her head even one centimeter. Her stance was so confident and impressive. Cali knew she would never be like that.

Ruby tensed up but smiled. "Absolutely."

Keagan stared at Ruby. "Are you the one I replaced?"

"Yes."

Keagan held out her hand and Ruby held out hers. Keagan grabbed it and forced her to shake. Ruby was angered since Keagan acted like such a leader, something that Ruby would never be, something that the 'C team' didn't have. Although Justice was trying her best, she still was not a leader. She just thought that as the oldest, she should bear the responsibility.

"Nice meeting you, Ruby. I'm sure we will play together next year," Keagan spoke with that formal tone of hers.

Ruby forced a smile.

Keagan pulled her in and talked into her ear, "I can tell you're faking it. I know you're jealous, but let's get over ourselves."

Ruby shook with anger as she pushed Keagan away. "Stop acting like you're perfect!" Ruby gripped Keagan's shoulders.

Cali realized that Ruby had on her sharp black fingernails. Keagan's face stayed calm the whole time.

What Ruby said next made the air go cold, like a ghost passing through a room, "I want you to remember what you made me go through. Forever. This is for taking something from me that you didn't need, track star."

Joy ripped Ruby away from Keagan and Connor ripped Keagan away from Ruby. Keagan's warmup ripped as they were peeled away from each other.

"YOU TORE HER WARMUP! ARE YOU INSANE?" Erie shook Ruby.

Ray and Cali peered at each other. "I thought she stopped wearing those."

Cali thought back to the night when she discovered that her brother was a criminal. Ruby said that she would never use her nails again on Cali but would use them if she needed to make someone remember her. "She told me she would use them for this specific purpose, but I didn't think she was crazy enough to use them on Keagan," Cali yell-whispered.

"Of course, she would, Cali!" Ray snorted.

Ruby was shaking too much in anger to speak. Keagan kept her head up and refused any help from Connor.

"Forgive her. We can at least try to understand her. She had something close to her heart suddenly ripped away in an instant, and I am to blame. Do not hate her. Instead, try to understand her." Keagan nodded at Ruby.

Ruby stared at Keagan with daggers, a killing type of stare. The same one Ray had when she attacked Cali.

"Ruby. Please."

Ruby backed away. "Remember my name!" She hissed, "Ruby Aurthur."

CHAPTER 14

"They finally got the flag back up," Ray commented as they walked onto the school yard.

"They never had it up before? Why not?"

"The drama kids kept taking it down due to the disrespect they were getting. It's sad," Ray mumbled coldly.

Cali had grown much closer to Ray over the past month, but still had to keep guard around her emotionally. It seemed to Cali like Ray was getting more and more mentally unstable since Sienna's disappearance, but she refused any help. This annoyed Cali since Ray always said that she wanted to die. Ray promised to stop saying this so much, but every time something small went wrong, Ray would claim that the sentence just "slipped out." Cali had to deal with it since Ray was all she had. She couldn't escape. The words affected Cali deeply due to her past. Cali had always wanted to just give up, but she never did for whatever reason. She truly felt sorry for Ray, but Ray wouldn't stop, and took it as merely a joke.

"I want to get a closer look at the flag, I don't think I've ever seen it before." Cali jutted her head towards it.

"Alright!" Ray smiled and trotted over to the flag.

Cali hated Ray's predictably unpredictable nature. She had severe anger issues, but how far would things go before Ray exploded to a point that no one has ever witnessed before?

They walked across bright green grass that was most likely fake, by statues, rocks, tables, and other students. It was early in the morning, 7:45 a.m. They were there relatively early. The sun was just stretching over the horizon. The mighty grey steel flagpole protruded into the sky, displaying a mighty flag that flew gracefully into the sky.

"They don't destroy the flag; they just take it. So, the school uses the same one over and over. Actually, they've been using the same one since the school was established. I'm surprised it lasted this long." Ray pointed up at it.

A shadow cast upon the two. It was Keagan. There she was, standing tall and confident. "Hello."

"Hello," the two said in unison.

"I know you guys did something at the festival."

"We didn't do anything," Ray spilled.

Cali turned her head toward Ray, staring at her with a look of annoyance. "Don't snitch now," Cali grumbled.

"You two didn't do anything except guilt by association, you know. Ruby was the one who did it, I know, Talivikki told me," Keagan sighed. "You know Swallowsville is basketball 'central,' right? If you want to be known, you come to this high school."

"We know that," Ray said.

"I just wanted you two to know that I know. Don't tell Ruby any of this. Talivikki wants Ruby to . . . I don't know how to explain it. She wants her to keep at her goal of taking me down." Keagan fiddled with her custom-made hoodie from Harlow. "However, she will never win. One's success will not always take away from yours."

"So, we will not be put up on the 'B team', and Ruby will never be back on varsity?" Cali asked.

"You will. Ruby will be put on varsity, but I will always stay. That's all." Keagan nodded.

The two looked at each other. The flag seemed to fly directly above Keagan, a sunrise in the background showed peace.

"I don't hate you guys." Keagan smiled. "I don't hate Ruby, either. I think this is kind of fun . . . but how did you two know that I don't want to play basketball?"

"Your brother, Nick. Ruby got ahold of him."

Keagan stayed calm, but her eyes showed panic.

"Nick. Of course. He's like Ruby, jealous of me." Keagan stared off into the distance.

"Why are you talking to them?" Ruby asked as she approached the trio.

Keagan stepped down from the pole's platform. "I just wanted to talk." Keagan walked past them. "I'll see you later," she said.

"You can tell she and Harlow are working together." Ray pointed at Keagan. "Her hoodie is one-of-a-kind. You can tell that because there is a white star hand-stitched into the sleeve."

"So, what does that mean?" Cali observed Keagan's sleeve as she walked. There was a white star on it.

"I don't exactly know; I just feel like Harlow is going to help Keagan get known."

Ruby screeched and threw her beanie onto the ground. "God, I messed up so bad with Harlow. I'll never be well-known! After I graduate, I'll probably go back to being a thief! I don't want that! I love you guys and I want you guys to be proud of me."

"You won't. You can't be!" Ray forced her morals onto Ruby. Cali drowned this out as she saw someone in the distance sitting alone at a picnic table not too far away.

It was Eliza. She had an expression of "here we go again" plastered all over her face. Eliza was right; she was always in the wrong place at the wrong time. She heard everything. Cali wondered how much she knew and how traumatized she was from everything she knew about everyone in the school. Cali couldn't imagine hearing all of those conversations. Eliza gave a thumbs-up and went back to her phone.

"Cali and I are going to go to homeroom." Ray nudged Cali.

"I'm going to stay here for a bit."

Ray and Cali quickly walked away to the school.

"Remember, we have Roze to talk to tonight at the café."

"What café?" Cali raised an eyebrow.

"Oh, it's a cat café," Ray shrugged. "Of course, like all the rest of the restaurants, it's downtown."

"Isn't it supposed to rain or snow tonight?"

"Either way, we're walking." Ray turned. "You know what? Let's skip school but still go to practice."

"Why?"

"Everyone will be talking about the festival. I'm not ready to hear anything, *hah*. It will be overwhelming."

Cali sat next to an orange cat in the back of a café where the three of them could talk privately.

"Do you think she will actually show up?" Ray mumbled.

"We've been sitting here for ages."

"Look, she probably had practice, and the drive here takes over forty-five minutes." Ruby laid back in a seat, swatting away the cats trying to climb on her.

"Hey, don't swat them." Cali rubbed her fingers together to get the swatted cat toward her. "All you have to do is pat them on the head and put them down."

Ruby rolled her eyes.

Ray was nervous around the cats. "I don't want to accidentally hurt them," she said under her breath.

Cali squinted. "Is that so?"

Ray nodded. "They're so small, knowing me, how reckless I am."

"Ray," Cali sighed. "How come you admit your recklessness sometimes and other times you refuse to believe it?"

Ray shrugged. "I don't know."

"Anyway," Cali picked up the orange cat and laid it on Ray's lap. "Just pet it."

Ray looked down at the cat, overwhelmed by its purring. "How is it purring? I haven't laid a hand on it!"

"Well, you're probably warm. Those sweatpants of yours may be comfy too." Cali pointed.

"You always give weird answers," Ray grumbled.

"But it's the right answer."

"It's almost 7:00! Where is this woman?!" Ruby slammed her phone down into the table.

"You don't seem happy," Ray said.

Ruby kept her eyes glued on the doorway. "I'm so sick of Keagan. I just want her gone."

"Well, be careful what you wish for, I guess." Ray took a sip of her cola. "She seems like a really nice person!"

Ruby grabbed Ray's coke and threw it at the wall. Thankfully, it was empty. Ruby stared down at Ray angrily.

Ray was unphased. "You should probably fix your hair."

Cali peered down at the soda. Ruby was always getting angry at the slightest hint of disrespect or at the mention of Keagan. Just like Ray, Ruby didn't like disrespect. Cali didn't truly know their personalities; she still couldn't grasp it. Ray could switch from being happy to angry in an instant, and sometimes she didn't react to anger at all.

"Ray." Ray turned to Cali. "Why do you react to anger and other times you don't," Cali asked once again.

"Why are you asking me so many questions?" Ruby hovered over Ray behind her.

"You're so weird."

Ray cocked her head. "Is that an insult?"

Then it hit Cali. *Could Ray understand others all that well?* She understood that they were angry, but did she fully understand *why* they were angry? All she must take away from anger is that they're disrespecting her. But what about the theater incident? *God, Ray was so strange.*

"Never mind," Cali said.

"Sorry we're late." Roze stood tall, looking down at the three. Alli stood beside her and tried to stay still, but it was obvious she was excited.

"I had to bring Alli with me. I didn't have time to take her home. I hope you don't mind."

"No, it's fine, sit down," Ruby scoffed.

Roze nodded and sat down. Cali couldn't help but notice she always looked down at others, which was very true to her personality. Roze retrieved a pen from her pocket and began to shake it slightly. It sounded somewhat like a rattlesnake.

"So, what exactly are we going to talk about?"

"Well." Ruby sat back. "I want to know what your relations are with Keagan. I want to know everything that you know about her."

"She used to go to Blackridge before homeschooling, then came to Swallowsville. That was because of me." Roze pointed to herself. "She stepped over me all the time. You can see that through multiple text conversations I had with her. Once I exposed her to my classmates in my freshman year, her parents made her the victim and forced her to homeschool." Roze slid her phone forward. "These are from years ago; I doubt she's changed. The environment she was in probably wouldn't admit her any break from her 'victim's' way of thinking."

Ruby took the phone and scrolled through the messages. Ray and Cali almost climbed over each other to read them.

"She does seem very manipulative." Ruby looked up. "I wouldn't see someone like you as the type to be pushed around. You're twice her size."

"I grew up with Keagan. We were friends since kindergarten. I trusted her and blindly followed her around, agreeing with everything she did and everything she did to me. I believed that I deserved it, until my parents went through my text messages." Roze ran her hand through her hair. "They told me what was really going on, so I got my revenge and told everyone about her."

"People can change," Ray muttered. "What makes you think she hasn't changed? It's been years, and she seems nice."

"Have you not learned from Harlow? It's just a façade," Ruby sighed.

"What I am going to do is . . ." Roze scratched her chin. "You guys have a Halloween Dance, right?"

Ruby's eyes lit up. "You're going to show everyone at the dance?"

Roze smiled mischievously. "Yup."

"Is that all?" Ruby asked.

"Yeah, but I might as well get some food." Roze shrugged. "I drove awhile to get here, so I might as well stay a bit."

Ruby looked at Cali and Ray. "We might as well plan what we are going to do up until then. There's also the winter festival that she will speak at again. We'll just do the same thing."

They laid out their plans with just four weeks to go until the dance. On the first week, they would steal her jersey. The second week, they would break into her house and steal anything that they could use against her. The third week they really didn't know yet. They couldn't come up with any ideas.

CHAPTER 15

"I really wonder who the Masked Demon is?"

Cali prodded the guys talking about the fall festival. "Who is the Demon?"

"Yeah, that's what we're talking about."

"No." Cali shook her head. "I mean, what is the Masked Demon?"

"Were you not at the fall festival?" The guy leaned forward. "It's the dude with the really deep voice who tried to slander Keagan!"

Cali nervously laughed and backed away. "Sounds like a fairytale."

"If you were there, you would believe it!"

Cali raced off to find Ruby and Ray, texting them while walking to her next class. Soon after the bell, they met up in the restroom. Ray sat on the sink, and Ruby leaned up against the sink while Cali stood facing them. "Ruby, it looks like you've created some fairytale in the school."

"I mean, it's cool, and real so," Ruby snickered. "Is that all you wanted to talk about?"

Cali shrugged. "People are probably going to go on a manhunt for you, Ruby."

"Yeah," Ray hung her feet off the side of the sink, "There actually was a new club founded because of it."

Ruby and Cali glanced at each other. Ruby pushed herself away from the sink. "What? What is it called? How old are the members?"

"Well, they're all young freshmen, our age." Ray leaned against the mirror with her hands behind her head. "From what I saw, there were four of them. The only lead they got is that you got moved down from varsity. I'm sure they're out searching for you, Ruby."

Ruby kicked the ground. "Damn."

"Is that all you have to say?" Ray jumped off the sink in front of Ruby. "You don't absolutely have any plans?"

"If I hide from everybody, they won't be able to find me." Ruby covered her mouth with her hoodie.

"Ruby," Ray grabbed Ruby's shoulders. "There's probably going to end up being a schoolwide manhunt for you. You aren't going to hide from anyone," Ray laughed.

Ruby slammed her hand down onto the sink. "I'll be fine."

"It's been a quick minute since Ruby was ever late to practice," Milan mumbled, looking down at her watch. She paced back and forth. "Once again, Piper is not here. Has anyone tried to get her to come to practice again?"

"She won't listen to any of us. She blames basketball for Sienna's disappearance instead of the people who caused it." Justice shrugged.

"She thinks it's all because of Keagan. She believes Keagan had something to do it with it too." Justice pointed at the two. "Ray and Cali, they were with them.

Harlow began to slander them for hanging out with Ruby and—"

Milan interrupted, "Look Justice I didn't ask for a whole novel." Milan threw her hands up. "I'm just wondering where my players are."

"She's stressed," Eliza whispered to Cali. "She's just taking it out on us."

Cali rolled her eyes. "She shouldn't be, she's supposed to help us through this, isn't she?"

"She's just our coach."

"Hello, is Piper Hester in here?"

Everyone turned to see Talivikki standing in the doorway.

"Her sister, Delilah Hester, told me she was great friends with Sienna Campbell. I wanted to see her so I could tell her some things."

Milan glanced at the ground beneath her, terrified. "She hasn't been coming to practice." Milan bit her lip.

Talivikki blinked and walked over. "She's having a rough time; you'll have to forgive her. Was she coming before or did you say something to get her to stop coming to practice?"

"I can't think of anything I said that would ever stop Piper from coming to practice."

"You said that we shouldn't be sad about Sienna, since we weren't losing much," Eliza yelled from beside Cali. She then covered her mouth and hid behind the team. A smirk crept up her face from behind her hand.

Milan's heart seemed to drop to her feet in an instant. Milan looked up at Talivikki.

Talivikki glared at her. "Is that true, or is your team trying to mess with me?"

"They're just trying to mess with you," Milan laughed nervously.

Talivikki snorted and and leaned down, but still was not level with Milan.

"The one time I come to practice, oh my God." Piper stood in the doorway, pulling her braids. "The varsity always comes to intrude on everything!"

"I'm guessing your sister texted you." Talivikki rose.

Piper stepped forward. "Delilah texted me. I'm going to leave right after."

Talivikki stared at Piper with a blank expression.

Piper tilted her head. "Stop staring at me like that, Talivikki." Piper climbed onto the bleachers so she could be eye-to-eye with Talivikki. Piper held onto the rails and held herself off the bleachers. She put one hand on her hip. "So, what did you want?"

Talivikki walked over. "I wanted to give you some advice about losing someone. I'm in my forties. I've lost some people in my time, even as a teenager."

"God, I thought I was going to get some gift or something, not pity!" Piper shook her head, causing her braids to slap her face. "I don't want to talk to you. I'm leaving."

Piper let go of the rails and dropped to the floor. Comparing Piper to Talivikki was like a mouse compared to a lion. No one on any of the teams was near Talivikki's height at all. Talivikki liked to round her height to 6'5", when in reality she was nearly 6'10".

"She doesn't like uneven stuff, but I guess multiples of five are okay." That's what Ray and Cali figured out over the weeks since mid-September.

Milan stared at Talivikki in disgust.

"Milan, are you disgusted that she cares about our well-being more than you do?" Justice stared directly down at Milan. She hovered over Milan.

Cali had never truly taken in how short Milan was. She was about Ray's size, 5'4", but a little taller, closer to 5'5". *Why was height the only thing she could think about?* Cali was very small, just barely reaching 5'0", and everyone was taller than her, except for Piper.

Every tall person used height as some type of weapon—Ruby, for intimidation; Keagan, for authority; Roze, to put others down. It was all funny to Cali.

"Cali, stop spacing out." Eliza waved a hand in front of Cali.

She jutted her head over to Piper and Talivikki. Piper was trying to get out of the gym while Talivikki held the door shut. "Give me a chance."

Talivikki's eyes were always framed by dark circles and bags. This gave Talivikki an unhinged appearance, which made her even more intimidating.

Piper rolled her eyes. "I'm sorry, no. This is why I hate everyone on the varsity. You are all so pushy!"

No one sane would talk to Talivikki in that way. Piper must have had a death wish.

"I'm sorry you see it that way, but you need help."

Piper took this as another insult to her pride. "I don't need any help at all! I am perfectly fine! Can you *pl— ease* respect that?"

"Very well. I am sorry for your loss, and I hope you can get through this time."

"Cut the pity, old woman."

Talivikki chuckled and stood up. "I'll see you, the 'C team' later. You as well, Milan." She pointed as the door shut.

Milan slowly turned toward Eliza, who fearlessly, stepped up to Milan. "Do you planned to be benched next game?" Milan slammed her clipboard down, sending papers flying.

"Wasn't I going to be benched anyway?" Eliza cocked her head sideways.

Everyone glanced at each other nervously. Eliza had always been bold, but never this bold.

"Because of you, I probably lost my job." Milan seemed like she wanted to lay hands on Eliza but contained herself.

Eliza raised her eyebrows.

"Milan, if you put hands on her, the cameras and all of us," Justice said as she stepped between Milan and Eliza, "will see it all. Choose wisely."

Milan was appalled by Justice's sudden rise to power. "Since when did you develop some authority?

Considering your ear, you aren't the greatest one to rise to power." Milan pointed at Justice's stitched-up ear.

"You aren't the best either." Justice stepped on Milan's papers, scattering them across the floor. "I will be glad when you leave." Justice turned toward the team, still keeping her shoe on the papers as Milan tried desperately to grab them. "Let's go."

Ray threw herself in front of the team. "We can't just leave!"

As much as Ray wanted the team to stay, they were already heading over to the locker rooms to pack up their stuff.

"Do none of you take basketball seriously?" Ray tried to pull Eliza back.

"I think I will once we get a more sympathetic coach," Eliza said.

"Why does sympathy matter?"

"Do you have no sympathy? One of your teammates died! Can you not feel bad?" Eliza uttered calmly.

"I think Sienna would want us to play."

"You're *very* wrong." Piper sat under the bleachers on her phone. "She would most definitely not want us to play under a DICTATOR."

Piper slammed her phone onto the ground. Then she quickly scrambled toward it to make sure it was still functioning.

Milan sat in the gym, trying to take in what just happened. As Milan and Piper made eye contact, Piper flipped her off.

Cali stopped and stared down at the floor. "Ruby still hasn't shown up."

"I'm sure she's fine," Ray said, pushing her into the locker room.

As they got close to their lockers, Ray leaned towards Cali. "You don't think she's doing something horrible, do you?"

"GET YOUR GRIMEY HANDS OFF OF ME!" Ruby struggled against the tape wrapped tightly around her hands.

In front of her stood four figures, all standing just over five feet tall. None said anything as one of them continued to wrap tape tighter and tighter around Ruby's wrists. Ruby tried to kick them away, which prompted the taper to secure her ankles.

"Are none of you going to say anything?" Ruby squirmed around. "What do you want from me?"

"You are Ruby Aurthur, right?"

A girl with dark blonde hair that hung down in two big pigtails turned on the light to reveal the others. The one with the tape was also a girl, in fact, they were *all* girls.

Ruby stared in disbelief. "Are you all five?"

They looked at each other. "We're sixth graders. The middle school ran out of rooms for clubs, so we had to impr . . . improvissse," The tallest one slurred.

How did I allow herself be taken down by a gang of eleven-year-olds? Ruby thought in disbelief.

One girl with long, spiky hair perked up. "It's '*improvise!*' How did you get out of elementary, Alyssa?" She repositioned her black beanie.

"I'm sorry!" Alyssa stomped her foot down, barely missing Ruby's ankles.

"We should probably introduce ourselves." The smallest one stopped taping up Ruby. She had neatly combed brown hair, black glasses, and ironed clothes. She wore a black mask with a flower pattern and looked to be of Asian descent. She also looked more mature than the rest and was most likely the one who organized all of this. "I am Kikuko." She pointed to herself.

Ruby opened her mouth and was met with a stomp to the ankles. "OW!"

"Don't say anything." Kikuko pointed to Alyssa. "This is Alyssa, this is Molli." she pointed to the girl arguing with Alyssa before and then to the girl sitting in the corner. "And this, this is Blaze."

Blaze rose slowly and stared down at Ruby. She could feel the air grow colder around her as she stared into Blaze's cold, eerie eyes. Ruby hated that she was being intimidated by sixth graders. Blaze's bright natural red hair stuck out among the rest of them. Her hair seemed spikier, but it had been brushed before. She stood at an angle; something was wrong with her ankle.

"Her real name is not Blaze, but we don't call her Blaze for personal reasons. Also, she does not talk, but if you even slightly disrespect her, she will stomp on and break any bone she desires."

Blaze then showed her prosthetic leg. Ruby noticed that at the end of the toes were long, sharp screws. Blaze raised her hand up and pointed to the black glove on her hand. She took it off to reveal another prosthetic with screws on it. Ruby could tell she had to take this seriously at all costs.

"So, what do you guys want?" Ruby asked.

"Were you the one who was behind the fall festival thing?" Kikuko fixed her glasses again. "You are one of the suspects that we have. Well, one of them died, so . . ."

Ruby bit her lip, trying to hold back a snarky remark. "Who are the others?"

"Why would we tell you? Maybe you would try to frame them! That's what she said, at least." Alyssa pointed at Kikuko.

Kikuko sighed, "We aren't going to tell you the others. Yes, Alyssa is right. What if you do try to frame them?"

"What if I help you?"

Kikuko raised an eyebrow. "Help us?" Kikuko stood by Blaze. She laughed. "At what price are you willing to help us?"

"I think I have my suspicions as to who sabotaged the fall festival." Ruby smiled.

The four leaned in.

"Who?" Molli asked.

"Erie Barret," Ruby snickered. "She has been jealous of Keagan ever since she joined."

"How do you know this?"

"I used to be on varsity before I was kicked off, right? They kept their ties with me for a while. Erie was very jealous."

Kikuko glanced back at the rest of the crew. "We never suspected her. If you are lying to us, you can say goodbye to your ankles, if you aren't, well, sorry about all of this." Kikuko ripped the tape off Ruby. "You will help us from here on out, got it?"

Ruby nodded. "I understand completely."

"So you're telling me that you got kidnapped by a bunch of eleven-year-olds?" Ray yelled through bursts of laughter as she rolled around on the floor.

"Yes," Ruby grumbled.

The three sat in Ruby's kitchen. Cali sat spaced out as she observed the scene. Ruby said that her father was going on a business trip, so it was perfectly fine that they came over. That is, if he wasn't *lying*. Apparently, sometimes Ruby's father would fake business trips to try and catch her doing something wrong.

Cali hated that none of their parents were present in their lives. Cali knew she really wasn't the worst off, but her life still wasn't good. It seemed so cheesy that all of their parents were absent, but she didn't mind. It somehow pulled them all together subconsciously.

Cali shook her head, trying to snap herself back into reality. She had been thinking about that too much lately.

Ray pulled herself back onto the chair. She sighed and rested her head on the table and pointed at Ruby. "You got attacked by a bunch of kids. *Wow*."

Ruby slammed her hand down on the table. "One had screws on her prosthetics and I was taped to a chair. I couldn't do that much. And I guess she has the literal strength of *God*."

Cali and Ray's eyes widened.

"Say that again?" Ray leaned forward.

"One has screws on her prosthetics," Ruby sighed. "Now that's not what I'm here to talk about."

"Okay," Ray mumbled. "Then spit it out, this is really interesting."

"I may have thrown the blame on Erie in a desperate attempt to save both my ankles."

Ray and Cali stayed silent for what seemed like minutes.

"YOU WHAT?" Ray jumped up from her seat. "Now we have even more moving parts to all this." Ray threw her phone down angrily onto the table. "Why didn't you come clean instead of blaming someone else?"

"I did it in the heat of the moment." Ruby covered her face in embarrassment.

"Oh my God, Ruby." Ray sat back down and laid her head down on the table.

"They were really terrifying middle schoolers," Ruby yelled.

"Who were they exactly? I know some kids from the laser tag area." Ray shrugged. "I knew about the club; I didn't know the kids. I also didn't know that they were middle schoolers. I thought they were high schoolers."

"Alyssa, Molli, Blaze, and Kikuko," Ruby listed them off.

"Oh, I know Alyssa and Molli. We aren't friends, but we always play laser tag together," Ray said.

Ruby blinked. "You do?"

Ray nodded.

"Oh, well. That's nice to know."

An awkward silence fell over the three, as no one knew what else to say.

"So, you blamed Erie. Why?" Cali sat back.

"She was the first one that came to mind and the person who made the most sense to blame!"

"Do you guys want to commit arson?" Ray asked blankly.

"What?" Ruby asked, leaning forward.

Ray shrugged. "When are we going to break into Keagan's house?"

"Okay, wait, wait." Ruby held up a hand. "Let me make us some food first."

"You? Cook?" Ray got up with Ruby and went to the kitchen next door.

Cali, once again, spaced out at the table. Ruby, even as tall and strong as she was, was taken down by eleven-year-olds much shorter and weaker. Cali got up and walked into the kitchen.

"Ruby, do you happen to be meeting up with them soon, or no?"

Ruby turned to Cali. "I'm guessing so. Why do you want to know?"

"I want to ask them a few questions." Cali shrugged.

"Questions?" Ray and Ruby looked at each other. "Like what? What are you planning now?"

"Ruby, how did they take you down? Do you remember?" Cali rested her arm on the counter. "Like, did they exploit any weaknesses of yours?"

"Weaknesses?" Ruby scrunched her face. "All they did was trip me while I was walking."

"But you didn't see them because you're so tall."

"I mean, I usually look down when I'm walking. I saw them right before they tripped me. I reacted way too slowly for whatever reason. They didn't exploit any weakness."

"So, you didn't react fast enough? You don't have fast reactions?"

Ruby ran her hand through her hair. "No, I have decent reactions, trust me. They just caught me way off guard, that's all."

"So, all they did was catch you off guard? No exploiting of weaknesses?"

"No exploitation." Ruby turned back to cooking. "They caught me off guard."

Cali nodded.

CHAPTER 16

"So, how did you two find Keagan's house?" Cali asked.

"A little bit of research!" Ray chuckled and looked ahead.

They finally went out around midnight. The streetlights illuminated the sidewalks and cast eerie shadows as the teens walked.

"Keagan's house is just out of town. It's going to take us a while to walk there." Ruby walked beside Cali, being careful not to step too far ahead due to her stride. "The moon is pretty bright tonight; I don't think we even need the streetlights."

"You might think Swallowsville is on a big, flat plain. Well, that is partially true. It's going to take us about half an hour on foot to get to Keagan's house." Ray looked down. "Maybe I should try to explain to you the layout of Swallowsville. On the East side there is us, Cali, lower-middle class, and middle-class. Where Ruby is, the West side, is upper-middle class. Northwest, there is a small . . . *um*, valley?" Ray glanced at Ruby, looking for the right word.

"I wouldn't say it's a valley, I really don't know what is. People call it the 'Rich Resort' because that's where people like Harlow live. I thought Keagan would be like me, upper-middle-class, but I guess not." Ruby kicked at rocks as she walked.

"Of course, places like downtown and the restaurants are pretty neutral." Ray chuckled. "There used to be so many turf wars, but that calmed down years ago."

"Or so you think," Ruby mumbled. "The stupid police are acting like everything is good on the news."

Ray frowned. "Right."

"Why have we never talked about about this before?" Cali asked.

"I really don't know. It really bothers me when I go to Ruby's house especially," Ray grumbled.

"Sorry about that."

"It's fine." Ray smiled awkwardly. "*Ugh*. I wish we took the car now; this is too much walking," Ray changed the subject.

"I think it would be less obvious if we ran away from the scene than if we jumped in a car and raced off." Ruby shrugged.

Cali stared up at the sky, and could clearly see the stars.

"It's been a while since you could see the stars clearly in Swallowsville. That usually means that something is going to change, bad or good." Ray slowed down to let Ruby and Cali catch up. "That's just my experience with it."

"Strange," Cali mumbled. The last time Cali observed the stars was before the Fox Den incident. Perhaps Ray was right.

A few minutes later, Ray suggested that they took a backroad to get to Keagan's house. "I'm not sure if this is faster, but I'm sick of the streetlights."

The backroad they took was gravel and looked as if it came straight out of a horror movie. Cali even noticed fresh footprints but decided to keep silent. She suggested using their flashlights, but Ruby insisted that the moon was bright enough.

"So, this goes straight out of town, Ray?" Cali avoided touching any plants.

"Yep. We're getting away from the buildings now. We're going to go West for a bit and then begin to go North." Ray chuckled as she picked up a stick and waved it through grass.

"You seem like you've taken this route before? Have you?" Ruby pushed Cali forward, trying to get her to move faster.

"I have, only once. In middle school, my friends and I would always go to the rich side and throw stuff at them," Ray chuckled. "It was a fun time."

"You don't talk to them anymore?"

"Shut up," Ray said.

"I'm curious now, can you tell us, please?"

Ruby stopped Cali along with her. Ray clenched on the stick. Her face was still cheerful, however. She chuckled and then jabbed the stick into her own thigh as hard as she could. Her face was no longer cheerful but instead, furious.

Ruby and Cali both stepped back in shock.

Ray threw the stick to the side and gave the two a death glare. "I said no," she growled.

"Okay, we're sorry," Ruby said calmly.

Cali raised an eyebrow. This was one of Ray's over-reactions to something stupid.

Ray continued walking as if nothing had happened.

Ruby lowered her head. "Why did she freak out like that?"

"I have no clue." Cali shrugged.

They continued to follow Ray cautiously until they finally reached the last stretch of backroads on a hill that gave the greatest view of the biggest houses in Swallowsville. The light showed on their faces like they were opening a treasure chest that glowed from inside.

"Great. Now let's go down and find her house."

Ruby stopped Ray before she stepped any farther. "It's really steep, Ray. Are you sure that we should take this path down there?"

"Absolutely." Ray smiled, pushed Ruby's hands aside, and continued her way down the mountain. Ruby carefully went down the mountain, following behind Ray.

Cali had to stop and stare at the valley. No wonder people flocked to Swallowsville. This place looked amazing.

Ruby suddenly grabbed Cali and forced her to walk down the hill beside her.

"You might want to be careful about the loose rocks. Those will get you killed in seconds," Ray said merrily.

They made their way down the valley side as quickly as they could with Ray's guidance.

"There are a lot of police out at night, so follow me. There's this old mine tunnel thingy that I think is still in service." Ray chuckled. "Don't worry, it won't collapse on us!"

Cali and Ruby glanced at each other nervously. Ruby stepped forward. "Ray, are you okay?"

"Yeah, I'm fine. No worries." Ray said.

"I don't think you are. Maybe we should go back?" Ruby slowly pushed Cali behind her in case Ray had an outburst.

Cali knew she needed Ray around, but this was getting out of hand. Now even Ruby was unsure and uncomfortable around her. Cali knew it was mostly because of Sienna's disappearance, but Cali believed she couldn't let Ray get too out of hand.

"Ray," Cali sheepishly stepped up. "I think you should maybe calm down more. You're making us uncomfortable."

Ray's eye twitched.

Ruby's mouth hung open, and frankly, Cali was getting scared as well.

"I'm sorry." Ray stood with her hands behind her back. She was frowning, but her eyes looked happy. However, looking deeper in her eyes exposed the strong pain that ravaged her, and her breathing was getting heavier.

"Ray?" Ruby stepped forward, holding out her hand.

Ray swatted her hand back and turned to the side, staring blankly at the ground.

"Did you break her?" Ruby yell-whispered to Cali.

Inside of Ray's mind, there was nothing. No thoughts or anything, nothingness. All she felt was the pain. Those few words caused Ray to shut down. She felt rejected. Ray knew that she had something wrong with her but never cared enough about herself or the others around her to reach for help. Her throat burned with tears as she stepped toward where she believed the old tunnel to be.

"Come with me," Ray muttered.

The tunnel seemed to stretch far underneath the valley. It was a small hill with a hole in it that was covered in tall grass. The entrance had old wood that blocked most of it, although the wood was long rotted. Ray stood in front of it with her hands on her hips.

"Yikes, it's dark." Ray pulled out her phone and turned on the flashlight. "You guys ready?"

"Yeah." Ruby nudged Cali ahead.

The tunnel was made of dirt, and no supports to hold anything up. It seemed like a death trap. Cali could only smell wet mud.

"I swear, it won't collapse."

The three walked through as far as possible until they stopped at a collapsed portion.

"*Aw* shoot. It did collapse. We took this part of the tunnel all the time. My childhood collapsed."

"Where did this even lead to?"

"It led somewhere on the other side of the valley," Ray sounded devastated. "I wonder if someone got caught under here." Ray touched the fallen dirt.

Ruby and Cali, once again, looked at each other nervously.

"Well." Ray turned around. "Let's go back and find Keagan's house the hard way." Ray pushed past the two and power-walked back to the entrance.

Ray, Cali, and Ruby peeked over a thick stone wall. The house in front of them was huge; it was bigger than the three of their houses combined. The house was made of white brick with a brown roof. Golden yellow light washed the house with a feeling of peace. The tremendous brown door had great white steps leading up to it, and the expanse of the front lawn boasted the greenest grass Cali had ever laid eyes on. For it being October, the grass surely had to be fake.

"This is Keagan's house?" Cali asked as she faced Ray.

"Yup." Ray had her eyes glued to the window of the dining room. "Keagan and her family must be having supper or something right now."

In the dining room, Keagan, Nick, and their parents sat in apparent silence as they ate. No one looked happy.

"It annoys me how big of a house they have for four people." Ray shook her head in disgust and looked at Ruby. "Your house is okay, Ruby, but this?" Ray threw her hand out angrily. "Greedy pigs, the rich."

"Maybe they have a reason, Ray," Ruby muttered.

Ray glared. "Four people in a house for thirty, in a valley that is reserved just for the lucky." Ray slammed her hand down on the stone. "Do you not see anything wrong with that?"

"Well, they worked for it. They can do what they want with it." Ruby shrugged.

"*Well*," Ray mocked Ruby. "I did some research while looking for their address. Her mother, Joel Perry, was one of the $10-million lottery winners in 2018. They didn't work for any of the money, and they are hoarding it."

Ray had a point. The resort for the rich in Swallowsville was a bit overboard. There was a clear divide in the town. Ruby peered into the dining room again.

"This is a perfect time to storm her house," Ray sighed. "If we go through one of the back doors, we should have a perfect way into the house." Ray put her hands into her pockets. "I also have these puppies." She pulled out the masks the two had used before, plus a new moth mask.

"How did you manage to steal those from me?" Ruby cocked her head.

"It was easy; you leave everything unattended," Ray chuckled. She dropped the two other masks recklessly on the stone wall. Ruby put on the butterfly mask while Cali put on the fox mask.

Ray suddenly jumped down the stone wall without warning, causing Ruby and Cali slight panic. They followed behind more carefully, and found a hedge to hide behind.

"They don't seem to have any pets outside." Just then, a small camera popped up from the ground. Ray patted it lightly. "But they seem to have a lot of . . . useless cameras."

Ruby spotted the back door and pointed it out.

"We aren't going to go through the backdoor," Ray grumbled. "Idiot."

"I thought you said we were?"

"No! We're going through that window." Ray jutted her head toward a window. Underneath the window was a series of bricks that looked as if they had been stepped on many times before.

"You want us to rock climb up to a window?" Ruby ran her hand through her hair, trying to calm herself.

"I'll go first." Ray sprinted over again, without thought or warning. Ruby and Cali stood under Ray as she struggled up the side of the house. She chuckled from the window, glaring down at the two with dead eyes.

"Now, you guys have to do it," she said, more loudly than she should have.

Ruby put her index finger over her lips to shut Ray up. Ray disappeared into the room, presumably waiting for them to follow.

After a few minutes of struggling, Cali climbed into te pitch-black room. "I don't think this is Keagan's room." Ray turned on the light. "This is a big closet."

Ruby cracked the door open; Cali could see a sliver of the tremendous hallway outside. "I don't see anyone," she whispered. "There may be hidden cameras you guys realize, right?"

"Yeah? They won't recognize us, though." Ray shrugged. "Let's go." Ray pushed away Ruby and headed out the door.

The hallway was larger than Cali's bedroom. It had a fancy rug running up the middle of it, the fake gold pillars stood high and mighty like tall evergreens. The walls were a heavenly white and dotted with strange old paintings framed in gold- and silver-gilt frames.

Ray seemed to ignore the mansion instead of being impressed with it all. "Which one is Keagan's room?" Ray turned.

A small camera began to slide slowly down the side of the hallway like a snake. Ruby and Cali frantically pointed at the camera. Ray turned quickly and kicked it, breaking it. It flew straight into the wall with a thud. Ray landed perfectly. Cali was blown away by how Ray knew how to fight.

"When did you learn to do that?" Cali asked, impressed.

Ray chuckled. "I knew you would be impressed with that! I was jealous by how good you could throw Piper. Also, we may need it later." Ray nodded and picked up the camera and waved it around.

"So, does this mean these are motion-sensors, or is someone watching us?"

"Well, we are already here, so it wouldn't matter anyway," Ruby shrugged.

Ray adjusted her mask. "Okay, so we better find Keagan's room fast."

They wandered the hallways for what seemed like decades. Up until this point, they had no problems like people or pets getting in their way. This seemed too good to be true. They did, however, have problems with cameras. Ray took care of them swiftly every time, until they came across one that would not budge. It was planted in the wall and, if it came out, would bring some of the wall with it. As if they weren't suspicious enough, this would be an instant clue that intruders were inside the house.

Ray pulled Cali aside and whispered quietly to her, "Keagan already knows what we are doing, why are we . . . I don't know how to explain it."

Cali shrugged. "I think we should keep going on like this. We should act like we have no clue Keagan knows."

Ray nodded and turned back to Ruby. "What do we do about the camera?"

In the distance, they heard footsteps. They all turned to see a shorter woman wearing nice clothes and light brown hair in a bun. She had a green broom she gripped in fear. "Who are you?" she screamed.

Ray suddenly ran at the woman; Cali and Ruby followed behind. The woman dashed inside a room. Cali could tell that everyone was terrified. Like a bull, Ray ran straight past it and slid on the rug, trying to stop.

Ray angrily tried to open the door before giving up and slamming her hand on the door.

"Look what you did to the rug!" Ruby threw her hands down.

Ray shook her head, ignoring Ruby. "She didn't lock it. She's holding it shut." Ray pointed at Cali. "You're strong; get it open."

"You're taking me over . . ." Cali stopped herself before she said Ruby's name. "You're taking me over Ruby?"

"Yes," Ray grumbled.

Cali hesitated before throwing herself into the door. It didn't work. Cali panicked; *she was strong, why couldn't she open the door.*

Ray cocked her head and went for the door handle again. This time, it opened. "She's hiding."

The room was a bedroom. Since it looked like a hotel room, it had to be a guest bedroom. The walls were white, like the hallways, the carpet was a blood-red hue with weird, random patterns. The bed was queen-size with black sheets. The room was certainly an eyesore. There was a cabinet at the back of the room, and a small bathroom in the tiny hallway which led to the main room.

"You stay by the door." Ray pointed at Ruby. Ruby reluctantly agreed.

Ruby shut the door behind her as the other two searched the room. Cali was searching under the bed when she heard a small voice . . . under the floor. Cali crawled further under the bed and listened with her head to the floor.

"Joel, please. Take me seriously!" The woman sounded frantic. "Yes, I did take my medicine. Please, I'm serious!"

Cali was utterly confused by how the woman was under the floor. She realized she couldn't call out to Ray or Joel would hear her in the background. Cali carefully crawled out from under the bed and glanced around for Ray. However, Ray was already moving under the bed, having heard the voice, too.

Cali could now see there was a trapdoor. Ray and Cali got down. They both silently argued about who would do the honors of opening it. Ray got impatient and flung open the trapdoor. Cali couldn't imagine the woman's fear as she looked up at the two kids wearing masks.

She looked to be about eighteen and as if she just got out of school not too long ago. Cali was too lost in her thoughts to realize that the woman had thrown her phone at Ray, who laid on the floor in pain.

The woman tried to scurry out of the trapdoor, but Cali quickly shut it down on her fingers and laid on it.

Ray rose slowly.

"What are we supposed to do?" Cali asked.

"I don't know!" Ray scanned the area for something, anything. "We should tie her up, that's our only option if we want to get through this house as fast as possible."

Cali nodded. The woman was putting up a fight, but Cali did not budge.

Ray called out to Ruby. "Look for any type of rope! We need to get her to shut up somehow!"

Cali could hear the woman panicking and throwing a fit under the floorboards. "What's the point of the trapdoor anyway?"

"Well, it was useful, but we wouldn't have found her if she didn't make any noise." Ray shrugged. "Not very smart," she said to the floor.

Ruby came over with a rope.

"Give it to me." Ray shooed Cali away from the trapdoor and opened it herself.

After a few minutes of struggling, they finally got the woman quiet. Ray crouched down in front of her. "You cannot say anything about us," Ray said forcefully. The woman said nothing.

Cali kneeled forward. "What is your name?"

The woman still said nothing.

"Perhaps you made the rope a bit too tight." Cali reached for the rope.

The rope fell gracefully off the woman, coiling beneath her as she grabbed Cali and put her in a chokehold. She pulled a pocketknife out and held it to Cali's throat. She gasped and tried to squirm out of the hold. She was more scared than anything.

Ray and Ruby stood up and stepped back in fear.

"Hey, hey now." Ray held her hands out. "If you let her go, we'll be on our way."

"I may as well use one of you guys for evidence or else they won't believe me!" The woman pressed the knife against Cali's throat; Cali's breath caught. "I am Oblivia. I am the cleaning lady and the Perry's thing to abuse. They act like I'm crazy. I want to show them I'm not."

"You can show them in other ways, just don't kill her. She's very special to us." Ray took a small step forward. Her voice was rough, and not calming at all.

"Very special to you?" Oblivia became more aggressive. "I want you to know how lucky you are to feel somewhat special to someone!" She looked into Cali's eyes. Cali was too afraid to speak.

"Please, we're here for a reason. If you let her free, we'll tell you the reason. You can even help us if you like."

Now Ruby stepped forward.

Oblivia calmed down but still didn't let Cali free. "Why are you here then?"

"We need to find Keagan's room. Keagan replaced me on varsity and I want revenge on her by stealing her varsity jersey and warmup." Ruby took off her mask. "Please. We need to know where her room is. We are going to be here in two phases. Right now, we are just learning the basic layout. We are on your side, Oblivia."

Oblivia thought for a second. Cali felt her grip loosen, she threw Oblivia's arm away and ran to the two of them. Oblivia didn't resist. "Follow me. I'll show you where her room is. I want to steal it with you."

The three smiled with relief.

"Sorry for almost killing you. What are your names?"

Cali and Ruby said their names; however, Ray was skeptical of Oblivia still. "You don't plan to do anything with those names, right?"

Oblivia shook her head. "Of course not. We're on the same side, as the tall one said." She jutted her head up at Ray. "You don't have to say your name, but I will still lead you to Keagan's room."

Ruby nudged Ray. "Let's just follow her already. We better hurry up."

Minutes later, the four were staring at Keagan's jersey and warmup on the wall. The warmup was white, Cali squinted.

"I can't help but feel like I have seen this type of set-up before. A white warmup hanging on the wall." Cali looked around. "This is the varsity warmup, right?"

Ruby nodded. "You may have seen it on the court, maybe."

"No, no." Cali sighed in annoyance. "I mean, I've seen someone's on a wall before."

"Well, it wouldn't be mine. I don't keep mine up." Ruby shrugged. "You may be seeing things."

"Yeah, you're just imagining things," Ray chuckled nervously.

Cali got into Ray's face; Ray stepped backwards. "It was in your house."

Ray shook her head. "You're wrong," she chuckled.

"Do you have any siblings or were you lying?"

"Why are you being so confrontational?" Ruby pulled Cali back.

Cali shook her head. "Maybe I'm wrong. Sorry, Ray," Cali mumbled. "I swear I've seen this before."

"Probably just some *déjà vu*, Cali." Ruby snatched the warmup from the wall with ease. "It still has the tear in it." She laughed.

Ray pushed past Cali. "Now, where is the jersey?"

Oblivia was already going through her drawers. She pulled out a purple jersey. "Here, it is, wasn't too difficult to find."

"Can I take a look at it? I'm curious if the varsity jerseys are any different," Cali asked.

Ruby grabbed the jersey and spread it out. "It's the same as your jerseys. Although, you see this line running up the shorts and the jersey?"

Cali and Ray nodded.

"Well, there's one stripe instead of three stripes. On the 'B team', there are two. On your heart, there is a white star. On the home side of the jerseys, it's just inverted with white and purple. The one stripe and star are only for varsity though." Ruby eagerly talked on and on about the jerseys.

"We should get going. Can we get down from her window?"

Ruby pointed to a huge window that took up most of the wall. In it was a glass door that led to a balcony outside.

"We probably can." Oblivia speed-walked over to the door and opened it. She waved the three over. "I mean, if you want, you can jump into the pond down there."

Down below, there was deep pond that was steaming in the cold air. The steam was lit up by the same white lights around the house.

"What about the jersey?" Ruby cocked her head.

"I think I'll be fine if I jump into those bushes right there. You guys can go for the pool." Ray snatched the jersey and warmup and hopped off the balcony.

Ruby tried to grab Ray before she jumped. "We didn't decide that that was the plan!"

"Well, it seems like you guys are going to have to jump in the pond," Oblivia said. "I will too."

"Are you coming with us?" Ruby asked.

"Oh, of course." Oblivia smiled. "I want to see what you guys do with the jersey. I can come with, right?"

Ruby shrugged. "Sure, it wouldn't hurt."

Cali looked down at the pond below. Ruby was already crouching on the railing. Ruby grabbed Cali by the shirt and pulled her over. "I can tell you're not going to jump. So, I'm going to throw you if you don't jump right now."

Cali blinked. "You're going to throw me?"

"Absolutely," Ruby said.

Oblivia took a running jump off the balcony, she fell with her arms out and back toward the water. From that, she turned it into a dive and landed in the water with little noise. That clearly wasn't her first time. Oblivia waved them down.

"Cali, jump," Ruby muttered. "You're not hesitant to jump out a window and almost freeze to death, but now you don't want to take a little jump off a balcony."

"There's a difference!" Cali got up onto the railing.

"We have to stop stalling."

The next thing Cali knew, she was falling toward the water with her arms flailing. She hit the water hard. Cali watched Ruby do a simple swan dive into the water as Cali climbed onto the ground. Ray laughed hysterically at Cali.

"That was the greatest thing I've seen out of you, Cali!"

Cali slapped Ray across the face. "Will you be *quiet*?"

Ray slapped Cali back. "Don't hit me," she growled.

Cali stepped back.

Ruby stepped between the two. "Now, what are we going to do with the jersey?"

Ray was already walking. "I have the greatest idea."

"Ray, you have to be secretive about this," Ruby called.

"Watch me!" Ray rolled her eyes and turned away. "Meet me at that tunnel."

Ruby sighed, "How hard did you hit her?"

The three stood around Ray, who was backed against the fallen part of the tunnel.

"Okay, so what are you going to do with the jersey, Ray?" Ruby and the others looked strikingly concerned. Ruby whispered to Cali, "She better not have a gun or something."

"Oh, I don't have a gun." Ray shifted through her hoodie pocket. "I have a lighter." She flicked it on, lighting up the tunnel and her face, making her look even more sinister than before.

"We can't burn the jersey in here!" Ruby pointed to the rotting wood. "It'll catch fire!"

Ray put the lighter closer to the jersey and warmup. "That's the point. I want to end one of my eras for sure. They will not be able to get her a new jersey by the next game." Ray laughed.

"Ray, you're not making much sense," Cali muttered.

"I want to burn in this tunnel. I want to burn with my past," Ray grumbled. She put the lighter to the jersey and warmup. They lit up in a fireball that consumed Ray's hand fast. Ray screamed and tried to run away from her own pain.

The burning clothes landed on the dry wood and exploded into flames. Oblivia panicked and sprinted out of the tunnel. Ruby grabbed out to her but missed her completely.

Ray slammed her hand against the wall, finally putting out the flame. She then sat down calmly. Cali saw they didn't have much time, as the fire was spreading to the entrance. Cali grabbed Ray and tried to run out, but Ray was dead weight.

"RAY!"

Ruby grabbed Ray's other arm and pulled her up.

"I don't want to go!"

"We aren't going to leave you to burn!" Ruby picked Ray up and ran out, even though Ray was squirming and kicking like crazed madman. The three ran out of the tunnel just as the wood fell behind them. Ruby put Ray down and they observed the scene.

"Ray," Ruby turned. "You need to get your head together. We're going to have a serious talk when we get back to my place."

"I don't need help."

Ruby glared.

CHAPTER 17

Keagan walked into her room after the long dinner of discussing what she would do in college, what she would major in, and what her family wanted for her. She sat down on her bed and held her head in her hands. Keagan wanted to stay strong in every situation, even being alone, but she couldn't help this one time, but to cry.

She was *Keagan Perry*, the new face of Swallowsville High. She knew that letting Ruby run around with no repercussions would come back to bite her, although Talivikki wouldn't let her do anything about it. Keagan knew if Ruby got hold of some horrible past information, she would be over for sure.

Keagan felt a breeze hit her back. She turned to see the door to her balcony open. Confused, she walked over and shut it. Before she shut it, she heard sirens. She ran out to her balcony and scanned the land fearfully. However, she could see no fire.

Her door opened.

"Keagan, there's been a fire at the old tunnel," Oblivia said, out of breath.

Keagan wiped her tears and stood tall. She turned to Oblivia after closing and locking the balcony door. "Do they have a cause for it?"

"No," Oblivia glanced to the side nervously. "Your parents wanted you to come with them down there. Since your parents are kind of, you know, the big ones."

Keagan could smell smoke on Oblivia. "Were you down there already?"

She glanced to the side again. "No."

"I can smell smoke on you." Keagan sighed and looked over to where Oblivia was looking.

"What were you glancing at anyway—"

Keagan's heart stopped as she laid her eyes on the empty space where her warmup jersey once was.

Oblivia went into full on panic. "Oh no, your warmup! I wonder where that could have gone?"

Keagan kept her composure. "Oblivia. Tell me the truth." Keagan refused to look down at Oblivia. "Were there three girls here earlier?"

"Three girls? Heaven's no!" Oblivia slowly backed out of the room. "I have no clue what you are talking about. Anyway, your parents want you downstairs lickety-split! I washed your coat for you earlier. It's cold outside."

"Why is your hair wet?" Keagan asked while opening her closet.

"Just got done with a shower!"

The door closed. Keagan sighed. She knew that someone had been there, most likely Ruby. Keagan tried to clear her mind as she put on her coat and walked downstairs. Keagan agreed subconsciously that her house was way too big. She wanted to be like Harlow and give away some of the money. However, the difference was that it was her parents' own money and not Keagan's money. All she wanted was to have a normal high school life and be a track star.

"Keagan," her mom, Joel, called out as she reached the top of the stairs. "We need you to hurry up. I hope the cleaning lady got word to you. If it didn't, there has been a fire at that old tunnel that we decided to close up years ago. The police asked the elites of the place to come down and decide, again, what we want to do with the fire."

Keagan rolled her eyes. She was sick of the word *elite*. It was now leaving a bitter taste on her tongue.

"Keagan Perry do not roll your eyes at me! Do you hear?" Joel pointed aggressively as Keagan reached the foyer.

"Sorry, Mom." Keagan fluffed up her coat. "That old tunnel? They closed that up because of those kids terrorizing the rich years ago, didn't they?"

"Clearly they didn't collapse it enough because they came back!" Joel angrily got out her phone. "Your father is outside waiting for us; he's called me multiple times already! Let's go."

Minutes later, Joel and Keagan arrived at the tunnel. Keagan's father looked horrified but kept his composure. Keagan felt terrified when she thought about mentioning that someone stole her jersey.

Her parents were not told about the plan with Ruby at all. They were only told that she would be granted a basketball career. They were indeed told that she would bring some attention to Swallowsville, but only in her basketball career alone. Keagan decided not to say anything and to go to Talivikki's house later.

Keagan inherited most of her physical traits from her father, but her personality traits came from both parents. Her mother raised her to be nice and kind, though she did have anger issues and no patience for standing around. Her father taught her how to stay calm in situations; however, he taught her to step over others to get her way. Keagan subconsciously took on both sets of personality traits to make her very own.

Keagan shook her head.

Five people stood around by the fire trucks, eight in total. Four of those five people were two couples, and one was single. They all had one thing in common: they were all lucky with their money. They all either made it big with a corporation, or they were jackpot winners that resided in urban North Dakota. Keagan thought that any millionaire who moved to North Dakota was crazy. *Why not go somewhere else? Maybe for political reasons?* Keagan would never know since she had already lived in Blackridge, North Dakota.

The first couple was Mr. and Mrs. Brown. They moved from Jersey City, New Jersey. They had won a jackpot in New Jersey just like Keagan's family did. They were the older residents of the area, having moved there in the 1970s.

The second couple was Mr. and Mrs. Fox. They moved from Los Angeles after Mrs. Fox made a name for herself as a successful writer. They had the least amount of money of the group, but were still millionaires.

The last person was Mr. León, the near-billionaire. He had been a successful dentist for years in Las Vegas. He moved from Mexico to Las Vegas with friends because they all thought it would be fun. Mr. León said they were fortunate enough to actually have money. Keagan, though, would never truly understand. During one of his gambling nights, he won multiple jackpots. He almost moved out of the resort after everyone kept pressuring him to marry someone. He always said that he had no interest in ever having a relationship. Mr. León didn't care at all what the others thought, as he was content with his life and didn't need the negativity. Keagan had a pleasant friendship with him.

"What should we do about this?" Joel nodded in greeting.

"Well, I think we should have the whole tunnel covered up. Just in case the perpetrator comes back for round two." Mr. Brown ruffled his expensive coat.

Mr. León stepped up. "I think we should leave it. Those kids will have some great memories."

Everyone glared at Mr. León.

"Cody, our homes could have been burned down and you think we should keep it just so some mentally ill kids can laugh at old memories?"

"They could have directly burned down our homes, but they decided to burn an old mine that was far away." Mr. León pointed to the mine. "Maybe the person was peer pressured, or they absolutely had to do it. You can't just assume that the person was ill in the head. Maybe they were ill, but we can't say for sure that they were. There could've been other factors."

"Cody, could you please speak more properly," Mr. Brown asked.

"Why don't you address me as Mr. León," Mr. León grumbled. "Look, this is no place to fight. We need to come up with a decision."

"Keagan. You're an adult this week. What do you think we should do?" Joel smiled warmly at Keagan, but behind that smile was obvious annoyance, not for Keagan but for Mr. León. Keagan snapped back into reality.

"I agree with Cody." Mr. León only let Keagan call him Cody since they were friends. "We should keep it up. Plus, it's a part of this town's history."

They rolled their eyes.

"Maybe let's not ask the liberal kid."

"What?" Keagan shook her head.

"Keagan, why don't you go inside and go to sleep?" Her mother laid her hand on her shoulder.

"The adults will talk about this one. Sorry for dragging you out here."

Keagan nodded and reluctantly turned around. She could hear Mr. Fox talking about how much of a disappointment she was. As she walked into the living room, Nick hopped off the coach and turned off the TV.

"Hey, Keagan."

"Don't talk to me, Nick." She held a hand in front of her face.

"Keagan, I'm sorry." Nick stopped her. "I had to."

"You did not *have* to. Nick, I promised to land you in a good college despite our parents."

She pushed past him and walked up the stairs. She turned and lashed out, "You betrayed me."

Nick stared up at her. Keagan looked into his eyes, hurt. She shook her head and continued up the stairs.

As Keagan was out of hearing range, Nick took a vase and threw it into a wall. Nick had messed up his future. He knew he had to take down Keagan with Ruby.

Keagan knocked on Talivikki's door. Keagan had gone down the same path Ray took. Talivikki lived middle-class. Keagan always thought about how people lived and was quick to label them due to the guilt she had for being fortunate.

Keagan rang the doorbell multiple times before Talivikki opened the door. Talivikki looked at Keagan, confused. "Keagan, what are you doing here? It's almost midnight."

"I have to talk to you about something. It's urgent," Keagan said calmly.

Talivikki looked back into her house. "Fine."

Keagan sighed in relief. "Your accent is acting up, Talivikki."

"Yeah, yeah, shut up about it," she mumbled sarcastically. She turned on the main light. "Sit at the table in my dining room."

Talivikki's house was a bit strange. To get to the dining room you had to go through the living room, then through the kitchen, and then turn.

"What did you want to talk about?" Talivikki sat down with a beer.

"Don't be mad but—"

Talivikki rolled her eyes. "Oh boy."

"Someone stole my jersey."

Talivikki spat out her beer. "WHAT? Those take weeks to get replaced!" She sat back. "What are we going to do? Do you have any ideas who did it?"

"Well, it was definitely Ruby." Keagan crossed her arms and sunk into her seat.

"Oh, Christ. That's way too far." Talivikki got down from her chair. "I'll call the school right away. How are you going to get home, by the way, and how did you get here?"

"I walked and I am going to walk back."

Talivikki rested her head against the wall above the phone. She sighed. "Keagan, you have to remain in perfect health. I and the team can't afford to have you come down with an illness."

Keagan shrugged. "That's what I've been doing every time. I thought it was weird you never asked."

"It's because it's usually later when you drop by."

Talivikki picked up the phone. "I'm going on the phone now, *vær stille*."

Keagan nodded. After hanging around Talivikki for a while, she had learned bits of Norwegian. Keagan thought this brought them closer, Talivikki felt like a mother to her.

Since Talivikki was so tall, the things in her house were adjusted accordingly. The doorways were higher, the chairs were bigger, everything was modified. Keagan felt bad for her, even though Talivikki was content with her living.

They were very close. However, Talivikki had never told Keagan the reason she never went to the WNBA. Keagan suspected that it had something to do with her ankle.

Talivikki stood with her weight shifted onto the opposite, unaffected ankle. She had always changed the subject when anyone asked about her limp.

"Keagan." Talivikki snapped her fingers. "We need your jersey number."

"Eight." The number associated with achievement. Keagan had always picked that number since she was a kid.

She thought back to middle school in Blackridge. She was a horrible person, but was never truly punished for her actions. She lost a good friend, but she believed she should have been punished more.

Keagan shook her head.

"Alright, the order is in. You'll get it ... after the first game of the week," Talivikki sighed.

"What ... What will I do?" Keagan asked.

"Four. You're going to have to wear the number 'four' for a while."

"Isn't that the number of death?" Keagan cocked her head.

"It's just a jersey number, Keagan." Talivikki shrugged. "I know you believe in numerology, but really, it's just a jersey number."

Keagan squinted. "Fine, I will take it," she said hesitantly.

"Alright, Keagan. Four it is."

Keagan swallowed. She genuinely believed she was about to die.

CHAPTER 18

"So, what you're telling me is, Ray burned Keagan's jersey and warmup without warning, and then almost got you killed?" Eliza tilted her head.

"Yes." Cali nodded.

After Ray's attempt at killing them, Cali had decided she should talk with Eliza. It was around 1:00 a.m. on October fifth, a Saturday. Cali had been drained more by Ray and so cautious around her since the fire that it was killing her. Ray was, at first, the person at school who first looked after her. Now, Cali was looking after Ray and trying to keep her alive. That wasn't what Cali wanted.

"It seems like Ray is . . . how do I put this . . . suicidal." Eliza shrugged. "She's not at the level of 'suicidal' to keep it to herself. She maybe doesn't outright say it, but she is still suicidal."

"Well, yeah. I could tell."

"Since it is in her nature to be selfish, she doesn't care if her attempts bring down others with her," Eliza said. "There's something not right with her. But also, please remember that the majority of suicidal people are not like Ray. They aren't selfish. Ray is just a different case."

"Who can help her?" Cali sat back, feeling hopeless.

"Well, a therapist." Eliza took a sip of water. "I don't want you to think she is entirely a bad person; she just needs help. Everyone likes to support mental health until someone says that they are manipulative, and they need help. I don't know if that resonates, it's just on my mind." Eliza leaned in. "Her father is not the nicest person, you know. It could stem from that."

"She tried to get us killed. I don't have any pity for her."

"She didn't entirely know what she was doing. Her head was so clouded with death that she didn't comprehend her own actions." Eliza scratched her head. "You're going to have to have a talk with her."

"We already tried." Cali looked at the ground.

"Well, how did that go over?"

"Ray, you almost got us killed and aren't even apologizing?" Ruby had Ray trapped in a closet, as she was trying to run from the conversation. Cali had gone home and was too angry with Ray to even look at her.

"You guys didn't have to stay with me!" Ray screamed.

"You mean something to us, why can't you see that?" Ruby rolled her eyes.

Ray snorted. "I know that!"

"Then why do you keep trying to get yourself killed or hurt! You almost got us killed too!"

"You had a choice to save me or not! Will you shut up?"

That's what Ruby said had happened. Knowing Ruby, Ruby most likely told the truth.

"Ray always said that you copied her. Why did you?" Cali cocked her head.

"She copied *me*," Eliza chuckled.

"What?"

"She copied *my* personality." Eliza shrugged. "I will never know why. Everyone says that Ray is the comedian, even though she literally is me. There's one thing she can't steal: my ability to be a therapist. She has trouble expressing empathy, it seems like. Doesn't mean she can't feel it, though."

Cali was at a loss for words. "What is wrong with her?" Cali laid her head on the table in defeat. "Why didn't you talk to her?"

"She didn't want to talk to me, trust me, I have." Eliza shrugged. "Of course, I will never know what Ray has, but whatever, I guess."

Cali felt torn. "I think I'm just going to try to ignore it."

Eliza raised her eyebrows. "Okay. What have you found out about the shooting and Sienna?"

"Oh, I completely forgot about that!"

Eliza chuckled, "How in the world?"

"I didn't forget that it happened; I just forgot that I was supposed to be finding stuff about it."

"Have you found anything out about weaknesses?"

"Ruby got attacked by a bunch of sixth graders."

"What?"

"Let me finish. They were all smaller and weaker than Ruby. They didn't use any weaknesses of hers, all they did was catch her off guard."

"Let me guess. It was the middle schoolers that came over?" Eliza laughed. "So, what did you learn from it?"

"You don't all need to use weaknesses."

"You're going to have to use some weaknesses." Eliza leaned back. "You're how tall? 5'0"?"

"I'm 5'1"." Cali sighed, clearly lying. "If I don't know the culprit, how will I ever know their weaknesses?"

"You do have a point." Eliza's pet kitten jumped onto the table. "My cat has three legs; it wouldn't survive in the wild. That's a weakness that it has. If it learned to exploit small things, it may have a chance to live some. Now, if you take a perfectly fine cat, it wouldn't have that disadvantage. The predator would have to catch it off guard, right?"

Cali nodded.

"I don't think we have anything else to talk about? Is there?"

"Well, you know, you seem very suspicious. I mean, in the case of Sienna's disappearance."

Eliza laughed for a second. "Oh, you're being serious? Well, I can tell you right now. You actually aren't too off, but it isn't me."

"Why won't you tell me?"

"It would make it less exciting." Eliza got up. "Anyway, would you like to spend the night or go home? Again, I don't think we have anything else to talk about.

Oh! One thing. This weekend, Justice invited us to the arcade in Blue Sun."

"Blue Sun? Where is that?"

"Oh, it's a small town northeast of us." Eliza shrugged. "I think Justice is burning herself out with her mindset of 'I have to be the responsible one.'"

Cali got up from her chair. "How will we get there? Neither you nor I can drive."

"Right." Eliza yawned. "Only Mel, Justice, and Ruby can drive. We're going to be meeting them in the school parking lot, and we're going to drive up there."

Cali nodded. "Alright, how was this even decided?"

"Well, the whole team has a group chat. Were you ever added?"

"Nope."

"Well, I'll add you right now." Eliza picked up her phone. "Anyway, I think it's better that you stay here for the night. It's late."

Cali nodded reluctantly.

CHAPTER 19

Ruby had to drive with Ray, Cali, and . . . Piper. Piper stayed silent the whole way, but everyone could feel she was tense and judging everyone around her.

"So, Piper." Ruby was acting like a middle-aged mom. "Why don't you ever talk to us?"

Piper snorted, "You guys are weird. Especially Cali."

Cali raised an eyebrow. "How exactly?"

Piper stayed quiet and stared angrily at the others.

Ray smacked Piper on the side of the head. "Can we not fight?"

Ruby rolled her eyes. "This day is supposed to be fun for the whole team. No drama today. We don't have to worry about anything."

Minutes later, the three cars pulled up in front of a huge building.

"This is Blue Sun's game house." Ruby nodded at the house. "It has tons of games for everyone, including dodgeball. Varsity came here a couple of years ago after we won the championship, and Blue Sun was here too."

"No one cares about varsity. Shut up," Piper grumbled.

Ruby ignored her. "Varsity all loved dodgeball, does the 'C team'?"

"I've never been here before. I mean, I love dodgeball, so I do at least."

Ray crawled over Piper and opened the door. Piper whined. The team gathered outside of the building. Everyone was excited and talking. For the first time in a while, the team wasn't fighting. Justice had somehow brought the team closer. The only problem was Piper's bitterness, although, no one paid any attention to her except Eliza.

"We have to play dodgeball when it gets later. That's the main attraction here, we can't just *not* play it," Ray chuckled while talking to Kimberly and River. The two didn't seem too grateful for Ray's conversation.

Justice held the door open for everyone. Cali nodded in thanks to Justice and laid her eyes on the arcade.

Ruby nudged Cali. "You've never been here?" She brought Ray over. "So, I'll explain the place to you. There are three floors. The first floor you see here is the arcade floor. The second is non-contact sports, and the third is contact sports. I won't show you the dodgeball arena yet, but I can assure you; it's the best thing you'll ever see."

Justice stood in front of the team. "I will be paying for all of you." She smiled warmly. "Go have fun, guys."

Ray grabbed Cali's arm. "We're going to be staying on this floor."

"I'll be staying with you guys," Ruby uttered.

"I'm going to be putting my name in every single one of these arcades!" Ray ran off.

"Oh, by the way. We will be meeting down at the cafeteria at 3:00." Justice called out to Ray. "I will be paying for that too."

Everyone split up into the three divisions. Cali didn't really enjoy playing the arcade games. She did enjoy talking to Ray and Ruby, though. Cali noticed that quite a few people were there, mostly other teams of other sports.

"Why can't I get the high score on this thing. I'm doing everything I can to beat this, but I can't," Ray whined.

"Maybe try a different one?" Ruby offered.

A ping came from Cali's phone. "It's almost 3:00. We should be heading to the cafeteria."

"We got here at like what? 1:00?" Ruby snickered. "Ray, you were distracting us."

"I know, I'm just *so* attractive," she sneered, flicking her ponytail.

Ruby blinked. "Anyway, I'll take us to the cafeteria. It's not too far off."

Ruby led them down a longer hall to a huge room. "There are multiple stands that you can choose from ... different restaurants."

"So, this is exactly like a mall?" Ray cocked her head.

"They added this like two years ago. Blue Sun is so small, and they only put their money into this thing."

Justice pushed past Ruby. "We're going to be sitting at table fourteen. Also, if you're going to buy something, ask me for money."

Ruby held a thumbs up as Justice walked away. The team was gathered over by table fourteen . . . arguing about who would eat first.

Eliza stood beside Cali. "It was inevitable for the team to argue, it's long overdue," she chuckled.

Justice freaked out. "EVERYONE SIT DOWN."

The team shut up and looked at Justice.

"I will start with the youngest three. Who are those people?"

Ruby stepped up. "That would be Eliza, Ray, and Cali. The next would be Hayden."

Justice nodded. "Thank you for helping, Ruby. I appreciate it."

After about thirty minutes of more arguing, everyone was at peace once they got their food. The team sat in a big circle so that arguing was easy.

Cali piped up. "Does anyone know if the police had any leads on Sienna's case?"

Cali felt everyone's stares pierce into her. Piper threw down her sandwich and left the table. Eliza elbowed her.

"Why would you ask that? That's what we are trying to avoid," she whispered.

"Why are we trying to ignore it?"

"Cali, you're not a president, please shut up," Mel mumbled.

"The police clearly aren't doing anything. Why aren't we doing anything? We know her better than the police."

"Stop." Eliza pulled her down. "This isn't the time to force your morals on everyone during a time when we are trying to get our minds off something."

Cali blinked. "*Hm*." She refused to apologize.

A muffled sound like the low hum of music from a speaker was in earshot of the team.

Ruby laid her head on the table. "No. No, please don't let it be them."

"Who?"

"The Blue Sun Royals."

"HEYYYY LOSERS!"

The door flew open, kicked by a tall woman with short hair held up by a bright red headband with a sun on it. Four other teammates joined her, all wearing multicolored team headbands.

"We saw the Swallowsville Swallows stickers on those cars out there. So we decided to assert our dominance!"

"You are really loud," Ruby said.

The second girl had black locks in a ponytail. She had a red-orange headband. The third girl had short, light brown hair and was short but athletic. She also looked like she could do no harm. She wore a yellow headband. The fourth had long, ginger hair in a high ponytail. She had many piercings all over her face, and wore a green headband. The fifth had medium-length hair that was a very light blue, almost white and wore winged eyeliner that gave her an intimidating look. She had a blue headband. The sixth had her hair up in a bun with indigo roses surrounding her bun and didn't wear a headband. The seventh was the shortest. She had long blonde hair with violet streaks and didn't wear a headband either. It truly was a diverse, inclusive team, and they wore identical blue varsity hoodies.

"*Ah*! I remember you!" The one with the red headband walked over to the table. "We kicked your butts in that game of dodgeball a few years ago! How's it going, Ruby?"

Ruby had her head down in embarrassment. "How in the world do you remember my name?"

"We have a list of everyone, every town, every team we've beat." She cackled. "Do you even remember our names?"

"No, of course, I don't remember your names," Ruby mumbled.

"I am Rowan. The one with the orange headband is Amber, the yellow headband is Goldie, the green headband is Chloe, the blue is Azul, indigo is Aura, the violet is . . . Thunder. That's a nickname."

Ruby rolled her eyes. "This doesn't look like the varsity as it was years ago? What happened? They look super young!"

Rowan messed with Cali's hair which resulted in a slap of the hand. "Ouch. Fierce too." She shook her hand.

"This is the 'C team'," Justice nodded.

Ruby glared at Justice.

"You have to be truthful."

STOLEN

Rowan burst out laughing obnoxiously. "You? Ruby Aurthur? On the 'C team'?"

"Yes," Ruby grumbled. "I don't even know you that well! Why are you making fun of me anyway?"

"You were a big thing back when you were a freshman. Did you get burned out?" Rowan sneered, pushing up her black hair.

"No, I was never burned out."

"Then why were you put on the 'C team'? What happened?" Rowan put her hands on her hips. "Don't you guys have like . . . the best coach around? Did you make her mad?"

Ruby rubbed her face due to the bombardment of questions.

"It's quite a simple answer."

"She got replaced, now screw off," Ray yelled.

"Is there no supervision in here?" Eliza whispered.

"There are other groups in here, why us?" Cali shrugged.

"Then what's the answer?" Rowan scratched her head. Rowan was so animated that it gave Cali motion sickness. "Can your goldfish brain not answer it?"

Kimberly spoke up for once. "Oh, I hate to butt in, but goldfish are actually relatively smart. You would want to call her Sloth or Turkey brain instead since they have the lowest IQs." Kimberly nervously starting sweating.

Rowan scrunched up her face, offended that an outcast such as Kimberly would speak down to her. Rowan sighed in annoyance. She put her foot up onto the table, splitting Ray and Cali from each other. "Swallowsville 'C team', I would like to challenge you to a dodgeball game."

Ray chuckled loudly. "We'll slaughter you and send you to a manufacturing plant," Ray taunted.

Ruby bit her lip. "You guys take dodgeball more seriously than you take basketball."

Rowan chuckled and ruffled Ruby's hair, taking her foot off the table. "Meet us there in thirty minutes. Good luck!" Rowan waved and left cackling.

Eliza was taking medicine for a headache. "Oh my gosh. Why are other teams so annoying!"

Cali glanced away nervously.

"I think I need to explain the dodgeball arena to you guys. I haven't been there since my freshman year, so things might have changed." Ruby ran her hands through her hair. "It's a laser tag arena, with capture the flag and dodgeball."

Ray gasped in amusement. "Oh, that sounds so cool!" She held her head in her hand, her eyes sparkling.

"You are split into two teams. Each person on their own team goes into a room that is literally like a Colosseum room. You know what I mean?" Ruby cocked her head. "Each single person will get a different colored dodgeball, and you can only use that color of dodgeball. You have to put on a vest, if you get out by the other team, the vest will turn off, and you will have to go to a room. In that room, there will be colors signifying the dodgeball colors. If the person who got you out gets out, your vest will turn back on and you can go back in. It isn't until the last ten minutes of the game where you cannot go back in at all, or if everyone gets out."

The team blinked.

"I didn't catch any of that," Piper mumbled. "What happened?"

Ruby slammed her head into the table.

"So, what strategies can we use?" Eliza raised her eyebrows.

"Well, I have no clue." Ruby lifted her head up. "You guys are all really smart, so I think you can figure it out yourselves. There's a map outside the arena if you want to study that."

Ray instantly popped up and grabbed Cali's arm. "We're going. Everyone should come."

Everyone shook their heads.

"C'mon, Cali!" Ray tugged her. "Please?"

Ray mimicked those stupid puppy dog eyes and somehow made them seem human. Was she even human?

"Fine."

Cali sat on a comfy black chair in a black room with neon shapes painted against the black. Ruby was right. It was just like a laser tag game. Cali had the vest on; she had gray. It wasn't the worst color ever, but she wished she had her favorite color, purple.

Ray texted Cali about how excited she was to have a cool color like black. *How was someone even supposed to see black in the arena?* Ruby answered Ray, saying that black was an overpowering color.

Ray then asked what color Ruby had: she got purple. Cali groaned, she wanted purple. It was childish to be annoyed over your favorite color. Maybe Harlow was right, maybe she was still immature.

Where was Harlow right now? She hadn't hung out with Ray since the incident, and Cali hadn't heard from her since the festival. Perhaps Ray was disappointed that Harlow was a horrible person. Ray hadn't said anything about money until Sienna told Harlow off. Harlow was powerful.

Cali blinked; something clicked in her head.

"T-minus sixty seconds. The door will begin to open at ten," a woman's calm voice came over the intercom. The intercom was directly over the timer. Cali felt nervous. Those girls were beasts . . . some of them at least, but Cali knew that it was wrong to judge someone based on their size.

Cali wondered what colors the other team members got. Piper most likely got red, mostly because of her short temper.

There were three layers to the arena. Cali decided that she would use the bottom layer and hide because she was small. Cali guessed the bottom layer was where the taller people would be since they really couldn't hide anywhere. They would just be out in the open. Cali, though, did not know the layout that well, she would be different and use her small self to her advantage.

"Ten . . . nine . . . eight."

The door began to open, and Cali stood up in front of it shaking her head.

"Six . . . five . . . four."

Cali's vest flickered on.

"Three . . . two . . . one."

The door was open now, and Cali could see the arena completely. It was strangely cold. Cali walked out slowly. The rest of her team did too. They were wary, not knowing what to do first.

In the distance, Cali could see Rowan strutting confidently towards them. *Where were the rest?*

Cali heard a pitter-patter of feet above her. The door closed behind her.

"THEY'RE IN THE WALLS," Ruby screamed and ran off.

"THE WALLS?" Ray frantically ran off with her.

Cali ran off with them and heard a wall of flying dodgeballs and multiple buzzers. They were now under a top-floor building. "I'm going to the top floor. It seems like they're up there, so I'm going to need you two as backup."

"We're going to lose," Ray mumbled.

"That's a horrible way to put it . . . loser." Ruby smiled and prodded Ray's shoulder.

That triggered something in Ray to go absolutely berserk. She ran off screaming. "I'M NOT A LOSER! I'LL MAKE BLUE SUN LOOK LIKE ONE, THOUGH!"

Cali blinked in surprise. "What?"

"Swearing works sometimes, I guess." Ruby shrugged.

"Helloooooo!" The smallest one, the most innocent one, the violet one swung down from the rafters and stared at them upside down. She held up a purple dodgeball. "Are you not going to run?"

"No." Ruby threw one of her purple dodgeballs at her.

She hoisted herself up just in time so the ball missed. She was incredibly athletic it seemed. "You really think that you can hit me?" She dropped down from the rafters and took Ruby by surprise and hit her with the dodgeball. The vest flickered off with a sad buzzer sound.

She got up and looked at Cali. The girl had no more dodgeballs. Ruby walked off angrily, leaving Cali behind.

The violet girl charged at Cali's ankles for her dodgeball. Cali quickly hit her in the back as they both fell. Her vest flickered off with the same sad buzzer sound. That meant Ruby was back in right away, and there she was, already coming back over.

"Ray has a lot of people out right now." Ruby snickered. "Blue Sun is not happy; they're targeting her right now. Let's go help her on the top floor."

The top floor had twists and turns that the two were cautious about; however, they had no trouble navigating it. They made it to the open area of the second floor which literal looked like a jungle.

A yellow dodgeball whizzed past Cali's head. It was one of the girls with the most average height of the team. In fact, Cali remembered her name well. It was Goldie, an ironic name.

Goldie swore angrily behind the bushes before she hopped out into plain view. "Aren't you going to throw anything at me?"

Cali had a strange feeling. "There are more in here!"

"You're correct." Someone laughed from above the door. She had a deeper laugh, meaning she was most likely older. "Look up!" She had what Cali would describe as a flirty type of voice.

Cali shuddered. "You talk weird."

"Excuse me?" Her face was hidden, and only the green vest lights shone. She snorted and attempted to hit Cali.

Cali successfully dodged.

"My name is Chloe, in case you forgot. You may want to look behind you."

However, Cali was already on it. Cali hit Chloe, took Ruby's dodgeball, and hit Goldie.

"That's cheating!" Goldie stomped her foot on the ground.

"And I just got back in," Chloe grumbled.

Ruby picked up her and Cali's dodgeball. "Jeez. You're doing well."

"I'm just trying to catch people off guard from now on."

Ruby blinked. "Okay, I really don't care, let's just win."

As Cali and Ruby rounded the corner to the third floor, she heard multiple screeches of anger coming from the room. Since Cali had seen little of the team, they had to have been up there. But Cali was horribly wrong. Swallowsville was being picked off one by one by Rowan and the orange girl, Amber. They were the tallest and strongest people on Blue Sun.

Cali and Ruby were not the only ones on the floor. Ray and Piper were working together for once to take them down. However, it wasn't working. Eliza hid behind the door, and pulled Cali down by her hoodie strings. "Cali, you are always going to lose against someone stronger than you, but remember to exploit peoples' weaknesses."

Cali nodded.

As she walked into the doorway, she saw that the third floor was themed like a Roman Colosseum. Maybe that's why Ruby called it a colosseum in the first place. Piper and Ray were both rolling, diving, and doing everything they could to avoid the death sentence of those girls' throws.

Rowan made eye contact with Cali. Cali swallowed as she saw a red dodgeball fly at her. She ducked and it stuck itself into the hallway behind her. Cali raised her eyebrows. Their dodgeballs differed from the others... they were *weighted*. A deep hatred arose in Cali's chest and throat.

"THEY'RE CHEATING!"

Everyone in the room looked over. "What are you going to do about it?"

Rowan was distracted, Cali subtly nodded at Piper. Thankfully, Piper understood and drilled a dodgeball into the back of Rowan's head.

Piper laughed and spit on her. "You needed to be humbled, you cocky varsity player!"

Piper was met with a hard, weighted, orange dodgeball to the face that knocked her into the wall. Piper got up, unfazed, but with a nosebleed. "Wow," she yelled and flung herself at Amber. She was like a cat, pulling and scratching at Amber.

Ray threw a dodgeball at Amber and got her out. Cali swallowed as the whole arena lit up with the Swallowsville colors, purple, black, and white.

The automated voice announced over the intercom, "Swallowsville has won!"

Ruby laughed.

The fight between Piper and Amber came to a halt as Amber threw Piper to the side. Rowan stood with her mouth open.

"Cheaters sometimes win, but not this time," Ray chuckled.

Eliza came out from behind the hallway and laughed. "Great teamwork, Cali." Eliza laid her hand on Cali's shoulder. "You distracted them."

Rowan and Amber pushed past the three at the doorway.

"Walk of shame! Walk of shame," she sneered, stepping over Ray.

Ray got up on her own, picking up the two black dodgeballs she had. "I'm so sore," she groaned.

"So, what do we do now?" Cali asked, turning around.

Ray and Piper caught up to them; Piper trailed a bit behind, however. "We just leave. Also, expect to be beat up outside. Our win here will be displayed for a month on the boards."

Cali laughed. "So, are you happy that we won against them?"

Ruby snickered, "Of course."

Ray was the last one to jump into the car and slam the door shut before any of the Blue Suns got her. Ray flipped them all off as they drove off. "Losers," she screamed out the window.

"Don't get too cocky yourself now." Ruby looked back at Ray in the mirror.

Ray shrugged. "I think this was justified."

"Justice told us that everyone was cheering us on in the out room," Ruby said.

"That's so awesome," Ray mumbled.

"Cali did help a bit." Ruby nodded.

"She distracted Rowan, which helped us win."

Cali shrugged and shook her head. "I just did what was instinctive. We were going to take them down ourselves. Ruby may have had a chance, but we weren't going to win unless we tried something else."

"Okay, brainiac," Piper grumbled. "You know I don't care for you rambling on about how good you are."

Cali shook her head and laughed. Swallowsville suddenly felt like home to her. She had great people all around her. She felt safe.

CHAPTER 20

"So, you are the eleven-year-olds who took down Ruby *single-handedly*?" Cali stared in astonishment. She knew they would be small, but the so-called leader was even shorter than Cali.

Ruby told Ray and Cali that she had to meet the middle schoolers today, and if the two were interested, they were welcome to come. They also had a game today, Tuesday, after school. They were supposed to be in the gym, but no one seemed to care enough to be there early anymore.

"Yes." Kikuko rolled her eyes. "I am so sick of explaining this."

Cali blinked. "Sorry." Cali glanced at her mask. "May I ask one more question?"

Kikuko sighed in annoyance. "It's about my mask, isn't it? I have a horrible immune system and a heart condition. Is that good enough for you?"

Alyssa patted Kikuko's shoulder. "She's had a rough day. She's angry that her IQ is just under above average."

Kikuko punched Alyssa directly in the nose. "Why would you say anything about that?"

"Hey, hey. Let's not punch each other," Cali warned.

Kikuko shrank into her chair and crossed her arms in anger. "Blaze."

Blaze woke up from her nap on the couch and stared.

"Come here." Kikuko treated Blaze like a dog. "Can you *talk* to this girl right here?"

Blaze shook her head.

"Why not?"

Blaze laid back down on the bed.

"Lazy," Kikuko muttered. "Anyway, I want money to go to the varsity game. We want to talk to Erie."

Ruby swallowed.

"Don't you have your own money?" Cali cocked her head.

"Do you think I have sixteen dollars on me right now?" Kikuko rested her head in her hands. "I don't always have money on me."

"Why do you guys need to go?" Ruby sat up more.

"We need to observe Erie," Kikuko mumbled. "Unless you have a way that we could sneak into the games."

"Literally, just run in," Ruby scoffed. "They don't care and will not go after you, trust me."

Kikuko cocked her head. "Really?"

"Yeah."

"How are we going to get there? Do you have any idea how we could maybe . . . sneak onto the bus?" Kikuko was already lost in thought. "Is there any way we could sneak onto the varsity bus?"

Ruby's eyes lit up, seemingly forgetting that it was her at the festival and not Erie. "You could sneak into the varsity bus's storage area."

Kikuko looked at the time. "We better get going if we want to get to the bus on time." She turned to Blaze. "BLAZE! Get up. We're going."

Blaze grumbled under her breath and reluctantly got up.

Cali, Ray, and Ruby grabbed their basketball bags and ran out the door, followed by the younger girls. "The storage is labeled storage; it won't be too hard to find. You don't need an access key, either."

Kikuko nodded.

Ray pushed open the front door to the school and ran out. The buses parked out in front of the school in what was called the "leaving circle."

The circle was in front of the school, down the path from the long entrance. The circle had two roads splitting from it. The 'C team' bus was the smallest, but still looked as nice as the others. The 'B team's' was bigger, and the 'A team's', (varsity), was the biggest. The buses were painted in royal purple with a white stripe through the middle spelling "Swallowsville Swallows." Under the words, there was a "C," "B," or "A" depending on the team ranking.

Kikuko and the rest split off on their own. Cali wasn't concerned about them, since they were awfully smart kids. It was Ruby she was worried about. *How would Ruby pull this off? She couldn't. There was no way she could keep pointing to Erie.* Cali shook her head and got on the bus.

Everyone greeted them as they took their seats. Ray and Cali sat together while Ruby claimed her own seat beside them. In front of them were Eliza and Piper, both in the opposite seats. Mel and Justice were in the back of the bus, while Kimberly, River, and Hayden, were in the front. Milan usually rode with them, but that was no more after the talk with Talivikki. Milan said she didn't know how long she would even keep her job, and would lose it sooner or later. Cali guessed that Milan would be let go after the season.

"Hey, Cali, Ray, and Ruby," Eliza said. "So what were you guys doing with a bunch of eleven-year-olds?"

Cali swallowed.

"Oh, Ray knew them from laser tag downtown," Ruby said confidently. "No worries, we weren't doing anything."

Cali gave Ruby a look.

Eliza raised an eyebrow, looking directly at Cali. "Okay." She turned away and went back to her phone.

In front of them, the 'B team's' emergency bus door opened, and two girls ran out while laughing hysterically. Harlow emerged from the entrance, clearly angry. Piper punched the seat in front of them. "We need to get going, but the 'B team' can't sit still for two seconds."

Eliza chuckled, "I've always wondered why Harlow is on the 'B team' and not the varsity team."

Justice and Mel sat behind Cali and Ruby. "When I spoke to Harlow a couple of years back, she said it was because she didn't want to take away from others."

Ray sighed angrily, "She's trying to be *so* nice. She's a horrible, but powerful person."

"Do you not think we know that? Everyone can see through her. The only people who can't are the new people, like the freshmen." Justice nodded at Ray and Cali. "You didn't know, did you two?"

"Cali definitely didn't know, I didn't either. Harlow and I hung out all the time." Ray laid her head against the seat in front of her. "We've hung out since I was in eighth grade."

"How did she treat you?" Eliza leaned closer, poking her head around the seat. Piper poked her head over her own seat and looked down at Ray.

"She treated me nicely, like Cali saw. She was with us, at my house, during the Fox Den thing." Ray shrugged, trying to suppress her pain. "I thought she was a good person, since she treated me great, you know."

"She treated you like that because she knows how unstable you are. If she treats you like crap, everyone will hear about it," Justice mumbled.

"Unstable?" Ray sat up straight.

"Ray, have you not seen how you act?"

Ray shook her head. "I act perfectly fine, thanks," she nodded.

Ruby glanced at Cali.

"So, she wanted to keep her reputation up with me, so she treated me ever so kindly."

"Yup." Justice gave a thumbs-up.

"What is the main difference between the buses?" Cali changed the subject quickly.

"The 'B team' bus is just like ours, only bigger. The varsity's though, oh boy," Piper mumbled. "I was told that it has a table with magnetic stuff so they can play board games while on a trip," she growled.

Justice nodded and gave another thumbs-up. She seemed tired of talking.

"Why, though?"

"Because they could. The table and board weren't originally magnetic, though." Piper giggled manically. "Their pieces used to fly off every time they went over a bump. Also, since they're competitive cavewomen, people usually got a board to the head. They had to nail down the board."

Cali blinked. "Oh?"

Piper smiled. "Absolutely."

Ruby snickered. "That's true." She stared ahead at Harlow, dragging the two girls back inside the bus. "Though, only the 'more popular' girls would play. They never let me."

"Right, you were a varsity player," Piper got up in Ruby's face. "Are you ever going back, because frankly, you're more annoying than Ray."

"Hey," Ray hissed.

Justice pushed Piper away from Ruby. "We've had days without fights, we're doing better, so can we *not* fight?"

"Okay, mom." Piper glared. She quickly spun around and curled up against her window.

"Dude, we're like a literal family. I'm going to be sad once we graduate," Mel spoke up.

Justice looked down sadly. "Oh right, we're graduating this year. I never had a chance on varsity."

"At my old school," Cali winced, "The seniors would always play on varsity, whether they were . . . good or not."

Justice laughed, "Thanks for calling me bad at basketball, Cali."

"Sorry." Cali smiled.

"I would have loved at least a chance at varsity," Mel said, putting her beanie over her eyes.

The bus moved.

"Who were those two running out of the bus?"

"Fern Cook and Ivy Buck." Justice squinted.

"Who are on the 'B team'?"

"Too many I don't know." Justice shrugged.

The bus pulled out of the leaving circle and the teams were on their way to a new, unheard-of town, Canola.

"Let's go Dra-gons!"

Stomping and clapping rang out from the Canola high school's student section. The Swallowsville student section was relatively quiet. Talivikki was yelling from the benches, mostly at Keagan.

Swallowsville was having it handed to them as Canola led by forty points. This was the biggest loss they had in years.

Keagan panicked, knowing that Swallowsville's embarrassment was because of her. She had been out of it ever since she got stuck wearing the number four. Talivikki yelled at her, not because she thought that four was the number of death, instead it was because of Keagan's mindset. Keagan gasped as the basketball was stolen from her yet again by one of the Bull sisters.

Keagan quickly high-tailed it in front of Alisha Bull, making a 'J' shape. Alisha smiled at her for a second before Keagan took the hardest charge she had ever taken, worse than the last. Keagan laid there with the breath knocked out of her. She wanted to cry but felt nothing.

Alisha looked down at her and held out a hand. "How are you alive?"

Keagan stared at Alisha's hand.

Talivikki warned Keagan about Alisha and Adley Bull. The Bull sisters. They both lived up to their last name. Some said that if you ever took a charge from them, you would never be the same person again. Keagan believed that was just a stupid tale used to scare everyone. Keagan had taken four. It didn't even give Canola any gain, it just hurt players. However, the refs didn't always call the charges, which was most likely a bias.

Keagan got up on her own, rejecting Alisha's hand. She stood tall and looked at the disappointed faces in the Swallowsville student section.

The refs called a foul, and Erie called Keagan back to get the ball.

"What in the world is going on in that head of yours, Keagan? *Huh?*" Erie shook her head angrily. "Get out of your own head. You're embarrassing us all."

Keagan nodded and took the ball.

Ray leaned against the student section bleachers. "Wow. Keagan's . . . messed up." Ray leaned towards Cali, who was sitting hunched over. "Do you think we did that to her?"

Cali shook her head. "I don't know. I feel horrible, even if that didn't stem from us."

Ray shrugged. "I don't feel bad, why do you?"

"Because all of Swallowsville is embarrassed by her! Wouldn't you feel horrible if you were in her shoes?"

"I would never be in her shoes!" Ray shook her head. "I don't see your point here?"

Eliza was right. Ray barely felt any empathy. Cali had forgotten what her original reason was for helping Ruby. She originally wanted Ruby gone, but now she felt like Ray and Ruby were some type of messed up, but great family. Cali sighed. As much as Ray was messed up in the head, the more Cali grew attached to her. Cali was greatly interested in Ray.

Cali completely forgot about her mental notebook. She cringed. *What in the world was that anyway?* She understood why she had it, but she realized she didn't need it that much anymore. She didn't know when she became her present self. She just randomly began to let go and move on.

"Oh, by the way, Cali." Ray chuckled. "We are going back to Keagan's house tonight. If you'd like to go."

Cali hesitated. "I'm sorry, Ray."

Ray frowned.

"I don't want to go with this time."

"What?" Ray sat up. "Is this because of me?" she growled.

"No. It's not because of you." Cali shook her head. "I feel way too bad for Keagan."

Ray looked defeated. "We need to be moved to the 'B team', Cali!"

"I will help. I just don't want to ruin her mentally again."

"Soft," Ray mumbled.

Cali glared.

Keagan was ordered to sit out and was being lectured hard by Talivikki. "GET THAT NUMEROLOGY CRAP OUT OF YOUR HEAD! YOU'RE STILL ALIVE!"

"*Numerology.* "Numerology?" Cali cocked her head.

"Isn't that like, a Chinese thing or something?"

Cali shrugged. "It seems like she believes in it." Cali's eyes widened. "Ray, look up what number four means."

Ray rolled her eyes and got out her phone. "Some sources say that it is the number of death."

"Death?"

Ray nodded with a blank expression.

"You guys aren't going to harm her in any way, right?"

"Absolutely not. I saw a stupid journal in her room. We're going to read through that tonight. I'll send you pictures if you want."

"No, Ray, I'm fine."

STOLEN

The buzzer went off for the fourth quarter. The game was finished and Talivikki was rounding up varsity to yell at them in the locker room.

Ruby came back from the concessions with a cookie. "I'm glad I'm not on varsity right now." Ray grabbed her bag and got up.

"Cali isn't going with us."

Ruby looked at Cali, confused. "Why not?"

"I feel bad for Keagan. Look at her." Cali pointed at Keagan. "She's destroyed and distraught."

"Cali, ignore that. We need to do this." Ruby sighed. "You don't have to go with Ray and me, but you still need to look past Keagan's feelings. We have to do this to make everything 'normal' again."

Cali shook her head. "I won't go on this one night. I want to think. You said even if I don't do anything, I will still be put on the 'B team' so I don't have to do anything."

"So be it," Ruby mumbled. "See you tomorrow, Cali."

"We're still on the bus together," Cali grumbled.

Ruby perked up. "Oh, right. Sorry to be so dramatic."

"*Psst.*"

Cali stirred in her bed.

"*Psst.* Cali."

Cali opened her eyes to see a silhouette standing over her. She gasped and scrambled to get away. "Who are you?'

The light came on.

"It's Ray," she whispered. "I'm here to talk to you about something."

"It's 2:00 a.m." Cali rolled her eyes and sat up. "What could you possibly want at this hour?"

Ray stared at Cali blankly. "Nice sports bra."

Cali threw a cup of water at Ray. "Ray."

"Okay, okay." Ray took off her soaked hoodie. "I want to show you something I found."

"It's from Keagan, isn't it?" Cali wrapped the blanket around herself.

"Correct," Ray sounded like a gameshow host. "You want a prize or something?"

"Why are you so grumpy?"

"You threw water at me."

"That's because you stared at me." Cali rolled her eyes and laid against the wall. "What did you find?"

Ray pulled out a small book with a red ribbon bookmark coming from the top of it. "This is the journal I was talking about. I've already looked at it, but I want you to see what she has been writing about us. It comes on around page thirty."

Cali glanced at Ray then down at the journal. "Why do you want me to see this?"

"She said she thinks she's been cursed, basically."

Cali read it.

"There's these three that I have been told that are trying to give Swallowsville attention through 'taking

down' me. Sorry for the improper grammar, I am not too happy currently."

Ray chuckled. "She was told by Talivikki, remember? Read more, skip a few pages."

Cali summarized the rest of the writing. "So, we did destroy her, mentally, with stealing her jersey." She threw the book back at Ray.

"That's all I want to know, nothing more. I'm glad my suspicions were confirmed." Ray caught the book. She saw the dream journal Cali had. "You have a journal as well? Laying right out in the open?" She walked over and opened it. "Did you ever figure out what that dream was about, even?"

"I figured out that the silhouettes were Ruby and Keagan. Never figured out what the stadium meant."

"I think I know what it means." Ray turned. "I think it means that we, well, maybe just you, are going to end up on varsity if we keep up like this. You were on the court, right? It says you were looking up at the fans."

Cali nodded. "I think, I don't fully remember."

"Well, that's what you wrote." Ray put down the book. "Only the varsity plays at the stadium, you know."

CHAPTER 21

It was Halloween and time for the Halloween dance. The 'C team' locker room was lit up with a new type of spark: The talk about partners.

"Justice has a boyfriend," Mel yelled, teasing Justice.

"You didn't need to tell the whole team," Justice giggled.

Ruby put her hoodie on. "Who is he?"

"His name is Alex." Justice put her earrings back in. "He's hot."

Ray gagged and coughed loudly from her locker.

"Ray," Justice rolled her eyes jokingly. "You've never dated before; do you like anybody?"

Ray tensed up and turned around, embarrassed. "I have never liked anyone before. That stuff is stupid." Ray messed with her ponytail. "Plus, I sound like a guy. I've only attracted girls before."

Justice raised her eyebrows, amused. Then she made eye contact with Cali. Cali glanced away and tried for the door. "What about you, Cali?"

Cali stopped. "No one," she mumbled.

"*Aww*, c'mon." Justice stepped in front of her.

Cali stepped back. "Can you stop?" she chuckled.

"Sorry," she apologized and stepped away. "You aren't planning to go to the dance like that, are you?" Justice looked Ray and Cali up and down.

"We are," Ray sneered. "We aren't going to attract anyone, so we are going casual."

"No costumes or anything?" Justice looked back at her own costume.

"What about the girls you attract, Ray?"

Ray angrily inhaled. "We are going with this."

Ruby stepped up. "I'm going as Ruby Aurthur," Ruby snickered. "You're going as a cat, I see."

Justice nodded. "Hopefully, it will distract from my screwed-up ear."

Ruby shrugged. "Anyway, see you at the dance."

The three left the locker room. Justice must have asked Piper about dating because Piper could be heard yelling at them all.

"Piper has been angrier than usual," Ruby commented. "I would say I'm concerned, but what would she even be capable of?"

"That's the first problem with her anger. People are underestimating her," Cali mumbled.

Ruby shrugged. "Do you underestimate my strength?"

"No, because you are strong."

Ruby glanced away. "I see your point, sorry."

Last week, Ruby came down with a cold, so they never messed with Keagan that week. They couldn't have since they had no more ideas. Still, Cali refused to steal anything from Keagan ever again.

The dance was in the varsity gym, the gym with the most space for thousands of kids. Varsity didn't have practice for the last week, so the student council and volunteers set up the dance.

Cali had never been to a dance before. Her old school had a dance, but only for the high school. However, if she ever stayed in Yarmen, she would never go to a dance, ever.

The three scaled the stairs with ease. Cali once again laid her eyes on the big hall of fame.

"I wonder if any of us would be able to get on there?" Cali mumbled.

Ruby and Ray stopped in their tracks.

"Excuse me?" Ray looked at the wall and then back at Cali. "Us?"

Cali shrugged. "Sorry, that was a dumb thought," Cali said, embarrassed. "It's just a 'what if' question, you know?"

"Do you think you're Travis The King?" Ray nudged her.

"No, I don't believe that." Cali laughed. "Maybe someone could get into here without basketball?"

"Everything you do here will always have something to do with basketball." Ruby blinked. "Can we get going to the dance now?"

"Talivikki looks so young."

Ruby groaned silently, impatient. "She was twenty in that photo. So was the rest of her team. That was the last time they ever saw one another."

Cali had only observed Ajorne, the old coach, and Talivikki before. She never looked at the other team members. "There were only five of them?"

"Yes." Ruby rolled her eyes. "Let's go."

Cali had her eyes glued to the wall and Ray dragged her away. *Only five? That is enough for a team, but wouldn't you need subs?*

"Hey, Daisy." Ray waved. "How are you doing?"

"It's going great, Ray, thank you." Daisy looked at Ruby, who was taking out the money. "You don't have to pay this year due to the incidents."

Ruby put her money away in her wallet. "Damn. Thanks, Daisy."

"No problem, go right on in." Daisy smiled warmly. "One thing, though. A couple of middle schoolers ran into the dance while we weren't looking. We couldn't catch them in time. So, if you see any young kids in there, please report them to us."

The three gave each other a look.

"We will!" Ruby said as she dragged the others in.

Cali stopped in her tracks. Ray did too, as they both observed the dance for the first time in their lives.

"I see they went all out this year," Ruby mumbled.

"Whoa," Ray said with her mouth open.

Kids were all over, and it was packed. Lights were flashing and music was playing. *How would they ever find Kikuko?*

"Should we split up and try to find the middle schoolers?" Ray offered, "I'd like to explore first. This is the first dance I have ever been to, and I'm guessing it's Cali's first as well."

Ruby glanced away. "Alright. We'll meet up later at the snack bar." Ruby walked off. "Have fun."

Ray nodded to Cali. "See you."

Cali was left alone. She looked around. Perhaps she would look at the bleachers. As she swam through the sea of teenagers, she finally came across the bleachers.

"Cali," someone with a husky voice called her name. Cali turned; it was Talivikki, who was drinking something out of a cup.

"Are you looking for Ray? She went that way."

"I'm not, actually." She gave a sham smile. "Why are you here?"

Talivikki sat hunched over. "I'm making sure none of my players make any stupid decisions." Talivikki looked around. "So far, so good."

"Have you seen any middle schoolers around?" Cali peered into the sea of people. "Daisy told us that there were middle schoolers running around. Ray thinks she knows them, so she was searching for them."

Talivikki raised an eyebrow. "Ray Eaton knowing middle schoolers with her child-like mind? Not surprising."

Cali glanced back. "Yep."

"No, sorry, Cali." Talivikki sat up. "I have not seen any middle schoolers."

"Alright." Cali stared curiously at Talivikki. "Why do you round your height to 6'5" instead of 6'10"?"

"Random question." Talivikki got up. "Tell me. Would you be more intimidated by someone who was 6'10" or someone who said they were 6'5", a more average height?"

"6'10"," Cali answered.

Talivikki nodded and sat back down.

"What about Ray? How much do you know about her? Why do you say that she has a child-like mind?"

"You ask a lot of questions, Ms. Horn. I like that," she mumbled.

"We all know Ray's fragile mind. It's impressive how she hasn't broken yet over the disappearance of Sienna."

"But why do you say that she has a child-like mind? How about me? What do you think of me?" Cali pointed to herself.

Talivikki blinked and shook her head. "I've been told about Ray before; I'm just going off of what people have told me. As for you, you seem like a smart young girl, just timid, but in other areas, you are aggressive. I have seen you play. You hate to take risks, like Ray, you don't deviate off the path, which is a habit thing of course, but you have been influenced by Ruby enough to break that by now. I'm going to ask you this; why do you not take those risks in basketball, but do in other aspects of your life?"

Cali squinted, trying to figure out what in the world Talivikki just said. "I don't know."

Talivikki laughed. "I think you know. You're scared to because you're small, Cali. You're small, but you can still do almost just as much as your taller teammates, don't be scared."

Cali nodded warily. "Thank you, Talivikki."

"You don't believe me, do you?"

"I d—" a crash came over from the middle of the floor, cutting Cali off.

"What in the world?" Talivikki got up and hurried over to the sound. Cali followed. The music was cut down to a much lower volume so people could chant louder.

Helped by Talivikki, Cali got to the front of the ring. It was Ruby fighting Erie. Erie had bruises all over her. Ruby had Erie pinned down while she gripped her shirt. Varsity stood around them, shocked. Olive, the other short-tempered one, looked angry and ready to jump in.

"Hey," Talivikki yelled with authority. "Stop the fighting!" However, Talivikki had no power over the hundreds of kids chanting over her. She fidgeted with her hands. *She was so powerful! How was she nervous?*

Ruby stared at Erie with so much anger, and that anger carried out through the punch at Erie's nose. A cracking noise rang out through the place. Erie's nose broke, and it was bleeding profusely.

"Oh my God," Cali mumbled.

Olive screeched and dove right into Ruby, sending them both sliding across the floor. Erie, despite her broken, bleeding nose, got into the fight as well. Varsity stayed back, knowing Talivikki was there.

Ruby was kicked and punched, although, there was nothing worse suffered than Erie's broken nose.

Suddenly, Keagan pulled Ruby away. Olive and Erie tried to rip her away but were only held back by Joy and Connor. Ruby looked up at Keagan. Keagan smiled down at her warmly, seeming to forget what Ruby had done to her.

Ruby snarled.

"You're just doing this for validation, aren't you?" Keagan shook her head and snickered. "We don't want any other players hurt."

Ruby glared. "Why are you like this?"

"Ruby," she whispered. "I know what you did to me. It's not a secret between us and Talivikki."

Ruby softened up right then and there.

"You know?" Keagan snickered again. "I wasn't allowed to tell you, but now you know."

Ruby began to cry. "Oh. Oh." She pushed Keagan away and ran off.

Keagan stared as Ruby pushed the crowd aside and ran out. Talivikki rushed into the circle and pulled Olive and Erie aside, furious. As she dragged them out, Olive and Erie whined about self-defense. Talivikki ignored them. Keagan followed.

"Cali, Cali!" Cali was shaken by Ray.

"We have to follow her."

"What about Kikuko?"

"We're here." Kikuko and the others stood behind Ray.

Ruby cried on Ray's couch in front of them. "I don't want to do anything to her again. I don't want to mess with her ever again. Please, I don't want to be on varsity anymore. I can't face them, I'm embarrassed!"

Kikuko was yelling in her face. "LIAR. You lied to us. It wasn't Erie!" Kikuko dug her nails into Ruby's skin. "Liar, liar, liar," she growled.

Alyssa slapped Kikuko. Kikuko stumbled back, holding her face.

"She's suffering already." Alyssa feared what Kikuko would do next.

Molli stepped in front of Alyssa to protect her.

Kikuko stared in shock. "What? Blaze?"

Blaze blinked at Kikuko and stood with Alyssa and Molli.

"Blaze," Kikuko growled. "You too?"

Blaze held out her hand to Ruby. Ruby reluctantly took it. Blaze jutted her head sideways. *She must have been implying a type of peace.*

Kikuko looked defeated. "She lied. What about the promise?"

"Blaze doesn't want to hurt, like she was. That's not what she wants," Alyssa mumbled.

Blaze nodded.

Ray stood silent with a blank stare. It was the same act of shutting down she always did when something went wrong.

Kikuko shook her head angrily and left the house, slamming the door behind her.

That woke Ray up. Her head snapped up.

"I think we should leave too." Alyssa watched Kikuko leave from the window. "We'll leave you guys to it. I'm so sorry about her." They headed for the door. "We will help you with anything you need. I'm not too sure about Kikuko, though. I think she needs time."

Blaze waved goodbye and closed the door behind her.

"Ruby, please, we have to get you back on varsity so you can be on the 'B team'." Ray leaned over to look Ruby in the eyes. Ray hugged her. "Please, Ruby. We can't give up now!"

"You'll grow older. You'll have the chance to be put onto varsity." Ruby stared at Ray with sorrow. "I, however, will not. I am done. My life is over."

"I will not get that chance, ever." Ray ignored Ruby's depressed comment. "You are my only hope."

"You don't have to hope on me." Ruby paced around angrily. "Stop acting like a useless toddler, Ray," she hissed.

Ray glanced down with a blank expression.

"Don't shut down and ignore me! Take some criticism!" Ruby threw her hands up. "Please, Ray. You have so much potential. Don't waste it."

Ray ignored her.

Ruby furiously yelled some nonsense and walked out, leaving Cali with Ray.

"Leave," Ray mumbled, sounding dead.

"I'm not leaving you."

Ray threw a soda bottle at Cali. It shattered on the wall behind her. "Leave." Ray got up and shoved Cali to the ground. "Do what I say!"

Cali remembered Ray's father. This had to be some type of mirror of him.

"Ray, listen." She held her hands up.

"No!" Ray stomped on Cali.

"Don't be like your father." Cali cringed. It was a horrible thing to say.

Ray's anger faded into a bout of crying. "God damnit, Cali," she sniffed. "Why did you say that?"

Cali slowly got up. "I'm so sorry, that was on impulse."

"You're right, you're right, though." Ray took criticism for once in her life. "I'm sorry, but please leave."

Cali backed up toward the door, keeping her eye on Ray. "You won't do anything stupid, right?" Cali asked as she opened the door.

"I won't do anything stupid, Cali." Ray headed upstairs. "Please, leave me alone. I promise you." The hurt in Ray's eyes was too painful for even Cali to look at.

Cali slowly shut the door behind her. A cold breeze hit her on the porch. It was the same feeling she had when that news car flew by her. She looked up. The stars were as clear as ever. Cali's heart dropped. The stupid stars were out. Something was changing. Cali started to run to Eliza's house.

"So, you insulted Ray and then expected her, as a suicidal person, not to do anything to herself?" Eliza inhaled. "Cali, c'mon now."

"Look, that's not the only thing I came here to talk about," Cali interrupted. "We aren't going after Keagan anymore."

"That was really predictable," Eliza mumbled. "Even so, you can still figure out what happened to Sienna, or the Fox Den."

Cali looked down. "I don't think I'm capable of that." Cali rested her arms on the table. "I'm *not* capable of that."

Eliza shrugged. "You are. You're very close to the culprit."

"Was it you?"

"No. It wasn't me." Eliza threw her hands up. "I can't tell you who it was. I just know the most suspicious person."

"So you really don't know?"

"I do, but I don't, if that makes sense." Eliza shrugged. "You should get going now. Goodbye."

"I wasn't done!"

"Too bad, it's late." Eliza pushed her to the window. "Ruby's birthday is coming up, and so is Sienna's. I think you may want to celebrate them in some way."

CHAPTER 22

"I have some people that I think you would like to meet." Ruby shuddered. "I have been thinking about this for a long time now. I think that it's finally time that you meet them."

It was Saturday, November ninth, the day before Sienna's birthday and two days before Ruby's.

"They want me to come over for my birthday. Early." Ruby gripped the steering wheel. "I know we were originally going to go to Ray's house, but is this okay too?"

"Of course." Ray smiled. "I'd love to meet them."

Cali nodded warily. Ray had been off ever since the incident with the quitting, but she had done nothing. Cali assumed that she was fine enough.

"Alright."

Ruby pulled out of her driveway. "I'm nervous about this. I'm going to need you guys to lay low."

"What do you mean by that?" Cali leaned against the door.

"They're very serious people." She snickered with an anxious undertone. "Don't say anything stupid."

"I would never," Ray chuckled.

"Mhm."

"What do you mean that they're serious people. They aren't criminals, are they?"

Ruby stayed silent for a few seconds. "Please, put that behind me. I just want you to meet my friends."

Cali squinted. "Ruby, you want us to meet a bunch of your criminal friends?"

"Yes," she hissed. "Don't call them criminals either. They'll freak out. That's all I ask of you."

"If I feel any danger, I am getting us all out of there," Cali said.

Ruby rolled her eyes. "You won't feel any danger if you don't mess up or show any weaknesses." She pulled up to a scary-looking house and parked. "We're here. Like I said, don't do *anything* stupid."

Cali swallowed nervously.

A dog barked from the inside of the house. Ruby waved Ray and Cali up to the door. A tall boy with a black mullet opened the door.

"Hey, Ruby," he mumbled. He peered over Ruby. "Who the hell are these guys?"

"I brought some friends if that's okay." Ruby pushed past him.

He rolled his eyes. "You can't just bring random people here without warning." He ran his hand through his hair. "Fine. Whatever. Let them in."

Ray pushed Cali in front of her, making her step in first. The place smelled heavily of marijuana. Cali almost choked but held it in.

They were instantly in the living room of the cramped trailer home. Two other boys sat around the small table in the middle. One was extremely tall, even taller than Talivikki, the other was more Ruby's height.

"I suppose I should introduce myself now," he said, annoyed. "I'm Reiser. The big boy over here is Truman, and the wimp is Cooper."

"Wimp," Cooper grumbled. "What are these bitches doing in here?"

"I don't know! Ask Ruby." Reiser pointed.

"I just thought they should meet you. They're my other friends." Ruby put her hands on both Ray and Cali's shoulders. Cali could feel Ruby's anxiety, her hands were freezing. Cooper rolled his eyes.

"This isn't good, Ruby, and you know why." He threw his hands out angrily.

"Why would this be bad?" Ray stepped forward. "I have never heard of you guys before."

Reiser whispered to Ruby. Ruby nodded multiple times. Reiser stalked off to a different room.

"Hey, you." Cooper waved Cali over, smiling mischievously.

Cali nervously looked back at Ray. Ray looked just as nervous as she did. Ray gestured for Cali to go.

Cali walked up cautiously.

"Scared?" He smiled. "I have a little something for you. I know you've been wondering about this."

Cali cocked her head. "What do you mean, that I've been wondering about this?"

He held up a jar covered with a red checkered cloth.

"Cooper, no!" Ruby stepped forward.

"I know you'll like this!" He removed the cloth. Inside the jar, a hand floated in formaldehyde. The skin tone was tan . . . like Native American skin.

Cali's heart dropped.

Ray tried to grab the jar out of Cooper's hands. Cooper swiped it away.

"I think she would be glad that you recognized her hand in this state!" Cooper laughed manically. "Are you going to hurt me now? What are you going to do?"

"You guys killed her! It was you!" Ray turned to Ruby. "You lied!"

Cali stood there, frozen.

Ruby grabbed Cali and Ray and ran to the back bathroom. She threw them in and shut the door and locked it. "Please, let me explain myself." She began to cry. "I have nothing to do with this!"

Ray glared, ready to jump at Ruby at any small mess up.

"You remember how my grandfather was killed?" Ruby was sobbing now. "Reiser. Reiser's father is the one who killed my grandfather. I was going to kill Reiser and his father, but then I got replaced by Keagan, met you guys, and changed. Now I don't know how to get away. I wanted this to happen. I'm sorry this is so sudden. They were also the Fox Den shooters."

Ray and Cali stared in shock.

Cali wasn't ready for this at all. *Should she do something right now? Should she fight them?* This wasn't how she imagined this would happen. She thought she would figure out who they were by herself. This was way too soon.

"Ruby?" Reiser knocked on the door. "All I heard was 'Keagan' and 'replaced,' who is Keagan?"

"It's no one." Ruby opened the door and reassured Reiser. Reiser didn't seem to buy this.

"Ruby, I can always tell when you are lying. Your body language always gives it all away." He stepped forward, trapping them. "Tell me the truth, right now."

Ruby stepped back. "I'm not lying."

"Then who is Keagan?" Reiser shrugged. "That's all you have to tell me."

"She's a girl that plays on varsity." Ruby cocked her head. "How haven't you heard of her lately? Do you not go to school anymore?"

"Why would I? I have everything I need right now. I don't need school. I'm stable." Reiser stared down at Ray and Cali. "Then who are these two? These guys are short, how are they on varsity?"

"They aren't," Ruby mumbled.

"You got replaced by this Keagan girl, didn't you?" Reiser glared. "We'll take care of her, don't worry." He stomped away.

Ruby followed him to the living room with Cali and Ray trailing behind. "What do you mean 'take care of her'?"

Reiser held up a rifle. "Well, we're going to kill her. What else would we do? What other way is there? Talivikki won't let up." Reiser pointed the rifle under her chin. "Do you want to save yourself or not, Ruby? Do you not want a good life, going to college, playing college basketball or maybe something more than college basketball?"

"I'm 5'9"! You need to be way taller to be in the WNBA. I really have no chance," Ruby sighed and slowly pushed the rifle away. "I will at least go to college."

"Are you kidding me, Ruby?" Cooper jumped up. "Please, keep trying."

"We're killing Keagan." Reiser paced around with his rifle. "We have to. We need someone to save us from this."

"Reiser, you just said that you were stable." Ray glanced at Ruby uncomfortably.

"Stable, but I would like to be more than enough type of stable." Reiser threw his hands out. "We've helped you through so much, and now you're just going to stop trying? You've also stopped stealing!"

Ruby blinked in shock.

"Do you not think we didn't realize that? You've changed because of these guys." Reiser poked Ray's face. Ray slapped his hand away. Reiser glared back.

"I don't need stealing anymore to live!" Ruby stepped towards the door. "You guys may need stealing, but I don't."

"What is Keagan's last name?" Reiser pressed.

"I really don't know. All I know is that her name is Keagan." Ruby seemed to want to protect Keagan at all costs now. The fight changed something in Ruby. Cali had never asked but she was now curious as to what made Ruby turn.

Reiser scoffed, "Alright." He looked back at Truman and Cooper. "Let's go, we're leaving. Now."

Cooper and Truman stormed out the door. Reiser caught the door from Cooper mid-slam. Reiser looked back and put the rifle to the side. "I will not let you give up so easily."

Ruby watched them leave in their pickup from the small grainy window.

"I recognize that truck. Wasn't that the one driven by the guys who yelled at us while we were walking, Cali?"

Cali gasped. "It is. It was them." Cali pointed. "They called us homosexuals way back."

Ray chuckled. "It all comes back around, doesn't it?" She shut the blinds. "Now, Ruby," she mumbled.

Ruby stared at the ground.

"We have to turn them in!"

Ruby perked her head up. "We can't do that!"

"Why not?" Ray rolled her eyes.

"I'd be guilty by association. We can't turn them in, or else I'd be going to jail just as long as they would." Ruby bit her lip. "I don't want to go to jail."

"But you're just as bad as they are," Ray mumbled. "You stole, they stole. They killed Sienna, and you hid that from everyone. They shot up the Fox Den, and you didn't turn them in!"

Ruby stared down. "I'm not, I'm really not."

"You are," Ray hissed.

Cali stepped in. "Can we please stop? They're going to try and kill Keagan. They will eventually slip up, then we can get them from there."

Ray glared. "She should be turned in as well."

"Why do you change so quickly on people, oh my God." Ruby ran her hands through her hair.

Ray crossed her arms. "I don't. You did something horrible. Why wouldn't I?"

"Ray, you, Ruby, and I are friends. I know you really don't want Ruby to go to jail. Can we go with my plan first, and if that doesn't work, we will turn them in?"

Ruby picked at her skin nervously.

Ray nodded. "Fine, but if it doesn't end up working, I am going straight to the police." She glared at Ruby.

"This is all your fault, Ruby. Why couldn't you just have been smart and gotten away from them right away?"

"You may think it's easy, but it's really not, Ray. Like I said, I was going to kill Reiser and his father, but I ended up getting cared for more than anything ever. Then I met you guys and I didn't need them anymore. I was content."

Ray sighed. "Whatever." Ray uncrossed her arms. "We'll try and catch them slipping up first, then if they don't, they'll be turned in."

CHAPTER 23

"They haven't done anything yet, but we have to tell Keagan. Or else, she will be off her guard and who knows what they'll do," Ruby fretted.

"They don't even go to school here," Ray mumbled. "They wouldn't be able to lay a finger on her. It's after school that's the problem."

"So why don't we try to warn her right now?" Cali pointed at varsity's claimed table. "We just have to get her alone somehow. They clearly will not trust us if we just go up there right now and ask her to speak with us."

"Keagan will eventually be at her locker." Ruby turned. "We could meet her there. She needs to pick up her books, you know."

"So should we meet her there now?" Ray slowly pushed herself up.

"Yeah. I think we should. Lunch is about to end." Ruby got up with Ray. "We'd better hurry."

Ray grabbed Cali and forced her up. They hurried to the second floor down the hall where the juniors had their lockers.

"How are we supposed to word this?" Ruby nervously ran her hand through her hair.

"Is that a new nervous thing that you picked up instead of annihilating your own skin?" Ray sneered.

"That's a random thing to ask. Never ask something like that again." Ruby felt her arms. "I'm very sensitive to people joking about my arms. That's a horrible habit that I have to deal with."

Ray rolled her eyes.

Cali glanced away. "Okay, but seriously, how do we word this? 'A bunch of rebels are trying to kill you'?"

"I mean, I guess so. How else would we word it? We don't want to sugarcoat it, but we don't want to scare her either."

The crowd of people split apart in Keagan's presence. The three panicked as they had yet not thought about what they wanted to say.

Keagan stopped before them and stared, confused. "Why are you guys at my locker?" She nodded at Ruby. "I'm not supposed to talk to you," she mouthed.

"We have to talk about something serious with you, Keagan," Ray said as she stepped forward.

"Seriously, please. I cannot talk to you guys; we cannot be friends, as rude as that sounds." Keagan unlocked her locker, opening it right in front of Ruby.

Ruby moved around the locker. "Why can't we talk to you? You talked to me at the Halloween dance, why can't you talk now?"

"I really want to talk to you Ruby. You seem like an amazing person, but I really do not want Talivikki to find out. She would kill us both if she found out you knew about the plan," Keagan sighed.

Cali couldn't help but admire Keagan's kind eyes. They weren't as kind as Delilah's eyes, but they were their own type of kind.

Ruby stood tall, standing up against Keagan, unlike how she normally stood next to her. She usually stood next to her with a downward lean that wasn't confident. "This is serious, Keagan."

Keagan shook her head and turned away. "Sorry to act so rude, but I don't want both of us in trouble. I'll see you later maybe when you are on varsity."

Ruby scoffed, annoyed. "Keagan, really?"

Keagan didn't reply and disappeared into the crowd.

Ray stared at where Keagan once was, furious. "She thinks she's too good to talk to us, huh?" Ray punched Keagan's locker, knocking her sign out of place. It hung sideways. "Gosh. At least she'll see soon enough."

Ruby opened Keagan's locker. "I'm surprised she keeps a pencil in here. I thought people would try to steal from it more." Ruby's eyes widened. She stuck her hand in the locker and pulled out a singular ticket. "She has a ticket to the rodeo. If we all buy a ticket, we can talk to her then."

"I didn't know she was the type to watch rodeos." Ray shrugged.

"Sometimes varsity goes to the rodeo together. I completely forgot about it." Ruby snickered. "We'll buy some, tonight at my place. Talivikki hates the noise of the rodeos, so she never goes to them." Ruby's heart seemed to drop. "But *they* like rodeos too."

All three girls' phones suddenly pinged at the same time with the same message on the group chat from Justice:

I've bought everyone a ticket to the rodeo for Sienna's birthday. I know we barely did anything for her birthday yesterday, but as most of you know she really liked the rodeo. So tomorrow, we are all going to the rodeo together.

"It's my birthday today." Ruby texted while smiling with snarky undertone.

Ray looked up. "I am so sorry, Ruby. I completely forgot about your birthday!"

"You're eighteen today, right?" Cali put her phone back into her pocket.

"Yeah. I'm an adult now." Ruby shrugged. "I don't feel any different, I guess."

"Wonder what we will be like when we are eighteen, Cali." Ray chuckled. "You'll look weird."

A bull's foot pounded against the dirt as it snorted aggressively out of its nose. It spun around in circles trying to buck off its rider. The bull was huge, bigger than three men combined. Cali learned that its name was Villain Vero. No one was ever able to ride that bull. It showed up year after year and made a name for itself outside of North Dakota.

STOLEN

Cali never had any particular interest in rodeos. She had never gone to one, in fact. Ruby was telling Ray and her about everything.

"So where do you think Keagan is right now?" Cali wasn't even watching the rodeo, but instead, she was scanning the area for Keagan.

"They should be here. I'm not quite sure where they are, though."

Ruby scratched her chin and sank into her seat. "The stadium is a pretty decent sized. They could be anywhere. You know who I see, though?"

Cali and Ray looked over to where Ruby was pointing. Reiser, Truman, and Cooper, stood in the front row. They were screaming, cheering, and jumping around in excitement.

Ruby told them that those guys liked a thrill and always sneaked into the bullpens the night before the rodeo. Ruby did it once and was almost impaled. Cali noticed that Reiser's shirt was ripped.

"They must have been with the bulls." Cali smirked.

"Yeah, we have to keep an eye on them."

"If *we* can't see Keagan, *they* can't either." Ray shrugged.

Cali scrutinized the crowd closely for any sight of Keagan and the rest of varsity. Then she saw her, a redhead with a messy bun in her hair. The post player, Delilah. They were sitting not too far away in the same row. They were hidden behind taller cowboys.

"I see them," Cali hollered.

"Jeez. Could you be any louder?!" Ray sneered. "Where do you see them?"

"Do you see those tall cowboys with mullets?" Cali pointed.

"There's a lot of tall cowboys with mullets. It's a rodeo, Cali," Ray mumbled.

"What row are they in? What number?" Ruby interrupted Ray.

Cali looked above at the numbers. "Twenty-two."

"Oh, there they are. How did you find them there? Also, Keagan is there. She's just sitting down." Ruby blinked. "At least we know she is safe."

"I still don't see them," Ray grumbled.

Keagan got up slowly and walked down the row. Delilah waved her off and pointed somewhere. Keagan nodded and went on her way. She passed Reiser and the others. Reiser jutted his head at Keagan, seeming to signal the others.

Ruby's eyes widened. "We have to go right now," she hissed. She pushed Ray into Cali, trying to get them to move faster over people. "Go, go, go, go, go!" she yelled.

They got down to the bottom row. Ray looked as if she realized how small she really was. Cali hadn't noticed at first, Ray too, since they were too busy trying to search for the varsity.

"Don't make eye contact with them. All we need to do is get Keagan safe. We're going to have to trap her somewhere." Ruby stood straight up, alert. "She's either going to the concessions or to the restroom. Beside both, there is a janitor's closet. I've been in them before, the one by the concessions is the least full, so hopefully she is going there."

Ruby stepped ahead of the two, stalking Keagan from behind. Ruby kept quiet. Her eyes were in a deep focus. Cali could ask Ruby a question and she probably wouldn't be able to hear her.

Cali walked cautiously, although she knew Keagan would never suspect her walk. The stadium was too loud for that. They followed Keagan until she reached a hallway Ruby never mentioned. Ruby didn't seem to know about it, either. Ruby glanced around.

Keagan turned. "I could feel your presence. You weren't that secretive."

"I was being as quiet as I could." Ruby cocked her head.

Keagan nodded at Ray.

Ray got offended . . . for whatever reason. "What? I was walking just like them! Is this some kind of insult?" Ray got closer and closer to Keagan.

Ruby took Ray and threw her back. Ruby stepped before Keagan, standing in that same alert stance. "Seriously, you are in *danger* right now. If you don't listen to what I have to say, you may die tonight."

Keagan blinked curiously, and softened up. "I suppose Talivikki isn't here, so no danger from that. What danger am I supposedly in?"

"My friends. They're trying to kill you because they figured out that I was replaced by you," Ruby spoke with small hand gestures, trying to get her point across. "They will not kill you right away, either."

"Your friends," Keagan muttered. "Those are the criminals you hung out with? Talivikki has known about those guys since they dropped out of school. They're trying to kill me?"

"Yes." Ruby glanced backwards.

"You don't want me to report them, do you?" Keagan stepped forward, staring at Ruby. "Guilt by association. I won't report them. We need you for varsity, Talivikki acknowledges that, she just wants the attention."

Ruby glanced away awkwardly, just wanting to protect Keagan. "Okay, that's good that you won't report them. I appreciate it. We don't have that much time."

"Are you Keagan Perry?" someone hissed from behind them.

Keagan snapped up. The other three turned instantly, knowing who it was.

There stood Reiser, Truman, and Cooper. They wore long, black trench coats and masks. The masks were all hog masks. Two were no different from the other, except for Reiser's—his was a true hog head, a *real* hog head. Cali felt sick.

"Perry." Reiser laughed manically. "It rolls off the tongue nicely. So very nicely," he sighed.

Cooper was shaking from excitement. "We finally found you!"

Cooper put his hands on his hog mask and leaned over. Reiser smacked Cooper on the head, and he straightened up. Reiser stared down at Keagan and walked forward. Cali and Ray were split away from each other as Reiser advanced. Ruby backed into Keagan and threw her arms out, trying to protect her.

Reiser stared down at Ruby. "What are you doing? Do you want to be on varsity or not?"

Keagan nudged Ruby away and stared calmly up at Reiser.

"Why do you care so much? Is she your only hope for a good life? Maybe if you all went back to school, you would have a second chance. Now you're trying to kill me for something that you can fix yourself," Keagan said.

Reiser, without hesitation, grabbed Keagan's hair and pulled her up. "You Goddamned women. You don't understand anything about anything. It's always you, you, you, YOU," he screeched.

Keagan winced but showed no fear.

Reiser threw her to the ground and brought out a nail bat. "I'll kill her right now! I have to LIVE." He raised the bat over his head.

Ray screeched and jumped onto Reiser. Reiser was caught off guard. Ray attacked Reiser like a cat, similar to how Piper attacked Amber. Ray must have copied Piper.

Truman and Cooper tried to tear Ray off him, but that clearly would not happen.

"HEY," a loud voice sounded like a rumble of thunder through the hallway. Cali turned to see Roze. She stood with a powerful stance, much like a bull ready to strike.

Ray and Reiser halted and looked over as well.

"Who the hell are you?" Reiser hissed.

"I will not say. In fact, who are you?" Roze stalked forward, always looking down at Reiser.

"You're a tall woman. What the hell?" Reiser shook his head in disgust. "Women aren't supposed to be as tall as you are. You're over my height, 6'1"."

Roze rolled her eyes. "You're sexist. That's not a surprise."

Ruby whispered to Cali, "He's not usually sexist at all. I'm guessing he held back since they were leeching off of me."

Cali nodded.

Roze and Reiser stared at each other for a few seconds. Reiser was trying to think of something to say.

Keagan got up and stepped between them. "We can all walk away from this."

Reiser once again grabbed Keagan's hair and flung her into the wall. Roze gasped and grabbed Reiser by his mullet and pulled as hard as she could. Reiser screamed as some of his hair came out in a big chunk.

"Remember who I am. Remember my face." Roze grabbed his head and stared right into the hog's eyes. Reiser shook his head. He ripped away from Roze and pointed at Keagan.

"You remember *me*. We'll be back. And your bodyguards can't always protect you," he snorted.

Reiser, Truman, and Cooper stormed off down the hall and out the exit door.

Ruby helped Keagan up. "I am so sorry for all of this."

Keagan smiled. "At least you protected me. Remember, I will always be fine. They won't be able to touch me if you're this cautious. I will do what I can to protect myself without telling anyone. Thank you, Ruby." She nodded at Ruby.

Ruby nodded back. "You're welcome. I will try my best."

Roze coughed.

"Roze." Ruby turned. "What in the world are you doing here?"

"I heard some ruckus, and I thought it might be you guys." Roze shrugged, fixing her cowboy hat. "So what happened? Why were you being attacked by mascots?"

"Mascots? They weren't mascots."

"I was joking, Ruby," she snickered.

Keagan recognized Roze instantly. "Roze?"

Roze raised her eyebrows and shook her head. "I'm surprised you remember me. It's been a long time. I thought you two were against Keagan?"

Keagan and Ruby stood next to each other.

"We're not against each other anymore for reasons," Ruby mumbled.

Roze kept her eyes on Keagan.

"You remember how Keagan replaced me on varsity?" Ruby made hand gestures.

Roze nodded.

"My criminal friends were leeching off of me, waiting for me to go to college so they could use my money.

Now, since I'm not on the varsity, I won't get any offers. So, they want Keagan gone."

"But is that not what you want?"

"I did earlier, but now I realize this is not Keagan's fault at all." Ruby held out her hand. "Do you want to help us?"

Roze stared at Ruby's hand and glanced at Keagan. "I'll help," she said, reluctantly. "If you need any intimidation, call me," she smiled.

Keagan sighed in relief and smiled.

"On one condition." Roze got down to Keagan's height and looked at her dead in the eyes with a serious gaze. "Can I get a welcome hug from you, Keagan?"

"You forgive me?" Keagan cocked her head. "After all I did? One thing and you forgive me for years of torment?" Keagan stared in disbelief.

"It's only the small things. I don't hate you." Roze smiled. "I'm glad to see you again." She held her arms out for a hug. Keagan hesitated before finally hugging her.

Cali's heart warmed. If only Cali could see her bullies again. *Maybe they could make up like this?*

"We have a game against each other soon." Roze winked at Keagan.

"I'll see you there." Roze stood up and turned to Ruby. "Will those hogs be there at the game?"

"I'm not quite sure if they know about the game. If they do, they will be there." Ruby shrugged.

Roze nodded. "I'll come prepared. They shouldn't be too hard to recognize. Or do you have a bunch of sexist hogs with mullets in Swallowsville?" She looked down at the clump of hair she pulled out.

"I don't know, not all of the dudes are like that in Swallowsville, I swear." Ruby scratched her neck.

"Alright."

The exit door opened.

"I told you not to take that turn," Piper whined. "Now we're late!"

Justice looked exhausted. "I'm sorry. I'm really trying my best."

"There you are," Ruby said as Keagan scurried off.

"This idiot made a wrong turn! How late are we?" Piper walked up with her hands on her hips.

"Not that late, you didn't miss too much, really." Ruby shrugged everything off.

"Oh good," Justice sighed and smiled.

CHAPTER: 24

"Someone tried to sand down my shoes," Keagan pointed at her shoes that had no grip left.

"That could have gotten you killed, and that would be a lucky kill for whomever, though. High chance of you not dying," Talivikki mumbled, scratching her chin. "Do you think that it was Ruby?"

"I highly, highly doubt that she would go this low, Talivikki." Keagan said nervously.

"Why do you look so nervous? Do you know of anyone who would do this? Are you lying to me?" Talivikki grabbed the shoe. "Did you perhaps . . . do this yourself?"

"I would never! I love basketball, Talivikki, you know that!" Keagan placed her shoes on the bench next to her. "Can we do anything about my shoes?"

"I always bring extra shoes. I'm not quite sure that these will fit you, but they'll have to do." Talivikki got up and rummaged through her bag. "Also, how is your new jersey fitting?"

"It's fitting me good." Keagan nodded.

Talivikki sighed. "It's *well* not *good*, Keagan. I'm native from Oslo and I know English better than you do," Talivikki grumbled, walking over with the shoes. "You can tie your own shoes, right?"

Keagan snickered, "Yes." She tied her shoes.

Talivikki watched her. "You aren't scared of that stupid number of death or whatever thing, right?" Talivikki seemed like she genuinely was concerned.

Keagan's eyes widened in embarrassment, and she stammered, "I am so sorry for that. I have no worries anymore. That was a stupid belief."

Talivikki shrugged. "Don't let me, in the spur of the moment, tell you what to *believe* in. Anything else, yeah." Talivikki pointed at her number. "Eight. What does that mean in numerology?"

Keagan perked up. "Oh, it's the 'achiever.' I've chosen the number since I was very young."

"I had the number thirty-five." Talivikki leaned forward.

"What does that mean?"

"I don't know what it means, but I've heard that thirty-five means that Saturn interferes with your efforts to be successful. He's like an old professor. He attacks you with accidents and stuff."

Talivikki blinked and looked at her ankle. "My ankle?"

Keagan raised her eyebrows. "Could be a coincidence."

"Most likely."

Piper awkwardly walked past the two, trying to stay as hidden as she could.

"Piper."

Piper froze and slowly turned. "Hello," she said, fearful that she had somehow done something wrong.

"Did you see anyone come into the locker room just before this?" Talivikki turned to her.

"No, I didn't see anyone. I just came in here to get my money."

"Oh, alright." Talivikki held up Keagan's sanded-down shoes. "You didn't do this, right?"

Piper's eyes widened. "No, I would never, Talivikki!" She nervously messed with her pigtails.

Talivikki squinted.

Piper slowly walked over to her locker. Talivikki turned back over to Keagan and talked to her some more. Piper quickly sorted through her backpack, got her money, and ran out. She hurried over to the part of the bleachers where the 'C team' gathered.

"Guys," Piper jumped beside Justice. "Someone tried to injure Keagan!" She giggled.

Cali, Ruby, and Ray all perked up. "How?" Ruby leaned closer along with the other two. "Did they ruin her jersey or something? She just got her new one, right?"

It was Thursday now. Thursday the fourteenth. Cali glanced at the locker room that Keagan and Talivikki just exited. Talivikki had to duck slightly under the doorway. Cali and the rest of the team found that hilarious, though they would never joke about it to Talivikki's face. Ruby said that it was fine to joke about her height, but Cali didn't buy it.

Ray waved a hand in front of Cali's face. "Now is *not* a time to space out," she hissed.

"Someone tried to sand down Keagan's shoes," Piper said frantically.

"Sand down her shoes?" Ruby shook her head. "What would that do?"

"I suppose it would cause her to slide around. If she didn't notice, on a layup she might've slipped and slammed her head into the wall. That's really unlikely, but she also could have just injured herself another way," Kimberly explained.

"It's a stretch, but it's pretty smart. It's very unlikely that you would die from that."

The team blinked as one.

"That's stupid," Piper mumbled. "So, what are the chances that you would die from that, though?"

Kimberly explained more to Piper while the others turned back to the game.

Roze waved to the three from the floor. Cali waved back. "Hey, Roze is waving."

"She's waving with quite the panicked face." Ruby cocked her head.

Roze tried throwing her hands at the bleachers, trying to show something.

The three looked at each other with confusion. Roze gave up and walked over when her coach wasn't watching. "Guys. You're really bad at taking hints, aren't you?"

"Cali is." Ray patted Cali on the head.

Cali rolled her eyes.

"Those guys, they went into the locker room," she yell-whispered. "I think I'm the only one who saw, I swear!"

"That's what I was guessing. They have no morals, do they?" Ruby whined.

"Well, they obviously don't. This is who we're up against." Roze shrugged. "I have to go before I get yelled at."

Roze hurried off back to her team.

Ruby got up and walked over to the hallway where the concessions were. "Come with me. We need to talk about this."

"Where are you guys going, and who was that?" Piper called.

"Someone we know," Ruby hollered back.

"Seriously, where are we going?" Ray asked.

"We're going to fight Reiser and them. We're going to end this once and for all." Ruby stomped ahead with anger.

"Why do you think walking down some random hallway is going to do anything?"

"I'm thinking about all of this," Ruby muttered. "If we walk alone, they will surely attack us soon."

Cali swallowed nervously. Ruby knew better than to pick a fight with those guys. They would fight to the end. "Ruby. They'll kill us."

"They won't if we fight hard enough," Ruby sighed. "Everyone has seen how strong you are. Why don't you use it in this fight?"

"I refuse to hurt anybody."

"Cali." Someone stepped out from the shadows. She seemed to have been getting a drink from the water fountain. "What's going on?"

Cali bit her lip. She hadn't seen Eliza in a while, and she hadn't told her at all about Reiser. "Well, remember how we weren't going to harm Keagan anymore?"

Eliza nodded.

"There are people . . . Ruby's friends . . . trying to hurt her."

"I told you that you were close to the culprit. I was right, wasn't I?" Eliza raised her eyebrows.

"Yes, you were right."

Eliza nodded. "Now, what's this about not using your strength?"

"I don't know them that well."

"Ruby does."

Eliza walked up to Ruby. "Ruby, do you know any of their weaknesses?"

Ruby hesitated. "Reiser hates when people get his hair. Truman is way too tall, so he isn't very agile. Cooper isn't all there. He will do anything to hurt himself, and he doesn't care if he hurts others. So, Cooper, I'd say, is the most dangerous."

Eliza glanced at Ray. "So that's his weakness?"

"He hurts himself a lot. It annoys Reiser the most, and Reiser will get mad at him." Ruby shrugged.

Ray stared away.

Eliza nodded again. "You guys just have to exploit those weaknesses if you want to win the fight. I have no idea who these people are, so Cali, I'd appreciate it if you came to my house tonight." Eliza touched her shoulder and moved along.

Cali nodded back at Eliza.

"You've been talking to Eliza?" Ray cocked her head. "I knew you were friends with her, but I didn't know she was your therapist."

"She's saved me a lot. She saved me from Roze that first time," Cali said. "I thought I told you before!"

"No, I never knew either. I guess it went over my head," Ruby mumbled.

The loud call of someone imitating a hog snort came from farther down the hall. The three faced the other three.

"Is that your new call, Reiser?" Ruby looked them up and down.

"It is." Reiser's hog mask's mouth hung open just enough so they could see his mouth. It wasn't like that the last time.

"Your hog mouth is hanging open wider, have you been using it more?" Cali asked.

Reiser stared. "What is it to you if I was using it more. It's fun to wear. I like being mysterious."

"What do you guys want?" Cooper growled. "You clearly provoked us."

Ruby nodded. "We know you guys sanded down Keagan's shoes. You went into the locker room to do it. Someone saw you. We can't let you get away with that."

Reiser frowned. "I thought she wouldn't be smart enough to check her shoes."

Cali looked down at her own shoes. Maybe she should start checking her own basketball shoes.

Ruby glanced away. "We want to fight you."

Reiser laughed. "Fight us? You know that is a death sentence, Ruby."

"We'll at least try." Ruby nodded.

Reiser looked back at the group. "When do you want to fight?"

Ruby thought for a second. "Thanksgiving night."

"Thanksgiving." Reiser raised his eyebrows. "Good. That's good for us. What time?"

The two negotiated like business partners. Cali stared at the shadows that Reiser's group cast. They looked tall and muscular in the shadows. Cali frowned and looked at hers. Due to the lighting, it looked smaller.

"Thanksgiving night. Midnight. At the school." Reiser nodded. "We'll discuss the rules when we get there. We will be standing down until then."

Ruby nodded. "Goodbye."

Reiser said nothing as they walked back into the shadows.

"Are we really going to fight them?" Cali shuddered.

"You can't be scared. We are in the right," Ruby muttered.

"Are we in the right though?"

"Of course, we are. We're protecting someone." Ruby walked back up the hallway. Cali looked over at Ray;

she looked somewhat scared as well. Ray was the average height for a woman, but still she was way shorter than the average height for a man in Swallowsville.

"Okay, Cali, I didn't actually expect you to be fighting those kids." Eliza pinched her nose bridge and leaned back. "I knew that you would refuse to hurt Keagan, and that would manifest into you not fighting those guys. But I was wrong, for once."

"You're way too confusing, Eliza. Please, what do you want me to do?"

"Well, I want you to make the least stupid decisions so you won't get yourself killed." Eliza shrugged. "You're going to need to match their energy and have even more energy than they do. It's like basketball. I know Milan doesn't speak much about it, but you have to play with more energy than the other team if you want to win a game. If you play lazily, you will lose. You should dress up like they do."

Cali blinked and stared down at the candle in the middle of the table. Its flame waltzed around, kicking light out in every direction. "What would we even dress as?"

"You would use the same masks. You should go with a certain animal. You want to use a scary and intimidating animal so that you don't look stupid. Judging by your guys' personalities, I suggest a lion or a cheetah. You guys are brave, fierce, fast, and strong, while they are like hogs." Eliza leaned sideways. "Do you think that's good?"

"Why can't we use the masks we already have?"

"A butterfly and fox look stupid. Just saying." Eliza held up her hands in front of her, doing that "don't be offended" thing.

Cali nodded in agreement. "I'll talk to them this weekend."

"You're going to need dark clothing, but don't make it too heavy, as you guys are lightweight, except for Ruby, and you don't want to hinder any of your abilities."

CHAPTER 25

"Nick?" Keagan called out to him as he was about to hop out of his window. "Where do you think you are going? It is not like you sneak out late at night like this and not tell anyone."

Nick sighed and looked back. "It's just unfinished business."

"You never changed, did you?" Keagan stepped forward. "I'm glad dad told me to come and get you. We still weren't done talking to Aunt Jene and Uncle Harris."

Nick stepped onto the ground out of his perched position from the window. "It's almost 10:00! They need to leave!"

"Nick, tell me where you're going," Keagan approached him.

"I'm going into town. Going into town with Reg, okay?" Nick threw his hands up. "Are you happy that I told you?"

Keagan sighed in annoyance.

"What? You get to sneak out with Talivikki all the time!"

Keagan's eyes widened. "How do you know that?"

Nick scrunched up his face. "That's super weird, Keagan!"

"We're friends!" Keagan rolled her eyes. "Why would you ever assume something like *that*."

Nick raised an eyebrow. "If you tell our parents that I snuck out, I'll tell them that you did too. It's not like they would believe me anyway."

"What is up with you? This is not like you at all!"

Keagan grabbed his sleeve.

"Keagan." Nick threw her hand off. "Get over yourself. Get out."

Keagan stared at Nick. Nick couldn't have gone back down the wrong path, and if he did, it was all her fault. She was a horrible person; she always had been.

She watched Nick jump down the side of the house and scurry off.

She had made up with Roze. She agreed that they would start again. Roze believed that Keagan showed a lot of change.

She looked in Nick's cracked mirror. She inhaled, stood upright, and stared at herself. "I am Keagan Perry," the melancholy sound of her voice surrounded her. She could hear the blood running in her ears. She exhaled.

I am Keagan.

How could one convince oneself that they were worthy of everything they had when it always seemed to be on the edge of crashing down on them?

Keagan never wanted this life. She would never force her children into sports, just for her family to leech off of them. She let go of everything because she wanted to protect herself.

Keagan felt for Ruby. They were almost experiencing the same thing: leeches.

Keagan sat back on Nick's bed, still staring. She had to follow Nick.

Back to her room she went, grabbing everything she needed to protect herself in the night. She grabbed her pepper spray, pocketknife, bandana, her coat, and her heavy-duty snow boots.

She looked at her own, uncracked mirror and smiled. *I am Keagan Perry.* She flicked open the pocketknife and suddenly felt scared. *What if she was being watched right now?* She inhaled and flicked the knife back in. "I will not go down without a fight. I won't give everything up."

She walked out to her balcony, passing her varsity jersey. She didn't even glance at it. Everything that brought her these problems was sitting there. The jersey was a burden to her, but there was no way she could get out of this all. She had to deal with it.

Keagan smiled at the pond underneath her. She jumped without hesitation.

Keagan didn't hit the pond, instead she hit the bushes next to the pond so she wouldn't get soaked. She stood up from the bushes, brushing off every leaf that stuck to her. She took a second to stare at one. It was all crinkly. Brittle. Dead. Keagan crushed it between her fingers and saw footprints in the snow. There was no way that Nick could have covered them, so that meant they would lead her all the way to her destination.

Keagan smiled and stepped into the snow. Every time she stepped; a crunch followed. She felt freer as she walked away from the resort.

"Ruby, you're not going to tell me why you are leaving? You know you're not allowed out after 5:00. It's 10:00." A tall man wearing a sleek black suit set a wine glass on the table. He had seen Ruby reaching for the door handle.

Ruby sighed, "I'm going to be with Cali and Ray."

The man's face scrunched up. "You know how I feel about Ray, she's wrong in the head."

"She just has treatable issues." Ruby glared. "Who do you think you are, dad?"

The man rose from his chair. He gave Ruby a glare that was more intense that Ruby's initial glare. Ruby stood tall. "Where did that confidence come from?"

Ruby twisted the door handle. "I'm eighteen. You have no more control over me anymore. I'm going to move out soon. After Christmas."

"What?" the man frantically asked. "What do you mean you are eighteen? I thought you were sixteen!"

"There's my reasoning," Ruby muttered. "I'm sorry for the disappointing news."

"Where will you go? You're still my child! You are going to stay under my roof until you go to college, Ruby!"

"I'm not." Ruby shook her head. "I'm going to get a job at the movie theater. I have friends working there that I already know." She nodded. "I won't regret this."

The man didn't know what to say. "I respect that. I didn't realize this was so soon." He nodded. "You can go, just come back safely."

Ruby's eyes widened, and she nodded goodbye.

As Cali walked to the school with Ray, she tried to drown out Ray's complaints about the snow. "Well, of course, you're so used to it because you tried to kill yourself with it."

Cali rolled her eyes. "Ray, at first, you seemed so smart. You seemed . . . okay. What happened?"

"I was always like I am now." Ray shrugged. "I just never showed it to anyone. Now I can't control it."

"You need therapy."

Ray chuckled, "You do too." She nudged Cali.

Cali couldn't help but smirk a bit.

Cali could feel the tension, even though Reiser and his group weren't visible. The three swore to stay silent until they heard their hog cry or saw the group. An ear-piercing squeal came from down the corridor. They had become too good at that hog cry.

Cali shivered. The tension rose as both groups stepped from the shadows into the dim light. Reiser nodded slowly in greeting. Ruby nodded back.

"I see you guys *copied* our style," he snarled.

"Matching the mood," Ruby mumbled.

Reiser smirked. "We should discuss rules. Here are our suggestions. We fight on the rooftop; we'll both go up to it on the opposite sides. We will stand at least fifty feet away from each other and wait until the moon is directly overhead."

Ruby nodded. "Anything else?"

"We can use weapons." Reiser flicked open a red pocketknife. "I thought it would be fair to you guys."

Since when did he care about being any type of fair? Cali shook her head.

Ruby nodded. "Are we fighting to the death?"

"We fight until someone is severely hurt with their life threatened, or if someone runs off." Reiser looked back at Cooper. Cali guessed that that was Cooper's input.

"We don't have any suggestions." Ruby nodded. "Let's head up."

The two groups passed each other. Reiser and Ruby bumped their shoulders together to raise fear in each other.

Ruby gave a pep talk. "We will not be the ones to run. We will fight until we die. No running and no backing down due to any injury. You hear that?"

Cali and Ray nodded.

"This is terrifying," Ray said under her breath.

Cali agreed with her through eye contact.

Ray smirked. "I wouldn't hate it if I died here."

Ruby said nothing and walked faster. Each step Ruby took was three of Cali's. It was two steps for Ray.

They soon got to a smaller door labeled "stairs." Ruby retrieved a small crowbar from her pocket and cracked open the door. Dust spilled all over them and they all hacked. Cali could see the dust finally settle on the ground through the dim grey lighting.

"Oh my God, it smells like wet moss," Ray exclaimed, scrunching up her face.

Ruby paid no attention to the complaints and went forward. The old metal stairs groaned as they trailed up them.

"Ruby, how far do we have to walk?" Ray asked.

"Quiet. No speaking until midnight, starting now." Ruby held a finger up to her mouth, trying to silence Ray. Ray glanced back at Cali and shrugged.

After a while, they reached the final door. Cali felt some type of emotion, one that said, *this is it.* Cali smiled, scared but hopeful. *Maybe this would end it all, or maybe it would end soon.*

The three stepped onto the roof. Reiser arrived at the same time. They stood fifty feet away and stared up at the moon.

Cali hesitated before staring up at the moon. She swore that everyone's breathing synced. The stars were showing.

"MIDNIGHT," an unknown voice screeched.

The three turned, confused, toward the voice. It was another guy wearing a hog mask and trench coat. He lifted up his mask. He had spiky, strawberry blonde hair.

"Nick?" Cali mouthed, perplexed.

It was a split second before the rooftop became bathed in everyone's blood. Masks were ripped, clothes were torn, knuckles were broken, teeth were shed.

Cali couldn't help but glance at Nick. He was just standing there. Cali got focused on fighting, so did everyone else, and she drowned out Nick's presence. Ray was against Cooper, Ruby was against Reiser, and Cali was against Truman. Everything she had gone through would help her in this fight. Cali exploited the height difference between them. Cali went for the eyes, but every time she did, he turned to run, and then hesitated but continued fighting. Cali was afraid to go up against someone like him, but someone had to take on the job. Cali trusted no one else to do it properly.

Cali was having the time of her life until a female screech rang out over the rooftop. Cali looked around frantically as everyone stopped. No one knew who it was.

Nick fell onto the ground, swearing. Cali looked up and saw a girl's long, curly, strawberry blonde hair whipping around in the wind. The wind seemed to get more aggressive with every second that passed.

"Keagan?" the three exclaimed happily and half in shock.

However, Keagan was in her own world, blinded by her anger. She had sliced off Nick's hog mask with her pocketknife.

Nick felt his face. He then put his hand back into the snow. The snow lit up with a bright red substance. Blood. Keagan had sliced Nick's face along with his mask.

"What are you doing?" he yelled.

Keagan stared down at him. Her lip curled. "You've betrayed me twice!"

Keagan stomped down on his chest.

Nick gasped.

"TWICE!"

They all stared in shock.

Nick struggled to breathe.

"Coward," she muttered. "Up."

She slowly took her shoe off of Nick. He shot up and gasped for breath.

"Nick," Ruby muttered sadly.

"Why in the world are you sad? Couldn't you see from the very beginning how bad of a person he was?" Ray took Ruby by the shoulders.

"He was good before. He just broke," Keagan muttered. She stood in a powerful stance, slightly turned to them with her head up, looking down at all of them. She sighed. "I don't have any regret for this. As much I didn't expect this to happen, I won't say that I'm at all shocked."

Reiser snorted.

"We were in the middle of a fight. You ruined it."

"I'm the reason this is all going down." Keagan pointed her pocketknife at the two groups. "If I was never forced into basketball, this wouldn't all be happening."

Nick slowly rose and looked at Keagan. Keagan adjusted her glasses.

"They look so similar," Cali uttered.

Nick gasped and fell to the floor, clenching his chest. "I'm hurt, you hurt me," he said through each heavy breath. "What did you do to me? We're siblings! Why would you do something like this?" He was distraught.

"You betrayed me." Keagan rolled her eyes. "This is too dramatic for my taste. Goodbye." She turned away from the groups and went down a separate flight of stairs.

"Where do you think you're going, Keagan?" Reiser called out furiously.

"I heard the rules." She didn't turn to look back but instead continued to descend the stairs. "Someone is severely hurt, threatening their life. The fight is over."

Reiser threw off his hog mask. "Goddamnit!" He stomped his foot. This was the first time Cali paid attention to his shoes. They were replicated hog feet. Cali shook her head in disgust.

"He's right, Reiser." Ruby nodded at Nick, who was still gasping. "Rules are rules."

"Since when was I actually going to play by the rules?" Reiser laughed in her face.

Truman put a hand on Reiser's shoulder. "We may be criminals, but rules are rules, Reiser."

Reiser stared at Truman. Reiser sighed and bit his lip. He stared down for a few seconds, trying to organize his thoughts. The wind whipped around; it threw up their hair and trench coats, making them all look evil.

"We'll be standing down. You will never know when we strike."

Reiser picked up his hog mask and put it back on. "See you sometime soon."

Cali, Ray, and Ruby stared at them as they strutted off to the stairs.

Cali glanced at Nick. He was lying down, but still breathing. Cali hesitantly walked over.

Nick looked up at her. "I'm sorry," he mumbled. "I wish I never went back. I messed up."

Cali stared down at him, not feeling anything. "You did this to yourself. You betrayed your sister. How could you ever do that to someone of your own blood, let alone your twin?"

Nick stuffed his face in the snow to curb the bleeding. Cali felt no sympathy. It was the same type of pain she felt when she realized Louis was a criminal. She felt betrayed, like her life was a lie, but that was when everything took a turn. She learned a lot from it. She couldn't bear to know what Keagan was feeling at that moment.

CHAPTER 26

"I am Keagan Perry," she said into the backstage mirror. She was wearing the same teal dress she wore at the fall festival. *Gosh, it was cold, so very cold.* She had always hated the winter festival. Whether she was on stage or on the ground. It was always cold.

The other schools would usually come to the winter festival because of the food, Keagan snickered to herself. That's why she always came to them, anyway.

"Keagan," someone put a hand on her shoulder. "You ready?"

It was Harlow.

Keagan nodded hesitantly. "Always."

Harlow nodded and walked off.

Then Talivikki walked over. "You know I've always disliked Harlow," she mumbled. "Don't repeat that."

Keagan nodded again. "I wouldn't dare. She scares me. Sometimes I believe she has way too much power."

"She does have a lot of power, but you do as well, Keagan." Talivikki shrugged. "Don't let her discourage you. Now go out on stage and talk." Talivikki gave her a half-smile. She was always bad at comforting.

"Thank you, Talivikki."

"This is going to the last time you'll speak for a while. Well, until the end of the school year. I hope you have a good speech. I wouldn't even doubt that you wouldn't."

Keagan smirked and nodded. Talivikki ruffled her hair.

"I've always liked to think of you as a daughter, Keagan. You are everything I ever wanted in a child." Talivikki stared at Keagan blankly.

"Why didn't you ever have children of your own?" Keagan asked. "I've always wondered that."

Talivikki raised her eyebrows. "Parenthood is not my thing. Coaching is the second-best thing to that, for me at least. I love basketball and kids," she confided.

Keagan nodded. "Would you be playing in the WNBA right now if your ankle wasn't ruined?"

"No, I'm almost fifty, Keagan." Talivikki shook her head. "I wish so much that I didn't injure my ankle. That was the worst night in my life."

"I've heard the story one too many times, Talivikki. You don't need to tell me again." Keagan smiled.

Talivikki nodded. "Alright. I'll be waiting."

Keagan watched as Talivikki limped away. *What if something like that happened to her when her shoes were sanded down?*

She ran her hand through her hair and stared into the mirror. She was definitely in danger right now. Ruby told her those guys would be standing down but the most obvious guess was that they would strike tonight.

"Keagan," the mayor came out from around the curtains. "It's time." He smiled.

Keagan looked at him through the mirror and slowly got up. She counted every step she took in her head until she reached the curtains. Keagan stopped her slump walk, stood tall, and held her head up so she looked down at everyone, but not harmfully or out of conceit. People told Keagan she never truly looked down at anyone, which was what she wanted. Of course, since she was so tall, she looked down at people all the time, but no one ever said they felt looked down upon.

Keagan took a deep breath and walked on stage. It was cold, but thankfully there was no wind. There were cameras all over, unlike last time. This was a big event. A homeschooled kid that came from Blackridge moved to basketball city and was now the most likely to get chosen by the WNBA. In the news's eyes, that was amazing. To Keagan, it didn't feel real and she didn't think she deserved it.

She walked up to the podium and spoke. "Hello, Merry early Christmas, everyone," she began. "You may know me, but if you don't, I am Keagan Perry."

Standing by backstage were Ruby, Ray, and Cali. Ruby stood with her arms crossed and her head alert. Ray spaced out because of the cold. Cali listened closely to Keagan's speech.

"If you hear any silent hog cries, tell me straight away," Ruby muttered.

Ruby had been stressed and so alert over the days. They tried to calm her down by going to different places, but it never seemed to work. She always wanted to leave right away, but she always agreed to go in the first place. Cali guessed she was always second-guessing herself.

Ray seemed better ever since she learned what happened to Sienna, but she was still her impulsive self.

Eliza and Cali had a few more talks, but they weren't much. Cali felt like things were finally coming to an end. Cali was sure that she was ready for everything.

"I am honored to be standing here today. I never would have been here if it wasn't for my coach, Talivikki Nykánan." Her calm voice echoed throughout the great field. "On a boring day, our doorbell rang, and I saw this Amazonian woman standing at our doorstep."

She smiled and looked out onto the laughing crowd. Talivikki chuckled too. She seemed proud, like a mother would be of her daughter.

In the bushes, a small fire fluttered to life. Reiser leaned back into the thick bush. He combed out his mullet. "Keagan is going to die tonight," he snickered. "Nick is always going to be allowed backstage, so that will give us easy access. We will take everyone backstage hostage. If all goes to Hell, we'll light it all ablaze and try to save us all."

Cooper smiled. "This is going to be fun."

"I just want our fair share of the money." Reiser shrugged. "I couldn't care less about Ruby; I just want the money."

"Women, *tsk*," Cooper mumbled.

"Is your mom out of prison yet?" Reiser cocked his head.

"She never will be; she tried to kill me! Don't you remember, you idiot!" Cooper slammed his mask on.

"You could've fought her off," Reiser sneered.

Cooper took the gasoline and matches and ran off.

"Cooper," Reiser called out. "Cooper, that's not the plan!"

Cali heard the crunch of snow and yelling coming from the small hill. Ray and Ruby heard too. Ruby jumped up and tried to get to the entrance before Cooper and the rest did. However, they were too late. Reiser, Cooper, and Truman got backstage first.

"Everyone down, now," Reiser hollered.

No one on the outside could hear the noise due to Keagan's speech. Ruby slammed open the door.

"Reiser," she growled.

Reiser turned. "Long time no see, Ruby." He smiled. "I've won."

A fire broke out behind him. It reached up to the ceiling and ate away at everything it touched.

Cali stared in awe at the beautiful fire. The curtains were one of the first things to go. In due time, the festival-goers would be able to see the fight.

Instead of stepping back and running, Ruby ran forward and punched Reiser, sending him stumbling backward. Just before his hog shoe touched the fire, he stopped himself and held his nose.

Ruby and Reiser continued to fight while Ray took on Cooper and Cali went for Truman. Cali stood in front of Truman; they looked at each other for a few seconds before erupting into a fight.

The stage crew took the time to run. Cali noticed a girl out of the corner of her eye. It was the same girl from the drama club. The one Ray had jokingly fought with earlier in the year.

Keagan's speech continued outside. "Whether you are fighting for anger or just acting out of aggression..."

Reiser punched Ruby and threw her to the ground.

"Whether you are fighting for your morals..."

Cali poked Truman in the eye, sending him reeling.

"Or maybe you're just doing what everyone else is doing."

Ray screeched and kicked Cooper in the side of the face.

"We all know that violence is a universal language in this city. But I will be sure of one thing, I will be the pride of Swallowsville. I will make this town look great..."

The crowd clapped and hollered.

"As I reach the end of my speech, I want you all to pay attention to the stars. Are they out?" Keagan jutted her head up. The crowd nodded.

"I've learned that every time the stars are out, something is changing."

Talivikki took the microphone. "Something is changing because there's a fire behind you," she said frantically.

The crowd gasped and the news crews went to work. Keagan's eyes widened as she saw the crumbling stage behind her. The fire's light fell onto Keagan, casting a big shadow onto the crowd. Keagan, for once, showed everyone another emotion other than her usual calm. She punched the podium and ran into the backstage with Talivikki following behind her.

There, Ruby, Cali, Ray, Reiser, Truman, and Cooper were all having the fight of their lives; bloodier and more violent than the one they had on Thanksgiving.

Cali took a brick, poured extra gasoline on it, stuck it in the fire, and slammed it into Truman's head. Truman's hit the ground cold. Cali stood there for a second, shocked. She, a 5'0" woman, took down this 6'5" man. She laughed and looked over at Ray and Cooper. It looked like Ray knocked him out as well.

They were winning! She laughed in astonishment. Ruby and Reiser were still battling it out. Ruby shoved him away. Reiser was yelling and cursing at Ruby, but the roar and crackling of the fire was too loud.

Or was it the fire cracking? Cali looked up just as a huge piece of flaming wood fell right onto Reiser. *What luck did those guys even have?* Reiser screeched as he burned alive with many broken bones. He reached out to Ruby with his melting black glove one last time. His crazed and scared eyes drilled into her. He knew he lost.

Talivikki rushed everyone out of the burning stage and out to the back before anyone else was injured or killed.

Ruby, Cali, Ray, Keagan, Talivikki, and the rest of the stage crew stood helplessly as the stage crumbled. Everything that was inside was smashed and on fire.

Cali could feel the heat on her face. *They won. They finally won.* Cali was in pure shock, traumatized. *Surely that attracted enough attention for Talivikki?* Cali looked back at Talivikki, who was horrified.

"Those guys are dead, aren't they?" Talivikki covered her mouth. "Who were they? Why were they wearing hog masks?"

"Those guys," Ruby inhaled and continued, "were the Fox Den shooters and the reason Sienna went missing."

Talivikki looked up. "What? How do you know? If they're dead, they'll never be held accountable."

"They're dead," Keagan nodded. "I think that's enough, Talivikki."

Talivikki shook her head in shock. "You saved Keagan. Didn't you? They were trying to hurt her because I kicked down Ruby."

She looked at the three girls.

"We'll talk about this on the way to the police station. Let's go. I need time to think about this; it all happened so quickly. I'm still in shock, I think everyone else is too. Obviously, everyone else is," she said under her shaky breath.

Cali swallowed and followed beside Talivikki.

Keagan stared back at the flames. "Where is Nick?" she mouthed. "Harlow?"

Cali's eyes widened in surprise. *Were the two there? Did they get injured?* Cali never saw them leave. Cali looked up at the sky. *What about Kikuko? What were they doing? Why did Nick do what he did?* Cali knew one thing for sure; all the questions she had wouldn't be answered tonight.

Talivikki nudged her. "You never got your basketball paperwork in, by the way."

EPILOGUE

"**H**appy New Year!" the family shouted happily as they celebrated.

In her room, she flipped the calendar to January 1, 2020 and sighed angrily. She was isolated in the dark room only lit by a small candle on her desk. It illuminated reddish-orange light. It kept her on constant alert, which is what she wanted.

"They're on the 'B team'," she said, slamming her hands down onto the desk.

The door cracked open.

"Hey," a soft voice came through. "Are you coming to celebrate with the family?"

The room owner slowly turned. she glared at whomever dared to talk to them. "No." she shooed them off. "Close the door."

The person came closer to them. "Hey, I know you're angry, but you have to believe that you're great too."

"I am not great!" she said as she shoved the other person away. "Stop trying to give me false hope, you moron!"

"I'm sorry!"

She got up.

"You really seem like you need someone."

"I have myself," she growled. "Now get out."

They nodded and slowly tiptoed out of the room.

The room owner got up and stared into her mirror. She hated how they looked, how she was built, everything.

She groaned. *Why couldn't she just be built a perfect way? Like the varsity players? She deserved it all.* She was so very angry.

She broke. "I deserve it all. All of Swallowsville will see it with their very own eyes." She smiled and laughed. "I won't die like those idiots did."

ABOUT THE AUTHOR

Lindsey Undlin started writing when she was in fifth grade and self-published her first book at age thirteen. Now at fourteen, she is writing the second book in the Priders Series along with playing basketball, softball, and volleyball. It was through being part of a team and general school life that inspired her to create the Swallowsville Series.

Lindsey lives in Mohall, North Dakota with her family and plans on continuing her writing career with three more books in this series and two spin-off series which should complete about the time she goes to college.